Legal Theory Today

Law's Meaning of Life

Legal Theory Today

Founding Editor

John Gardner, Professor of Jurisprudence, University College, Oxford

TITLES IN THIS SERIES

Law in its Own Right by Henrik Palmer Olsen and Stuart Toddington
Law and Aesthetics by Adam Gearey
Law as a Social Institution by Hamish Ross
Evaluation and Legal Theory by Julie Dickson
Risks and Legal Theory by Jenny Steele
A Sociology of Jurisprudence Richard Nobles and David Schiff
Costs and Cautionary Tales: Economic Insights for the Law by Anthony Ogus
Legal Norms and Normativity: An Essay in Genealogy by Sylvie Delacroix
Consent in the Law by Deryck Beyleveld and Roger Brownsword

Law's Meaning of Life

Philosophy, Religion, Darwin and the Legal Person

Ngaire Naffine

• HART •
PUBLISHING

OXFORD AND PORTLAND, OREGON
2009

Published in North America (US and Canada) by
Hart Publishing
c/o International Specialized Book Services
920 NE 58th Avenue, Suite 300
Portland, OR 97213-3786
USA
Tel: +1 503 287 3093 or toll-free: (1) 800 944 6190
Fax: +1 503 280 8832
E-mail: orders@isbs.com
Web Site: www.isbs.com

Hart Publishing Ltd, 16c Worcester Place, Oxford, OX1 2JW
Telephone: +44 (0)1865 517530 Fax: +44 (0)1865 510710
E-mail: mail@hartpub.co.uk
Website: http://www.hartpub.co.uk

British Library Cataloguing in Publication Data
Data Available

ISBN: 978-1-84113-866-4

Typeset by Hope Services Ltd, Abingdon
Printed and bound in Great Britain by
Lightning Source UK Ltd

In memory of Paul Bourke

and for

Eric Richards and Margaret Davies

Acknowledgements

In the writing of this book, I have received a good deal of help. For their generous, robust and thoughtful comments on different parts and versions of the manuscript I thank Paul Babie, Judith Gardam, John Gava, Anna Grear, Emily Jackson and Catherine Kevin. For our many stimulating philosophical conversations, I thank Ian Leader-Elliott. For their helpful comments at a Roundtable on legal persons at the University of the West of England, I thank Mary Ford and Vanessa Munroe. I thank Kevät Nousiainen and Anu Pylkkänen for the opportunity to deliver work in progress at the Faculty of Law of the University of Helsinki. I am indebted to the students at Cleveland-Marshall School of law, Cleveland State University who allowed me to test many of my ideas. I also thank Dena Davis and Allyson Robichaud for their intellectual stimulation. For her editorial advice on the entire final manuscript, I thank Rosemary Moore. For her meticulous assistance with the manuscript, I thank Claire Simmonds. Margaret Davies has been a sounding board, kind friend and generous commentator throughout. For his sustained intellectual engagement with the argument of the entire book and his many detailed suggestions for its improvement, I am greatly indebted to Ben Berger. Finally and most importantly I thank Eric Richards.

I thank the *Modern Law Review* for permission to make use of parts of 'Who are Law's Persons? From Cheshire Cats to Responsible Subjects' (2003) 66 *Modern Law Review* 346.

I am also grateful to the Australian Research Council for funding the project of which this book is the outcome.

Contents

Table of Cases

Table of Treaties and Legislation

1
The Question: Who is Law For?

> [O]ur conceptual language tends to fix our perceptions, and derivatively, our thought and behaviour.
>
> Robert Merton[1]

The perennial question posed by the philosophically-inclined lawyer is 'What is law?' or perhaps 'What is the nature of law?'. The question is intended to stimulate inquiry into the fundamental jurisprudential problem of what makes law law: what are its sources, its characteristics, its limits, its purposes and its very basis for legitimacy. This has been called '*the* law question'.[2]

This book poses an associated, but no less fundamental, question about law which has received much less attention in the legal literature. It is: 'Who is law for?' or, more grammatically, 'For whom is law?'. To whom is it orientated and whom does it presuppose?

Is this the Right Question? The Question Disputed

To many lawyers, my question, 'Who is law for?', may seem to be the wrong question to ask of law. It may seem wrong-headed, misguided, even odd. Though it will generally be conceded, with little argument, that law is *for* 'persons', there are likely to follow strong words of caution about reading too much into this legal fact. For, in this received view, the term 'person' is simply the word law uses to designate its basic unit or coinage—the rights-and-duty bearer. The legal 'person', the one whom law is for, is imagined as pure abstraction, the basic conceptual unit of legal analysis. The 'person' is the formal subject of rights and duties: a legal idea or construct, not to be mistaken for a real natural being. The legal use of the term 'person' therefore should not be taken to entail any larger biological, philosophical or even religious claims or implications about the sort of beings law is for, claims which might render the question interesting and meaningful and worth asking.

Indeed, the question 'Who is law for?' may be thought, by such sceptically-minded lawyers, to carry with it a host of questionable and unfortunate

[1] Robert Merton, *On Theoretical Sociology* (New York, Free Press, 1967) 145.

[2] See, eg Margaret Davies, *Asking the Law Question: the Dissolution of Legal Theory* (3rd edn, Pyrmont, Law Book Co, 2008).

implications. One is that law's 'person' is always conditioned by the nature of real (non-legal) persons—the persons whom law is for—and that the legal task is always to determine, represent and respect that real nature; that the real natural person should fully and accurately sound in law. This sets law a very large metaphysical task. For it suggests that law is always confronted with prior natural subjects of rights (real persons before the law in both a temporal and spatial sense) to which personifying legal rights and duties must be fitted in a manner which honours their nature. The implication is that law must find, rather than make or conceptualise, its subject, its person; that law's task is to divine the true metaphysical person and attach rights and duties in a manner which is fully appropriate to, and consistent with, that nature. To such doubting jurists, this not only overstates the demands on law but misconceives the very character of the legal endeavour.

Another unfortunate implication of the question 'Who is law for?' is that such antecedent beings (those whom law is for) may not be everyone and anyone. Rather the implication may be that there are natural beings who are, or should be, highly influential because law is designed for them; perhaps they make law in their image. The suggestion here is therefore one of bias: that there are people to whom law is oriented in a partisan manner. Unless we accept that the answer to the question 'Who law is for?' is everyone and anyone (which is a perfectly reasonable response in a liberal democracy but renders the question banal), then the question seems to point to legal bias and partisanship.

Further, the question may also seem to be naïve and unattuned to the formal, artificial, technical and variable nature of the legal enterprise and the sometimes highly complex ways in which law constitutes legal persons through its endowment of rights and duties. It may seem to suggest some sort of simple or crude correspondence between the legal order (and law's population of legal persons) and the natural or social or human order (natural or moral persons) outside of law. But law, in this orthodox view, is not seeking to reflect or represent the non-legal world in any direct manner. This is not the legal task and so there is already a mistake built into the very asking of the question, for it rests on a false premise about the nature of law.[3]

To many lawyers of this sceptical disposition, the law is in its own realm. It operates within its own universe of meaning; it has its own guiding principles, precepts and purposes; it has its own conceptual resources; it works within its own intellectual and disciplinary confines. It does not even

[3] Eg, in his short treatise on legal personality, Alexander Nekam decried 'the confusions of the law-of-nature ideology' and its misguided belief that 'it is the human personality which somehow is the natural substratum of every right'. He thought it wrong '[t]o think that the human being is a subject of rights by the force of its nature'. Alexander Nekam, *The Personality Conception of the Legal Entity* (Cambridge Mass, Harvard University Press, 1938) 22.

purport to reflect the real world outside it in any direct or obvious manner which would make it sensible to say that law is for 'x' or for 'y'. Rather, we should appreciate what Lawson has called 'the separateness and completeness of what we may call the legal plane'.[4] Law operates in its own 'artificial world', much like a hot-house flower.

Thus (in this view) it is wrong to think of law as trying to divine and reflect the true nature of humanity or, in the alternative, as orientated, in any simple fashion, to a particular constituency. Law's purposes are too varied and complex to be characterised in this way. Law has no one type of person in mind. The question 'Who is law for?' may well be regarded by such lawyers as a political, sociological or even philosophical question which the members of these other disciplinary groupings are entitled to pursue; but it is not a specifically legal question which lawyers need to ask.

Matching Law to Life: the Question Affirmed

And yet it is not uncommon for judges and lawyers to ask whether a range of natural (and unnatural) beings have the necessary qualifying attributes to constitute legal persons. There is often this endeavour to match a non-legal being with the legal concept of the person, to check the degree of fit or correspondence—in effect, to ask who law is for. This is an important way in which jurists think about the legal person which begins to undermine all of the arguments above.

For example, the question is typically put: Does the foetus or even the embryo have the right characteristics to be thought of as a legal person? It was once asked: Do women? It is still being asked about animals. This is also precisely the question and way of thinking which has dominated much corporate theory. Thus, it is still being asked if the corporation is the right kind of entity to be called a person. Does it achieve personhood only by dint of its similarity to natural persons or by a fiction? Does it degrade the concept of the person to have the corporation included in the category? These are all still live questions in corporate theory.[5]

[4] FH Lawson, 'The Creative Use of Legal Concepts' (1957) 32 *New York University Law Review* 907, 913.

[5] The view that corporations are not moral persons and so may not properly be regarded as legal persons has been advanced, in different ways, by Michael Moore and Elizabeth Wolgast. To Wolgast, 'it is implausible to treat a corporation as a member of the human community, a member with a personality . . . responsibility and susceptibility to punishment' and further that 'treating corporations like persons is morally hazardous': Elizabeth Wolgast, *Ethics of an Artificial Person: Lost Responsibility in Professions and Organizations* (Stanford, Stanford University Press, 1992) 86, 88. To Moore: 'It is only persons like us . . . who are obliged by moral norms and thus have the capacity to be responsible' and so he questions whether corporations should be thought of as persons: *Law and Psychiatry: Rethinking the Relationship* (Cambridge, Cambridge University Press, 1984) 62. See also Michael Moore, *Placing Blame: a General Theory of the Criminal Law* (Oxford, Clarendon Press, 1997).

If we accept that the meaning of terms resides in actual use and practice (a view which will be endorsed in this book), then it is significant to know that it is common juristic practice to try to match law's persons with natural persons, variously conceived. It is important to know that when making their determinations about legal personhood, lawyers and judges often feel obliged to consider whether the being in question has the necessary intrinsic or attributed characteristics to qualify for legal being; whether it is the right kind of being to be thus legally endowed. Is it considered sufficiently intelligent? Does it feel enough pain and pleasure? Is it sacred? Does it possess intrinsic value? If it is the community which is thought to endow it with value, then is that social value sufficient for legal personification?

As we will discover over the course of this book, there is a good deal of evidence that many jurists think of the legal person as possessing a variety of inherent and natural, and even supernatural, characteristics which make some kinds of beings suitable for legal personhood but make others ill-suited. Such jurists therefore do not conceive of their person as pure abstraction. Instead, they operate with some model of a real natural or supernatural being and it implicitly or explicitly influences their practical determinations about the distribution and denial of rights and duties and the resulting constitution of the community of legal persons. As John Dewey observed in an early and highly-influential paper on the nature of persons in law, 'discussions and theories which have influenced legal practice have, with respect to the concept "person", introduced and depended upon a mass of non-legal considerations'.[6]

These considerations have included the 'popular, historical, political, moral, philosophical, metaphysical and . . . theological'.[7] Especially when faced with difficult controversies about who or what should be a legal person, judges have tended to support their decisions 'by appealing to some prior properties of the antecedent non-legal "natural person" '.[8] Such decisions, as Dewey remarked, go beyond the 'strictly legal sphere' and draw upon 'non-legal theory'.[9] They rely on a postulate, albeit unconscious, 'that before anything can be a jural person it must intrinsically possess certain properties, the existence of which is necessary to constitute anything a person'.[10]

Given this strong legal tendency to endow law's person with a variety of non-abstract characteristics (a tendency which will be explained and illustrated throughout this book), it is sensible and meaningful to ask the question 'Who is law for?'. Again to draw upon Dewey for support here, 'some theory [of the jural subject] is implied in the procedure of the courts

[6] John Dewey, 'The Historic Background of Corporate Legal Personality' (1926) 35 *Yale Law Journal* 655.

[7] *Ibid.*

[8] *Ibid* 657.

[9] *Ibid.*

[10] *Ibid* 658.

and . . . the business of the theory of law is to make explicit what is implied'.[11] It does not 'become jurisprudence' simply to maintain 'a position of legal agnosticism, holding that even if there be such an ulterior subject per se, it is no concern of law, since courts can do their work without respect to its nature, much less having to settle it'.[12]

If we turn to consider some of the most pressing problems of current law, we begin to see the pertinency and purchase of the question 'Who is law for?', as well as the many uncertainties and controversies which persist about the nature of law's person. Doubts and disagreements about who law is for are particularly evident in the laws governing life before birth, where the nature of law's person is discussed to an unusual degree. The legality of embryonic stem cell research, for example, depends on the legal status of embryos which in turn depends on whether they are regarded as the sort of beings law is for. And yet there are serious differences of opinion about the moral and legal status of the embryo.

Law sets the terms and the limits of reproductive technology (how it can be done, with what gametes, and for whom) and this too arguably depends on the sort of creatures law is thought to be for. Law can now permit or prohibit some kinds of being from coming into existence (notably cloned beings or beings of mixed human/animal species). Abortion laws are shaped by judicial and legislative views of the type of beings law is for. Decisions must be made about whether the pregnant woman is to be the law's primary or even exclusive concern and whether the foetus should come into consideration as a protected party. The highly-protected legal status of young children and adults of impaired mental capacity seems to depend on law eschewing a view of its subject as necessarily capable of reason. The legality of withdrawal of life support at the end of life can depend on whether the being in question is thought to have any interests worth protecting: is it the sort of being that can be owed a duty of care?

During life and even after death, prohibitions on commerce in human body parts and tissue at least partly depend on a legal view of us as the sort of beings who cannot be owned or sold, in whole or in part. (By contrast, animals can be treated in this manner because of the way in which their natures are legally understood.) The broadly-accepted legal view is that there can be no property in humans because of a particular, but often unstated, understanding of the kinds of creatures that we are, as moral and legal beings.

From just this brief list of current legal problems, it should be evident that judges and law-makers must constantly make difficult and controversial decisions about who law is for and that these decisions have a direct influence on the assignment of legal rights and responsibilities throughout our

[11] *Ibid* 660.
[12] *Ibid.*

lives, including before birth and after death. There is no avoiding difficult judgments about the meaning and significance of human life, which have a direct bearing on law. However, the nature and the operation of law's human preferences and discriminations are quite difficult to grasp, and even more difficult to explain, expound and defend.

Competing Views of Human Nature and their Implications for Law

Much of this problem of interpretation, I suggest, is to do with the presence within law of coexisting, competing and shifting understandings of human nature and human value. There are further differences of legal opinion about the role law should adopt (if any) in reflecting that supposed nature and value. Law's preferences and discriminations do not necessarily entail any legal malice or even positive and conscious endeavours to favour some over others. They are more to do with concomitant and conflicting fundamental metaphysical views operating within the field of law about what makes us what we are and who should therefore matter and why.

To illustrate my point in a very preliminary way: there can be a great cultural gulf separating those who adopt a secular, rationalist, humanist view of human beings and those who adopt a religious view of human nature. The religious believer is likely to regard human sanctity as the most defining human characteristic and to feel that law should positively recognise this attribute. The secular humanist may regard the human capacity for reason as that which most defines and dignifies us and also look to law to reflect this fact. These different understandings of human beings, *both* of which are to be found in law, may create sharp tensions in legal determinations about who law should be for.

On the legal status of the foetus, on whether law is *for* foetuses, for example, the holders of these different views are likely to differ greatly. The religious believer is much more likely than the secular humanist to invest the foetus with moral and legal interests and to regard it as a type of moral and legal person. Religious and secular thinkers are also likely to disagree about whether law should treat pregnant women in precisely the same way as it treats never-pregnant men, especially when the enforcement of the rights of the woman endangers the foetus. The extent of the disagreements between the religious and the secular, and the degree of fixity of their various positions, may in turn depend on the particular variety of religious belief (and in this book I will focus on some of the more influential varieties of Christian faith). When religious and secular views of human beings coexist within the one legal case, as they often do, then the resulting jurisprudence can confuse.

Moreover, different understandings of human nature seem to permeate different parts of law. Thus, for instance, in medical law one is regularly confronted by the religious idea of human sanctity. The patient is often described in these implicitly spiritual terms. Judges consistently invoke and endorse a common law principle of human sanctity, regarding it as the moral basis of the endowment of the most basic human rights, especially the right to life, but also the right to bodily integrity, sometimes religiously termed 'inviolability'. For this reason, patients can always say 'no' to any physical interventions (unless perhaps they are pregnant and there is a sacred foetus at stake) but cannot ask for positive assistance to have their lives ended.

By contrast, in criminal law, the capacity for reason is strongly accentuated. Here one is much more likely to encounter the liberal, rationalist belief that human beings are most defined by their capacity for reason: they are essentially and by nature rational choosers which makes them legitimate subjects for the assignment of responsibility and blame. In this rationalist account of our natures, those of diminished reason may not be regarded as authentic, complete legal actors. They may not be considered true subjects of law and justice because they can neither give justice nor receive it.

The Concept of the Person and its Problematic Nature

The concept of the person is central to the question posed by this book because it is the technical term lawyers use to designate their subject *and* it is the term also often used by those who believe in the natural basis of rights and who use the term to dignify and give value to its designates. That is to say, the term 'person' is used in ordinary *and* legal language to mean a human being and it is also used, inside and outside law, to endow with value and demonstrate respect: 'You don't treat *persons* in certain ways'. Thus, part of the problem of defining law's subject seems to be the very word used by lawyers to designate it: 'the person'.

When lawyers employ this term 'person' in its most formal and technical sense, they endeavour to expunge these moral connotations from the term and to invoke simply the right-and-duty bearing unit; anyone or thing that the law is willing to endow with the capacity to bear rights and duties becomes such a person, such a unit. There are no logical or formal limits to who or even what might be considered a suitable subject for the bearing of rights and duties in this view. And so the strictly legal term 'person' is highly compatible with the liberal idea that law is indeed for anyone: there is nothing inherent to the concept which suggests a preference for one type of rights holder over another, for one type of person over another. The concept is in fact so ecumenical that it does not even demand a human subject of rights (witness the corporation). However, the more naturalistic and moral conceptions of the person are not so ecumenical, precisely because they demand certain moral or natural characteristics of their person.

To a liberal moral philosopher, for example, a 'person' tends to mean a moral agent, that is, a being who can reason and reflect and make rational choices. This is a connotation of the term 'person' which has had a particularly strong influence on legal thinking and is especially in evidence in criminal law, with its idea of a responsible agent who can be held to account for his crimes. To the religious believer, a 'person' is a sacred being, and the population of protected, sacred beings tends to include human foetuses, but to exclude animals. Medical law often invokes this sacred being. To those lawyers who are constitutionally opposed to such metaphysics, a person can simply mean *any* being or entity capable of bearing rights and duties. There are no necessary moral limits to the concept.

Animal advocates have endeavoured to take advantage of several connotations and characteristics of the term 'person'—its formally open abstract nature and its supposed basis in the natural attributes of its subjects—and have sought to have some animals included in the category of legal persons (rather than as property, essentially their current legal status). Consistently, the argument is that biologically, and even cognitively, human and non-human animals share many characteristics and that the law should recognise these commonalities through a conferral of legal personhood on at least the most intelligent animals. Law, they say, should be for animals as well as for humans and there is no formal reason why it cannot be. Animals as well as humans should be able to go to law. So far, animal rights lawyers have not succeeded in this quest. There is profound legal resistance to the idea that law is for (non-human) animals and that animals should be rights holders and therefore legal persons. This still strikes the vast majority of the legal community as a preposterous suggestion.

The advocates for foetal personhood have used similar arguments, with greater success. In their case, they have tended to invoke the supposedly sacred nature of the foetus or its biological similarity to born human beings and have demanded that law recognise that nature by an appropriate endowment of legal rights.

These advocates for new rights holders are therefore making their own strong assumptions about how law's concept of the person works and about who law should be for. They appreciate the formally ecumenical nature of the concept. But they also typically assume that the inherent nature of the entity or being they seek to represent necessarily dictates to law and its conception of the person. It follows that if the being in question can be shown to demonstrate some natural or supernatural capacity which is morally and legally significant (say the capacity for reason or the possession of a soul), then it too should be regarded as a 'legal person'.

It was tempting to write a book about the legal status of these various problematic beings and entities precisely because these debates are so lively and diverting. In fact this book had a few false starts. One entailed a study of the distribution of rights and duties over the human life-cycle: from embryos, to foetuses, to infants, to adults, to the demented, to the comatose, to the deceased. Another option was a study of borderline or controversial legal entities such as (again) foetuses, animals and the human dead. But both projects threatened to produce taxonomies of unusual or eccentric legal persons, rather than a critical understanding of the fundamental processes by which someone or something becomes a legal person. They turned out to be detours from the main endeavour, which was to work out how law creates its subject, its person and, more particularly, under what moral and intellectual influences. Both projects also seemed to suggest that there was something inherent in the nature of the being or entity which *necessarily* dictated the nature of legal rights and legal personhood. In other words, they naturalised the person and their rights, from the outset, and failed to appreciate the critical and creative role of law in the making of legal persons. In this book, I wanted to retain a focus on the artificial yet inventive manner in which law positively constitutes its subject, and for what reasons, and not simply document the legal characteristics of the resulting cast of characters.

Instability of the Concept of the Legal Person

The precise nature of law's person has proven remarkably elusive. The entire topic of persons in law, of who and what can and should bear rights and duties, is very slippery because there is so little carefully considered reflection about it in legal judgments and treatises and yet it is utterly fundamental to legal thought. This poverty of theory and fuzzy thinking is even true of the leading cases and scholarship which have endeavoured to tease out the problem.

Judges seem to use a variety of terms and meanings, often without any obvious awareness that they are doing so—that they are drifting from one meaning of the person to another, driven by an implicit metaphysics. Sometimes they import religious ideas, especially if they are themselves religious believers. Other times they rely on philosophical theory. Sometimes they talk like ordinary-language users about persons and sometimes they act like highly technical lawyers and invoke the concept of the person as a formal legal device: the bearer of rights and duties. As one commentator recently remarked:

> Judges not only fail to invoke philosophical support for their ideas of personality, but also inconsistently apply jurisprudential theory in resolving problems of legal personhood.[13]

They adjudicate disputes about law's persons, often without a clear idea of their underlying theories, even though they are necessarily guided by metaphysical views of their subject. Inevitably, they are always swimming in a

[13] 'Notes: What We Talk About When We Talk About Persons: the Language of a Legal Fiction' (2001) 114 *Harvard Law Review* 1746.

sea of existential controversy, for all these questions about what makes someone deserving of law's full or partial respect are subject to disagreement at the most basic level at which the law does its business.

In both legal judgments and legal scholarship, there is therefore a ready slide between different meanings of 'the person'. The term is thus highly unstable, and yet this instability is often not acknowledged. Instead, judges seem to draw from a particular repertoire of persons but often without reference to the positive choices they are making about who and what should count as a rights bearer and what sort of person they should be. The cast from which they draw seems to include the person as a legal rights-and-duty bearer (the formal technical usage favoured by the lawyers who opened this chapter), the person as human being (a biological species use), and the person as moral person, as a being of inherent value, but that value may derive from different sources, such as the capacity for reason (typically a secular humanist usage) or from the supposed human spirit (a religious usage). There is an easy slippage between legal and more ordinary-language meanings. The jurisprudence on foetuses demonstrates well this mutability of persons. Foetuses are sometimes regarded as little souls, sometimes as undeveloped humans, sometimes as future reasoners, sometimes as potential rights holders (say as beneficiaries of wills).

Because of this legal sleight of hand, different characterisations of the person are being employed, often with no obvious awareness of the changing cast of characters. Sometimes there are bold, even dogmatic and undefended statements about the sort of beings that are suitable for rights. Sometimes there are contradictory characterisations of the person within the one case, leading to great existential confusion.

When trying to emphasise the specifically legal nature of their concept of the person, jurists may prefer to use the term 'legal personality' rather than 'legal person'. They may also draw a conceptual distinction between the two terms, regarding 'the legal person' as the subject of legal rights and duties and 'legal personality' as the particular constellation of rights and duties held by any given legal person. However, this distinction can itself presume too much (and so settle the debate about persons prematurely) if it is taken to mean that the legal person and their personality are two quite separate things. For as we will see, many lawyers insist that legal persons are only their rights and duties, their so-called personality. In this view there is no separate, free-standing, legal subject or person (apart from their rights and duties) to which the rights and duties are attached. It follows that with the dissolution of all rights and duties (the personality) there is simultaneously a dissolution of the person in law. In this book, I will therefore not invoke this distinction. Instead, I will generally refer to 'the legal person' but also at times employ 'legal personality' as a synonymous term, often simply for the sake of variation and linguistic convenience and sometimes to reflect the actual uses of a legal scholar.

Social Significance of the Concept and its Implications for Justice

It is jurisprudentially interesting, in its own right, that jurists use their central term, 'the legal person', in such a rich variety of ways, often without a clear sense of their own inconsistencies. But my purpose here is not simply to engage in an intellectual exercise of exposing legal confusion about a basic legal concept, though there is some satisfaction in this. Rather, my more serious scholarly intention is to reveal, examine and evaluate the type of thinking that goes into fundamental legal determinations about who should count in our modern Anglophone Western liberal societies and to consider whether it is logical, fair and just.

Through its concept of the person, law helps to define who matters. The scope and nature of legal personification are both barometers of social and moral thought and the means of practically enforcing those ideas: of giving them the force of law. Law thus absorbs, reflects and expresses ideas in the broader culture about what and who is of value and why. These include religious ideas, philosophical ideas and even scientific ideas. And this is true for all the Anglophone common law countries which are the concern of this book: Australia, New Zealand, Canada, the United States and the United Kingdom. This is not surprising given their common legal and cultural heritage.

All of this means that something rather remarkable is happening when people enter the legal arena. They are being judged for their suitability as persons and so endowed with or refused rights and duties on the basis of ideas about who matters, ideas which often remain poorly articulated. Within the law, there is always this existential and ethical moment when it is decided whether someone or something is an appropriate subject for a certain type of right or duty—whether they are the right kind of being to enter legal relationships. Are they, for example, sufficiently rational, or sacred, or just human? Law thus helps to define the moral and the political community, for to be a legal person is to have political and moral as well as legal standing. If someone or something is a person, it tends to count in its own right. If the being or entity is not a person, its legal protections are dramatically diminished. Law therefore powerfully assists in the determination of the normal and the abnormal, the intrinsically valuable and that which is mainly for use, as in the case of animals.

Given that all this is going on in law, this tumult of moral and existential evaluations and judgments, it is perhaps odd that lawyers tend to speak of the legal person as if its exclusive moral and philosophical interest lies with the corporation as a person. Often the legal person as a human being is treated as posing few conceptual or moral problems. Indeed, the subject of the person is poorly developed outside of the study of corporate entities.[14]

[14] This point was well made in a recent note in the *Harvard Law Review*, above n 14.

And yet, as Lon Fuller once observed, the legal person, in whatever manifestation, corporate or human, always remains an invention of law and so represents an act of legal creativity with immense social and political import.[15]

Law's Changing Community of Persons

The type of beings who have been brought into law as legal persons has been steadily expanding and it is salutary to reflect on the changing ways of thinking about human nature and human value that have driven this expansion. In his *Descent of Man*, Charles Darwin told a story of the slow enlightenment of humanity as it grew less selfish and slowly expanded its circle of sympathy. He observed a gradual shift from an exclusive concern with oneself to a concern with one's 'fellow men'. And then:

> his sympathies became more tender and widely diffused, extending to men of all races, to the imbecile, maimed, and other useless members of society, and finally to the lower animals.[16]

Generally speaking, Darwin accurately describes also the trajectory of law, the expanding circle of its concerns, though law, so far, has baulked at the inclusion of the lower animals in its community of beings who seriously matter.

The long history of the common law can also be characterised, less forgivingly, as one of persistent and shameful stereotyping and exclusions in which the concept of the person has been quite obviously manipulated and the legal community of actors extended only grudgingly. Changing belief systems about what makes us truly human and worthy of law's respect have guided this legal development. As John Dawson observes:

> [c]hildren, married women, bankrupts, lunatics, Jews and foreigners have all been assigned a distinct legal status within the history of the common law, distinguishing their legal position from the norm of the adult, male, solvent, sane, Christian citizen.[17]

Sometimes this was quite explicitly achieved by careful deployment of the meaning of law's central term. Thus, the conferral and the denial of legal personhood have had profoundly social, philosophical and political implications and consequences.

We might even say that the evolution and the vicissitudes of the concept of the legal person have shaped the modern world. For example, the rejec-

[15] Lon Fuller, *Legal Fictions* (Stanford, Stanford University Press, 1967).

[16] Charles Darwin, *The Descent of Man and Selection in Relation to Sex* (2nd edn, London, John Murray, 1874) 119, 120–1.

[17] John Dawson, 'The Changing Legal Status of Mentally Disabled People' (1994) 2 *Journal of Law and Medicine* 41.

tion of slavery entailed the legal transformation of slaves from property to persons and so laid the foundation of modern universal human rights.[18] And again, modern capitalism has been legally enabled by the personification of the corporation (its constitution as an entity that can act in law, as a single legal unit, and independently of its members). Similarly, the eventual recognition of women as persons in the early part of the twentieth century immediately doubled the population of those able to participate in public life (as voters, doctors, lawyers and so on) and again reshaped the nature of our community.[19] Again, if the animal rights movement prevails, the legal community may once again be extended, this time to include certain animals. The possible personification of artificial intelligence would equally entail another major change to the complexion of our society.

This is not to suggest, however, that the expansion of law's community of persons is always a necessary good. For example, the consistent extension of legal personhood to foetuses would do great damage to the legal rights of pregnant women. It would mean that the woman's interests would always compete directly with the interests of her foetus. And the extension of legal personhood to all animals would mean that their interests would always vie with human interests. This might undo much of the good achieved by the human rights movement which has consistently sought to distinguish humans from animals.

The Mission

In this book I plan to reinvigorate the idea that law is always responsible for its subject, and not just in a narrow technical manner, and that in the making of legal persons it continues to set the very contours of the moral and political community. My task is to discover and evaluate the major influences on this process of constituting legal persons and so arrive at a better, more critical understanding of our legal natures.

The intellectual genre of this book is probably best regarded as jurisprudence, as legal theory, the philosophy of law. But as I have already intimated, the focus of this book is rather different from the usual set of jurisprudential concerns which tend to be the nature, sources, limits and legitimacy of law, often quite abstractly conceived. The concern of this book is not so much the nature of law and of legal legitimacy, but the nature (and legitimacy) of law's conception of its subject, law's person: whom law is

[18] Slaves were not in all senses property in that they were still protected against many of the offences against the person and also subject to them.

[19] The final persons case was *Edwards v Canada (Attorney-General)* [1930] AC 124. Here, the Privy Council finally conceded that women were 'persons' for the purpose of the right to be nominated to the Canadian Senate. A legal history of the British and American persons cases is to be found in A Sachs and JH Wilson, *Sexism and the Law: a Study of Male Beliefs and Legal Bias in Britain and the United States* (Oxford, M Robertson, 1978).

thought to be for; around whom it is organised; its basic presuppositions about us.

There is also quite a practical orientation to this book as it is interested in the way that ideas about human nature play out in law and result in real determinations about what we can do with ourselves and how we can live. These issues cut right to the bone. Most dramatically, they determine whether we have a right to live and a right to die.

This is therefore a study of law's deepest assumptions about the nature of human existence. It requires us to consider what and whom the entire edifice of law is thought to be for, to consider some of the most basic priorities, concerns and aims of law. It obliges us to consider law's basic values: how it orders the world of beings and things; who and what it regards as counting, as mattering, as having value. It compels us to think about law's hierarchy of beings and its supporting assumptions about what and who we are. The interest of this book extends to the more obviously perturbing possibilities and instantiations of legal personhood, such as the human foetus, comatose humans and intelligent animals. And this is indeed where a good deal of the legal action takes place. But it is also, squarely, focused on ourselves as rational, moral agents, as arguably, 'the primary subjects of justice'.[20]

This book is in one sense about the hierarchy of being created by those with sufficient influence to express and impose their values through law. It is about those whom law, as a consequence, embraces within its community of beings that matter and those it excludes and treats as the means to our own ends, and why. It considers how the concept of the person has been employed to endow or to deny status, the reasoning thus employed and the various forms of justification. This is therefore a book about the metaphysics of law: its understanding of what we are; the means by which it defines, explains, expresses and preserves life.

In another sense, this is a study of legal world views. It is an endeavour to identify, explain and evaluate the most influential ways of thinking about human nature and its bearing on the legal subject. The social hierarchy of beings expressed and imposed by law, generally through its concept of the person, derives its logic and legitimacy from these different ways of understanding our natures and our place in the social and legal world. Law thus contains and sustains multiple, and at times incommensurable, views of what we are.

Finding the Legal Person

So where in law do I go to find out about legal persons and the systems of belief that bring them into being? My study is focused on the common law

[20] Martha Nussbaum, 'Beyond the Social Contract: Toward Global Justice' in *The Tanner Lectures on Human Values* (Salt Lake City, University of Utah Press, 2003) 9.

Anglophone world: the United States and Canada,[21] the United Kingdom and Australasia. A problem I face from the outset is that the law of persons is not a discrete field of study in the common law world, such as torts, or contract or criminal law, but is a pervasive underlying concept throughout the different branches of law.[22] It is to be found in an extensive legal literature embracing case and statute law, learned commentary and legal scholarship. I have therefore to discover the nature of law's persons by surveying many parts of law, and then often deriving its meaning only by inference. Sometimes the nature of the legal person is presumed and implicit rather than expounded or defended. Some detective work is therefore involved.

I will place particular reliance on the writings of some of the most influential and authoritative legal scholars, the 'thinkers' in my story who represent the different perspectives. I will examine closely their understanding of the person and how they think it should be played out in law. My selection of jurists is based on the degree of their influence on legal thinking and also on the extent to which they have explicitly and positively engaged with the problem of law's person and endeavoured to make clear their own particular point of view. I am also interested in the fact that they stand for a position: a particular stance within a larger debate. Inevitably there will be those who disagree with my choice of theorists, who would replace them with others or would ask that I extend my population of thinkers. However, my task is to demonstrate the range of thought about law's person and to identify the main points of view. In view of the scale of my project, necessarily it is schematic and programmatic, not comprehensive and exhaustive. My task is to supply a conceptual framework for analysing and understanding the legal person.

I will also make considerable use of cases in particular areas of law which display well the different legal outlooks at work. These are cases which show the coexistence of very different understandings of human nature in majority and dissenting judgments; or they represent a test case in which a group is pushing for a change to legal meaning. These are common law demonstrations of collective thinking. There are also some legislative demonstrations, particularly in relation to the treatment of animals.

Certain beings and entities represent the location of tension between different types of thinkers and this is reflected in the often perplexing jurisprudence about their status. The beginning-of-life and end-of-life cases tend to demonstrate well the tension between often incommensurable views of the person which are present simultaneously in legal thought, as one type of thinker fights for the supposed sanctity of the being (life must be sustained at all costs), while another argues for the importance of reason and personal

[21] Canada of course is bilingual.

[22] According to Richard Tur: 'There is no general law of persons, but rather, a series of rules concerning relationships and liabilities'. See Richard Tur, 'The "Person" in Law' in Arthur Peacocke and Grant Gillett (eds), *Persons and Personality: a Contemporary Inquiry* (Oxford, Basil Blackwell, 1987) 123.

autonomy (say to have one's life ended). They tend also to lead to unconvincing decisions in which something seems amiss, compromised, unsatisfying, unresolved. There are two types of cases I will consider in particular: those which seek an essential attribute or character as the true locus of value for the person and those which argue from legal purpose and which insist on a separation of law from metaphysics.

There is a considerable literature on the nature of the legal personality of corporations.[23] Indeed, it may be said that the literature on the legal person is to a large extent preoccupied with the meaning of corporate personality. In the corporation, or the firm, we have a legal creation which is called a person, but which appears to lack any obvious moral status, precisely because it is a legal abstraction and not a flesh-and-blood human being. At first blush, the personification of the corporation might seem to lend weight to the proposition that law's person can be divorced from more naturalistic conceptions of the person.[24] And yet jurists continue to note the anthropomorphising effects of corporate personification.[25] As Nicola Lacey remarks:

> in both doctrinal scholarship and legal theory, the debate about the liability of corporations is marked by a sustained use of metaphors, contrasts, images which depend upon analogies and disanalogies between 'corporate' and 'human' persons.[26]

Some jurists go further and insist that corporations are literally both legal and moral persons.[27] Others go further still and say that because corporations cannot be moral persons, because they are not human, they should not be legal persons.[28]

[23] For a recent concise account of the competing theories of the nature of corporate personality and corporate responsibility, see Nicola Lacey, '"Philosophical Foundations of the Common Law" Social not Metaphysical' in Jeremy Horder (ed), *Oxford Essays in Jurisprudence* (4th series, Oxford, Oxford University Press, 2000) 17. There are numerous other accounts but see in particular the influential essay by Peter French, 'The Corporation as a Moral Person' (1979) 16(3) *American Philosophical Quarterly* 207.

[24] HLA Hart, for one, seems to say that there is little point to the sort of metaphysical exercise undertaken by many of the jurists discussed in this book, at least with regard to the corporation. Thus, in his inaugural lecture he assured us that we need not assume this 'incubus of theory': *Definition and Theory in Jurisprudence* (Oxford, Clarendon Press, 1953) 6.

[25] The anthropomorphising effects of the concept on corporations have been extensively analysed and decried by corporate jurists. See, eg Nicholas James, 'Separate Legal Personality: Legal Reality and Metaphor' (1993) 5 *Bond Law Review* 217.

[26] Lacey, above n 23, at 25.

[27] The view that corporations are moral persons is most closely associated with the work of Peter French. Roger Scruton has taken this argument further still, reversing the conventional wisdom, and suggesting 'that human individuals derive their personality in part from corporations'; that is, the corporation, not the individual human, should be regarded as the paradigmatic legal person. Roger Scruton, 'Corporate Persons' (1989) LXIII *Aristotelian Society Supplementary* 239, 240–41.

[28] For an interesting exposition of the reverse thesis, that the corporation supplies the template of the legal person, see Anna Grear, 'Challenging Corporate Humanity: Legal Disembodiment and Human Rights' (2007) 7 *Human Rights Law Review* 511.

The concern of this book, however, is not primarily with corporations and the well-documented controversies surrounding their moral and legal personification. Rather its interest lies in the study of those beings that are more obvious candidates for moral status (because, for example, they are sentient creatures or because they are so closely associated with live human beings) but who are not generally taken to be legal persons. Here, the jurisprudential controversy largely arises out of the denial, rather than the conferral, of legal personhood. There is a perceived disjuncture between legal and moral conceptions of the person which continues to disturb many legal theorists. The foetus is one such being and a number of the illustrations to be employed in this book will be drawn from the jurisprudence of the foetus and its legal status.

While the law of the person is perhaps most conspicuous when a case explicitly considers the legal personhood of a given being or entity, usually because of its troubling status, the nature of law's person is also to be discovered within the underlying assumptions about legal being embedded within the general principles of law. It is also to be discovered within the writings of legal scholars and other intellectuals, as we will see in the next chapter where I set out the major schools of thought about what it is to be a person in law.

2
The Debate: Legalists v Realists

> Whatever you may say . . . [you] must have ideological presuppositions and no matter how much you may fight shy of them, they are there, and you either hide them or you are brave enough to bring them out in the open and see them and criticize them.
>
> Charles Malik[1]

This book is about a fundamental contest of ideas being fought within the arena of law about the very nature of being human, about what gives us our defining value, and the role law does and should play in preserving and protecting that valuable nature, even setting the terms of being human. It is about who, what and why law should dignify with the appellation of 'person': who it should recognise as a legal subject and who should be excluded from this privileged legal status.

This often-undeclared battle of ideas is being fought by people with very different ways of thinking about the sort of beings that we are and about who (and what) is therefore worthy of law's protection. Some of these disputants about the meaning of life in law are willing to fight for their ideas in courts of law and in the legislature. Typically they go to law when someone or something they regard as deserving of law's concern and protection is excluded from law's community of beings that matter. They want to empower someone or something to act in law: to be rights holders, to be persons. For example, at the start of the twentieth century, women went to law to establish their right to be persons who could qualify for medical degrees and stand for public office.

The legal and political struggle about who should count as a person before the law is therefore not a new one. However, in recent times it has achieved new levels of public intensity and public rhetoric as North Americans hold elections on 'moral values' concerning the appropriate moral and legal treatment of embryos and the permanently comatose and as science creates new ways of making human beings and reveals new facts

[1] *Verbatim Record from the More Important Speeches and Interventions of Charles Malik*, Papers of Charles Malik (Library of Congress, Manuscript Division, 1946) 44. Malik addressed this point to Hansa Mehta, another member of the Commission established to draft the Universal Declaration of Human Rights.

about the human-like qualities of animals and even of artificial intelligence. As the terms of being human seem to be changing, those who have deep commitments to certain ways of viewing human beings go to law and seek to enforce their understandings.

The battle over what it is that most defines us and makes us worthy of law's concern and worth endowing with rights and duties is still being fought openly, even angrily, in certain areas of law. Abortion laws and animal laws tend to draw out the disputants and oblige them to articulate their positions. These areas of law are sites of explicit and heated engagement: here, the protagonists engage in vigorous debate about the supposed legal personhood of foetuses and of animals and whether they should be regarded as the bearers of legal rights. Such issues seem to galvanise the combatants in this existential battle into very public action. The debates about euthanasia also bring the contestants out in the open. The Catholic Church is a well-known intervener in such legal and moral disputes. There are minor skirmishes in other areas of law, such as the law of foetal inheritance (whether it is possible to be regarded as a beneficiary of a will before you are born). But the contention of this book is that strong ideas about what it is to be human and what constitutes the true basis of human value are to be found in most parts of law: they are there as often unexamined background understandings, largely unarticulated.

Why does it matter that we understand the assumptions about what we are which underpin the legal approach being adopted and which rationales are at work? It matters because the appropriateness and legitimacy of any conferral of status necessarily depend on the soundness of the underlying theory of the legal subject. That theory may guide us towards correspondence between law and life, variously understood, or it may drive us to look at specific and variable legal purpose. It is impossible to think clearly about the merits of any particular type of legal personification if we do not understand the basic presuppositions. And this matters for all determinations of legal status, even those that seem perfectly straightforward.

The Positions

The largest dispute, the biggest intellectual and moral battle, is between those who say that law *does not* and *should not* operate with a natural conception of the person and those who say that it does and should. I will call the first group the Legalists and their opponents the Metaphysical Realists. The Realists themselves then further divide into three families of thinker, in my account. They are the Rationalists, Religionists and Naturalists. This is the nomenclature I will adopt throughout this book.

Among the Metaphysical Realists, Rationalists put our reason to the fore. Religionists insist on our sanctity. Naturalists regard us as natural, evolved, biological creatures. By contrast, the Legalists resist all three ontologies and believe that law has its own artificial or constructed person who should not be confused with real human beings.

These are not the only schools of existential thought in law but they are the dominant ones. They exert the greatest influence. Their members do not belong in fixed and stable camps, always doggedly opposed to one another. Indeed, they often get along in law without too much animosity or open disagreement. When need arises, they are even capable of joining forces with each other. At other times, however, there is open warfare.

The Legalists

I begin my account of law's thinkers with the Legalists (the subject of Chapters 3 and 4) because they represent the orthodox, technical approach to law's persons. Legalists are characterised by their view that, as lawyers, they have no special insights into the human condition and that it is simply not the law's business to engage in such metaphysical, ontological or existential disputes and determinations. One's legal nature, therefore, should not be confused with one's nature beyond the confines of law, however that is conceived. The business of law is more practical, more mundane in some ways, and judges and law-makers are not philosophers. Law's business is the regulation and practical organisation of human affairs and the resolution of human differences which are highly variable and often have nothing to do with these basic existential matters. Although law has a legal subject known as the 'legal person', this is strictly a formal and neutral legal device for enabling a being or entity to act in law, to acquire what is known as a 'legal personality': the ability to bear rights and duties. It is not, nor should it be, a means of recognising or realising what is thought to be our true, essential natures—as sacred beings, or as natural beings, or as moral beings, depending on your legal and moral outlook.

For the Legalist, law is not engaged in such metaphysical or natural boundary setting and so, potentially, law's person has no natural limits. To some Legalists, anything goes, anything or anyone can be endowed with rights and so become a legal person, as long as it is compatible with the purpose of any particular law.

In this orthodox and analytical account of law's person, the defining attributes of a being—its capacity to think or feel or its sanctity—have no direct bearing on whether it has legal personality because the legal person is a construct of law. The defining characteristic of *law's* construct is the formal capacity to bear rights and duties. This does not depend on the supposed essential or even inessential attributes of the being to whom the construct is applied. Rather it depends on, and is formed for, specifically legal purposes. Law's person is not intended to mirror nature, however that is understood. Nor should it be. Instead the legal person is better understood as a piece of pure legal artifice, a clever device of law, law's basic unit of analysis.[2] Legalists therefore insist that the concept of the person is internal to law and essentially a matter of formal legal definition. Law, say the Legalists, is not about setting the moral or metaphysical limits of being human; or as HLA Hart once put it, lawyers should not be weighed down by the 'incubus of theory'.[3]

Legalists therefore regard law's person as an artificial legal device created for legal purposes which means that they are guided by legal conventions and norms in the definition and interpretation of law's subject. If you want to know about law's person, you have resort to law because law is fully responsible for the construction of its subject. The Legalists prefer therefore to stay within the legal realm of thought when they are conceptualising their person. It is unnecessary, and indeed undesirable, to go elsewhere to find law's subject: not to philosophy (with its moral agent), not to religion (with its sacred person), nor to biological science (with its natural being).

The Metaphysical Realists

By contrast, the Rationalists, Religionists and Naturalists all believe that the legal person is an expression of some important defining attribute of human nature and therefore it is important to go beyond law to work out what that nature is. They believe that law should find and reflect its subject which exists beyond law (and is variously defined by other disciplines, by philosophy or religion or science). They believe that law finds its subject beyond the legal realm and that law is to be judged by its success at finding and rendering this subject faithfully. The set of beliefs which determines the extra-legal nature of law's subject will depend on where one goes, in a disciplinary sense, to find out about one's subject.

The Rationalists

My first family of realist thinkers who believe that law's person should mirror nature, the 'Rationalists', draws upon what David Lodge has termed 'the humanist or Enlightenment idea of man',[4] which has grown out of the modern Western political and philosophical tradition. The Rationalists are convinced that it is reason which most defines and dignifies us and which law should reflect and preserve. Their paradigmatic legal person is the rational

[2] In *The Personality Conception of the Legal Entity* (Cambridge Mass, Harvard University Press, 1938), Alexander Nekam offers an entire book about the legal person in which he endeavours to empty the term of its metaphysical content and to reserve it for law. He even suggests that, in order to emphasise the pure artifice of law, and its technical mode of personification, we abandon such words as 'person' and 'subject' altogether, and replace them with the term 'legal entity', precisely to get away from any implication which seems to be contained in these words that law deals in natural beings.

[3] HLA Hart, *Definition and Theory in Jurisprudence* (Oxford, Clarendon Press, 1953) 6.

[4] David Lodge, *Consciousness and the Novel* (London, Penguin Books, 2002) 2.

actor, what once was called 'the man of reason'.[5] Creatures that are incapable of reason, some say, should not be a central concern of law because they are incapable of receiving law's communications and responding to them directly. Criminal law theorists tend to think this way about criminal defendants. In their view, it is appropriate to charge people and bring them to law and require them to give a reasoned account of their thoughts and actions because they are taken to be rational legal subjects: thinking agents who have it in their power to deliberate about their actions and to choose to obey the law or to ignore its dictates. Contract lawyers also tend to make the reasoning, even intelligent, subject the centre of their law of agreements.

To Rationalists (who will be the object of a sustained analysis in Chapters 5 and 6), the true legal person is the rational human being; legal rights in essence derive from the human ability to reason. Rights run with mental ability or capacity. The focus here is on human autonomy and independence as the basis of rights and personality. Law is for rational human subjects, for sane rational adults, intelligent agents who because of their capacity to reason can assume moral as well as legal responsibility for their actions and so enter into moral and legal community with others of a similarly rational nature. Only practical reasoners, persons who act for reasons, are the type of people to whom law directly communicates its norms.

Such thinkers necessarily draw a tight circle around their community of legal actors. Though they mostly believe that law does and should protect adults with impaired mental functioning as well as young children, they tend also to assert, without flinching, that such people are not authentic legal persons because they cannot truly participate in a moral and political community of equals.

The Religionists

My second family of realist thinkers, whom I call 'Religionists', believes that a religious idea of human sanctity most defines us and makes us deserving of law's protection and that our sanctity should therefore be fundamental to legal thinking. Creatures without souls are not the proper beneficiaries of law. (These believers in human sanctity form the subject of Chapter 7.) The guiding idea here emanates from the Judeo-Christian religious tradition. The mere presence of human life, it is thought, generates rights because all human life is divinely valued and valuable: we are all sacred. We all have the spark of the divine. (Divine) humanity (defined spiritually not according to the capacity to reason) is the hallmark of law's true person. In this view, all human beings are fitting legal subjects, whether or not they are competent to make their own legal decisions, because all humans are 'ensouled'. Human life alone generates legal claims that arise out of the

[5] This character is the subject of sustained analysis by Genevieve Lloyd in *The Man of Reason: 'Male' and 'Female' in Western Philosophy* (London, Methuen, 1984).

sheer fact of humanity. One does not need to be able to engage directly and in person as a rational agent with other rational agents to be said to be a fitting legal subject. It is sufficient to be human.

This is indeed a highly influential legal view and it is probably the main reason why even the profoundly mentally impaired, even the permanently comatose, are still regarded as legal persons: as legal subjects with rights but without responsibilities. Their loss of cognition does not lead to a loss of personhood. The idea of human sanctity is also the reason why voluntary euthanasia falls within the crime of murder. It also informs the demand, by some, to make foetuses legal persons, legal rights holders, a demand which has yet to find its way into law, though it keeps being pressed and remains politically volatile.

The Naturalists

My third family of realist thinkers comprises the 'Naturalists' who believe that we are best regarded as natural corporeal beings who can feel pleasure and pain, and who live natural mortal lives, and that this is how law should think of us. (The Naturalists are considered in some detail in Chapters 8 and 9.) To some Naturalists, law should preserve and protect our rights as essentially needy animal beings who spend much of our lives in a state of utter dependence. Here the emphasis is on our human frailty. To others, law should preserve our physical sovereignty, what is thought to be our natural bodily autonomy and integrity. Thus, quite different conclusions are drawn from the facts of our physicality. This third way of thinking about our natures is naturalistic and primarily scientific. It tends to advance a modern scientific understanding of ourselves as sophisticated animals, with certain species' needs; it is particularly indebted to evolutionary biology and to the insights of Darwin. However, the moral implications that are drawn from Darwin can vary greatly.

This third group of realist thinkers can be further divided into those who believe that the sentient being that law protects must be human and those who say that species should not count and that sentient non-human animals should also be part of law's community of persons. Indeed, among a number of Naturalist lawyers, emphasis tends to be placed on our commonality with other creatures, rather than on our distinctiveness, and this commonality is thought to provide the natural basis for a common treatment with other similar animals. Humanity is then rejected as the sufficient and necessary condition of being a person. Species are considered morally irrelevant and so implicitly they are legally irrelevant. Those who say that the sentient must be human appear to be influenced by a religious idea of human uniqueness, though there seems also to be a pragmatic concern that the divide between humans and other animals is needed on the grounds of utility. The concern is that the human/animal divide provides the floor, the minimum acceptable level, of moral and legal treatment.

Setting the Boundaries of Personhood

We might say that the first family of realist thinkers, the Rationalists, tends to regard law's true subjects as the intellectually able and tends to concentrate on the sophisticated thinker; the second and third families of realist thinkers tend to embrace the disabled (though not always). In the second and third views, human life (the religious sanctity argument) or human need (the naturalistic argument) generates claims and the fact that such claims may arise out of vulnerability does not necessarily detract from personhood, but rather positively constitutes it. One does not need to be able to engage directly, and in person, as a rational agent with other rational agents to count as a legal person. It is possible to participate in law's community with the aid of another person, such as a guardian. And of course the third group potentially embraces the animal kingdom as well.

As we move from one belief system to the next, the practical effect is to extend the community of legal beings. For each family of realist thinkers describes and defends a boundary or frontier between characters that matter in some important way because of their presumed innate characteristics, and those that do not matter, or at least not in the same way. These understandings of the proper boundaries of legal community are necessarily informed by particular world views, be they philosophical, religious or scientific.

With the Rationalists, the boundary runs between the rational and the irrational. With the Religionists, the boundaries are several: between life and non-life; between the sacred and the profane; and between human and non-human. With the Naturalists, the boundary is pushed out a long way: there can be animals that count and those that do not. Each family of thinkers is therefore engaged in legal and metaphysical boundary setting.

Disciplinary Influences

For each belief system, for each family of thinkers, there is a discipline which tends to be regarded as authoritative, as providing the necessary conventions, concepts and principles to capture and make sense of the nature of being. For Rationalists, who believe that human reason most typifies the legal subject, the authoritative discipline tends to be moral or political philosophy. A direct link is drawn between the legal person and the philosopher's person, with their common emphasis on human agency and the capacity for reason. For Religionists, the authoritative discipline is typically a variety of Christian theology. For Naturalists, the authoritative discipline tends to be biology and especially the principles derived from evolutionary biology. Here, the idea is that we should be regarded as natural creatures with animal dispositions and needs.

To the Legalists, however, law constructs, rather than finds, its subject and that subject is not intended to reflect, in any direct way, real beings in the real world. Therefore, the particular legal conventions which matter, which guide law's understanding of its person, will tend to depend on the legal disciplinary expertise of the Legalist. By contrast, those who subscribe to the belief that law must find its subject (already existing) in the real world beyond law will turn to the norms of the discipline which are thought to have the greatest insight into the human condition.[6]

To the Legalists, law is always engaged in a process of constructing its subjects for legal purposes. Always it is important to remind ourselves of this artificial nature of law, even though law is necessarily directed at a practical human problem and purpose. Legalists will be attentive to the specific norms and purposes of the particular part of law in which the term 'person' is performing its function.[7] They are likely to argue for the autonomy of legal concepts and an essentially interior (to law) analysis of law. Legal concepts, they will say, are to be understood legally. Indeed, a technical understanding of the legal person depends on a grasp of legal technology. This approach to law's subject completely opens up the possibilities of multiple and changing identities and an intellectual freedom from metaphysical thinking about the true nature of persons. One looks to legal purpose, not to human nature, for a proper understanding of legal identity.

Again by way of contrast, the Rationalists, Religionists and Naturalists tend to be engaged in a search for the intrinsic properties of the legal subject: a search for essential *a priori* moral or metaphysical human meaning. Law's task is to match its person to this true person, or true being, variously defined. It follows that there are proper and improper applications of the concept of the person. A good law is one which achieves fidelity to our essential nature, variously conceived. Law's person should be matched to the true non-legal person; the true legal application is therefore true to nature. Inevitably this means that the different families of realist thinkers will encounter great frustration with actual law when it fails to reflect their view of who matters. Animal rights' lawyers, in particular, have lambasted law and jurists for their treatment of animals as property rather than as persons.

Rationalists, Religionists and Naturalists therefore all tend to the view that law must start with some explicit and worked-out view of what we really are, of the metaphysical person,[8] before it applies its own label of legal

[6] These two attitudes to law's subject have their philosophical counterparts. There is the view that we are self-constituted (a strong liberal position) and the view that we are socially constituted.

[7] Eg, Peter Cane in *Responsibility in Law and Morality* (Oxford, Hart Publishing, 2002) adopts this legal sub-disciplinary approach in his analysis of legal and moral responsibility.

[8] By 'metaphysical person' I simply mean that which satisfies the metaphysical requirements of a person, about which there is considerable disagreement, as we will discover in this book. The term 'person', as Poole observes, 'is almost invariably used to collect together those

person or legal subject, especially when it is applying this label to beings that appear to possess some moral status. In other words, law must first establish both the necessary and the sufficient conditions of being a metaphysical person; it must then make further decisions about whether, and if so the extent to which, law should conform with, or deviate from, this conception of the person, according to its own specific purposes, when it is devising its own legal person. For such thinkers, law's task is to find the intrinsic properties of being and to ensure a legal correspondence with them. Law is duty bound to search for the essence of our natures, and then to translate them into law—to match law to life.[9] When it fails to achieve this correspondence, law is failing its true subject.

The Legalists dispute this. They are sceptical of metaphysics and say that this is not the purpose of law. They endeavour to be strictly legal in their characterisation of their subject. For the Legalists, law is positively constitutive of what there is in the legal world; law makes its subject and it does so for essentially legal purposes. Legal persons, in this view, are purely legal abstractions. They do not have arms and legs or human souls or the capacity to reason or a sex or indeed any human or moral or metaphysical attributes. The possession of any of these attributes is extra-legal and so necessarily extraneous to any definition of law's person, legally conceived. The legal person is a creation of law: it is a legal not a moral concept. It is not the legal task to get right our human natures and then provide mirror images of those natures in law. It is not the jurist's job to make sure that law corresponds to some assumed underlying reality.

The Legalists seek to remind us that even when it involves a human being, and not, for example, a corporation, the legal person remains a 'legal fiction', that is:

> A supposition of law that a thing is true, without inquiring whether it is so or not, so that it may have the effect of truth so far as it is consistent with justice.[10]

aspects of our existence which are considered to be most important, and then to designate what in some essential sense we are or, perhaps, ought to be'. Ross Poole, 'On Being a Person' (1996) 74 *Australian Journal of Philosophy* 38.

[9] See Maleiha Malik, 'Faith and the State of Jurisprudence' in Peter Oliver, Sionaidh Douglas Scott and Victor Tadros (eds), *Faith in Law: Essays in Legal Theory* (Oxford, Hart Publishing, 2000) 129 on whether law is reflective or constitutive of reality.

[10] *Mosley and Whiteley's Law Dictionary* (10th edn, Sydney, Butterworths, 1988). Lon Fuller in *Legal Fictions* (Stanford, Stanford University Press, 1967) explained the difference between live and dead fictions. With a live fiction, we are aware of the pretence entailed: that law is treating something that may not be true as if it were true and it is doing this for legal purposes only; because it is legally convenient so to do. With a dead fiction, we no longer have a sense of pretence and metaphor and the term seems to be applied literally and naturally. Fuller observed that the term 'person' was once a live fiction. We were well aware that it was a legal invention. He suggests that we are still aware of the fiction of the person when it takes the form of a corporation, but with the human being the fiction seems to have died. Legalists seek to revive the fiction.

They wish to draw our attention to the metaphorical nature of the legal person; they wish to denaturalise the concept so that we can see again the legal pretences of which it is made.[11]

The Thinkers and their Creation Stories

Still another way of understanding our different families of thinkers is in terms of story telling and creation stories. There are master narratives about who and what we are. These grand stories have different lineages.

For the Religionists, the creation story is the Biblical tale from Genesis[12] in which 'man' is created in God's image and is granted 'a unique place in creation'.[13] It is 'for Him that the heavens and the earth, the sea and all the rest of creation exist'.[14] This is the chronicle of God creating us as spiritual beings. In this account, our essence is our 'spiritual and immortal soul',[15] which distinguishes us from all other phenomena.

Naturalism has Evolution: the story of our descent from other animals. Evolution, as told by Charles Darwin in the late nineteenth century, is the story of our material, species natures which arise in an impersonal universe which is not shaped to, or organised around, our purposes. According to this story, our essence is our biological species' nature.

Rationalism has the creation story of the Social Contract and the emergence of the contractual individual. According to this story, our essence is our reason. The story of contract could be said to be the official, political account of the modern person in law, with its intellectual roots in the writings of Locke and Kant. Here, we have delivered to us the man of reason who contracts his way into law and society, somehow already fully-formed as a contractual agent; or as Lawrence Friedman recently put it: 'Modern law presupposes a society of free-standing, autonomous individuals'.[16] Here, we have modern political and legal beings in whom rights can be invested and who can be held properly to account as moral agents for their plans and their promises. These are the individuals of classical contract law

[11] 'A fiction starts as a pretence, and may, through a process of linguistic development, end as a "fact"'. Lon Fuller in *Legal Fictions* (Stanford, Stanford University Press, 1967) 77. My idea is to reverse this process.

[12] This story is shared by all three of the Abrahamic monotheistic traditions. But the particular interest of this book is the Christian development of this story.

[13] *Catechism of the Catholic Church* (Homebush NSW, St Pauls, 1994) 91.

[14] *Ibid.*

[15] Pontifical Council for Justice and Peace, *Compendium of the Social Doctrine of the Church* (Strathfield NSW, St Pauls Publications, 2004) 64.

[16] Lawrence Friedman, 'Is there a Modern Legal Culture?' (1994) 7 *Ratio Juris* 117, 125 and as quoted in Brian Tamanah, *A General Jurisprudence of Law and Society* (Oxford, Oxford University Press, 2001) 120.

theory.[17] They are also the individuals of influential parts of analytical criminal law theory.[18]

Though intended as an heuristic device of liberal political theory, the story of contract implicitly contains and communicates the idea that we have our own autonomous rational natures before we enter law-governed society. We are imagined as self-created, pre-social, individuals. Law's task is to order and constrain relations between these autonomous persons while guaranteeing and respecting maximum freedom.

So we have two modern tales and one that is traditional. The two modern stories are those of science and of rationalist philosophy. We have a traditional story in the Christian account of human sanctity. All stories, I argue, have currency in law's conception of its person.

Etymology of Persons

The history of the term 'person', its etymology, may help us further to appreciate the different ways of thinking about law's subject as well as the shifting usages of the term over time. The term 'person' once meant a mask, something worn by an actor, and donned and removed according to the part to be played. 'The earliest traceable meaning of persona', according to Duff, 'is a mask, such as Greek and Roman actors regularly wore on the stage'.[19] Over time, it came to denote the actual individual wearing the mask, the real person. As Keeton indicates: 'Originally it meant simply a mask. Later . . . the man who plays it'.[20] Finally, it came to mean, for legal purposes, 'a being capable of sustaining legal rights and duties'.[21] John Austin describes these transformations of meaning as a series of metaphorical shifts. He confirms that the term 'person':

> signified originally, a mask worn by a player, to mark the character he bore in the piece: and is transferred by a metaphor to the character itself. By a further metaphor it is transferred from dramatic character to legal condition. For men as subjects of law are distinguished by conditions, just as players by the characters they present.[22]

[17] See PS Atiyah, *The Rise and Fall of Freedom of Contract* (Oxford, Clarendon Press, 1979).

[18] See Andrew Ashworth, *Principles of Criminal Law* (4th edn, Oxford, Oxford University Press, 2003); John Gardner, 'The Mark of Responsibility' (2003) 23(2) *Oxford Journal of Legal Studies* 157; and Michael Moore, *Placing Blame: a General Theory of the Criminal Law* (Oxford, Clarendon Press, 1997).

[19] PW Duff, *Personality in Roman Private Law* (Cambridge, Cambridge University Press, 1938) 3.

[20] GW Keeton, *The Elementary Principles of Jurisprudence* (London, Sir Isaac Pitman and Sons, 1930) 117.

[21] *Ibid.*

[22] John Austin, *Lectures on Jurisprudence* (R Campbell (ed), 5th edn, London, John Murray, 1885) 164.

Those who say that there is a true metaphysical basis to the legal person, such as reason or sanctity or sentience, that there is a true type of legal being, seem to be saying that we should concentrate on what they take to be the real person behind the mask: that the legal person is, and should be understood as, the real or essential person, variously defined by reason or sanctity or sentience. He is the actual human player, or his essential qualities, rather than the legal part played or the legal mask worn.

The Legalists, however, tend to regard legal personhood more as a mask or as persona: the earliest meaning of person. It is something to be put on and discarded, according to the part played within any given legal relation. It can assume different expressions as it faces other legal persons, other mask-wearers. Legal personality is therefore shifting and variable. It depends on the legal part played and on the type of mask worn in order to play the part. For legal purposes, there is no real person behind the mask. The legal person therefore should not be confused with the flesh-and-blood being playing its legal part, wearing its legal mask, for legal purposes. Nor should it be confused with some essence of being, such as the capacity for reason or the possession of a soul.

The four families of thinkers which form the subject of this book (the Rationalists, Religionists, Naturalists and Legalists) all exercise an influence on general legal principle, but not in equal measure. This will become increasingly apparent as the stories of law's persons unfold. Some ways of thinking about who and what we are, and how law should reflect that understanding, are more powerful than others because they are so much a part of legal orthodoxy. Others represent relatively new and controversial ways of thinking about law's subject. It will also be my purpose to see whether the relative degrees of influence of these different thinkers are appropriate, productive, even just.

I will consider whether one particular way of thinking about our natures is too readily and too uncritically accepted because it has been around for so long. Is another more defensible? Would it produce better, fairer, more equitable results if we thought of ourselves in one way rather than another? Are we too complacent in our current thinking; too resistant to fresh but useful ideas about the human condition and the role they might play in shaping legal thought? Should it even be law's task to try to capture and preserve and protect what it takes to be our essential natures, to mirror life? Or should the life of the legal person remain an independent legal reality, not part of the non-legal world of fact, as the thinkers of the next chapter insist?

3
Strictly Legal Persons

> To regard legal personality as a thing apart from the legal relations, is to commit an error . . . Without the relations . . . there is no more left than the smile of the Cheshire Cat after the cat had disappeared.
>
> Bryant Smith[1]

I begin this inquiry into law's person with the internal point of view. This is the technical lawyer's intellectual approach to the subject of persons: the approach I have called Legalist. I begin here because this is where, I believe, we find the most intellectual and moral promise and also the greatest intellectual and moral frustration. It is also where technical lawyers would tend to start their analysis and where they would also swiftly grind to a halt and no doubt move on to what they would regard as more conceptually fruitful topics, because they would fail to see the rich promise of the subject.

The Legalist approach to the legal person is tantalising because of its insistence on the freedom of lawyers to define their own subject, their own person, without 'the incubus of theory':[2] without being constrained by the demands of naturalism or metaphysics. Great inventive possibilities seem to open up. We seem not to be tied to any one conception of the person. Multiple personality is perfectly possible. The approach is frustrating because of the dogmatism of many of its adherents. Not only do they claim that they are free to define their person as they wish, but they can be adamant that it is wrong, misguided, even poor lawyering, not to exploit this freedom fully. Law, they say, must not be beholden to the other disciplines. It is simply not the business of (Legalist) lawyers to explore the kinships which might exist between law's persons and their non-legal relatives, such as spiritual persons or rational human beings. This sort of exercise is not law; it is sociology or metaphysics.

As a consequence, the Legalist approach has tended to be fairly arid in what it has actually produced as a body of jurisprudence. Indeed, it is difficult to make the Legalist's person into an interesting character, so bent are Legalists on eliminating any trace of humanity or metaphysical speculation from their conception of their person. As we will see, some Legalists prefer to think of their person as virtually a number, a pure abstraction, a technical

[1] Bryant Smith, 'Legal Personality' (1928) 37 *Yale Law Journal* 283, 294.

[2] HLA Hart, *Definition and Theory in Jurisprudence* (Oxford, Clarendon Press, 1953) 6.

device within the great apparatus or machinery of law. 'Legal personality and legal persons are, as it were, mathematical equations devised for the purpose of simplifying legal calculations'.[3]

Legalists thus tend to erect a great conceptual wall between their own technical way of doing things and the more metaphysical approaches favoured by the Rationalists, Naturalists and Religionists. It is so high that they cannot see over it and they do not want to see over it. They are therefore often unwilling to contemplate the way in which other understandings of the person might find their way into law and influence real legal doctrine and real people who are regulated by law, which may thus enrich their understanding of their subject. They are also ill-equipped in their efforts to deflect such influences when they are unwilling to see how those influences work. For example, it is difficult to object to the Religionist's idea of the person and, for example, the idea of human but not animal sanctity, if the influence of this thinking is not first recognised and made explicit.

Legalism becomes arid and dull when it refuses to look beyond the formal intellectual borders of law and consider these other influences. For there is then a failure to appreciate the way metaphysical ideas about what makes us what we are necessarily inform fundamental legal decisions about who should be able to bear rights and duties in different legal relationships. Legalism even becomes irresponsible when it refuses to reflect on whether it is a good thing for Rationalist or Religious or Naturalist ideas of the person to determine the content of legal personality.

In this chapter I will examine the Legalist account of the person, strictly understood, and reveal the energetic endeavour to keep extra-legal influences out of law. In the next chapter I will discuss why it is impossible to keep out such influences from law's conception of its person and why it may even be morally and intellectually irresponsible not to consider the nature of these moral forces and to evaluate them critically.

The Person as a Purely Legal Creation

There are many authoritative legal theorists who have advocated the Legalist approach. For example, in his description of 'the elementary elements of jurisprudence' in 1930, George Keeton asserted that 'a legal system can personify whatever beings or objects it pleases'.[4] John Salmond, whose jurisprudential text, in its many editions, has spanned generations, said that 'a person is any being whom the law regards as capable of rights and duties'.[5] He

[3] FH Lawson, 'The Creative Use of Legal Concepts' (1957) 32 *New York University Law Review* 907, 915.

[4] George W Keeton, *The Elementary Principles of Jurisprudence* (London, Pitman, 1930) 118–19.

[5] John Salmond, *Jurisprudence* (Glanville L Williams (ed), 10th edn, London, Sweet & Maxwell, 1947) 318.

added that '[p]ersons are the substances of which rights and duties are the attributes'.[6] Salmond was keen to impress that '[i]t is *only* in this respect that persons possess juridical significance, and this is the *exclusive* point of view from which personality receives legal definition'[7] (emphasis added). In other words, the only attributes of legal persons are their legal rights and duties; or put another way, we might say that *legal* persons have only a *legal* personality, and no other.

However, perhaps the best exemplar of the Legalistic approach to legal personality is that offered by the influential German-American jurist, Hans Kelsen. In his aptly entitled *Pure Theory of Law*, Kelsen identified and rejected 'the concept of an entity different from, and independent of, the positive legal order'.[8] He also denied 'the existence of . . . legal subject[s] . . . whom the positive law must recognize as subjects of certain rights in order to preserve [its] character as true law'.[9]

Kelsen is indeed emphatically Legalistic in his portrayal of the legal person. He is intent on removing any idea that law's person should be thought of as a natural or metaphysical person. He therefore offers a particularly astringent account of law's person. And yet there is something almost magical in what Kelsen sees as law's power to endow with legal life:

> That the human being is a legal subject (subject of rights and obligations) means nothing else . . . but that human behaviour is the content of legal obligations and rights—nothing else than that a human being is a person or has personality . . . A legal person is the unity of a complex of legal obligations and rights. Since these obligations and rights are constituted by legal norms (more correctly: *are* these legal norms), the problem of 'person' is in the last analysis the problem of the unity of a complex of norms . . . The so-called physical person, then, is not a human being, but the personified unity of the legal norms that obligate or authorise one and the same human being. It is not a natural reality but a social construction created by the science of law—an auxiliary concept in the presentation of legally relevant facts. In this sense a physical person is a juristic person.[10]

Thus, Kelsen maintains a general insistence that the legal person does not reside outside the law, is never antecedent to and independent of law, but is always a creature of law.

As Roscoe Pound elucidates Kelsen's view of the person, it entails 'only a technical personification of a complex of norms, a focal point of imputation which gives unity to certain complexes of rights and duties'.[11] It is '[m]ore or less arbitrarily [that] the law individualizes certain parts of the legal order, establishing a certain unity in the rights and obligations

[6] *Ibid.*
[7] *Ibid.*
[8] Hans Kelsen, *Pure Theory of Law* (Berkley, University of California Press, 1967) 170.
[9] *Ibid.*
[10] *Ibid* 173–4.
[11] Roscoe Pound, *Jurisprudence* (St Paul, Minn, West Publishing, 1959) vol 4, 259.

pertaining to them';[12] or as Margaret Davies interprets Kelsen's person: 'it is a conceptual unity, not a moral or living entity'.[13]

Legal persons, in this view, are purely legal abstractions. For the sake of conceptual purity and accuracy, we must eliminate any sense that legal persons have arms and legs or human souls or the capacity to reason or indeed any human or moral or metaphysical attributes. The possession of any of these attributes would be extra-legal and so necessarily extraneous to any definition of law's person. The legal person is a pure creation of law.

As Alexander Nekam insists, 'those to whom the law attributes such a legal personality possess it entirely by the force of the law and not by nature'.[14] Indeed:

> [t]here is nothing in the notion of the subject of rights which in itself would, necessarily, connect it with human personality, or even with anything experimentally existing.[15]

For this reason, Nekam recommends the abolition of the term 'person' and its replacement with the term 'entity'.

Bryant Smith is another who presses for this strictly legal view of personality: a view which vigorously eschews metaphysics. Legal personality, for Smith, is a formal 'capacity for legal relations';[16] it is 'an abstraction of which legal relations are predicated, or . . . a name for the condition of being a party to legal relations'.[17] Clearly he is trying to get flesh-and-blood people and their dignifying or debasing characteristics out of the picture. It is only as rights holders or duty bearers that legal persons exist and relate to one another. Rights and duties are therefore the building blocks of legal relations and the sole constituent parts of legal persons.

We should therefore not think of the recipient of the grant of personality, the legal person, as a real (that is, non-legal) person, according to Smith and Kelsen. Rather, the legal person is purely 'an abstraction', a legal idea—not a being, or an individual, or even a thing. When there are legal relations, then there are necessarily legal persons involved, for only persons can be parties to legal relations. The one is logically entailed by the other. Legal personality, Smith insists, is 'one of the major abstractions of legal science, like title, possession, right and duty'.[18]

Richard Tur reminds us that it is this highly abstract, strictly legal, definition of the legal person which is pressed upon any new student of

[12] Roscoe Pound, *Jurisprudence* (St Paul, Minn, West Publishing, 1959) vol 4, 259.

[13] Margaret Davies, *Asking the Law Question: the Dissolution of Legal Theory* (3rd edn, Pyrmont, Law Book Co, 2008) 7.

[14] Alexander Nekam, *The Personality Conception of the Legal Entity* (Cambridge, Mass, Harvard University Press, 1938) 24.

[15] *Ibid* 26.

[16] Smith, above n 1, at 283.

[17] *Ibid* 284.

[18] *Ibid* 293.

jurisprudence (and, incidentally, has tended to be the kiss of death to the subject). Thus:

> [t]he first thing a jurisprudence student coming to analyses of legal concepts is told with respect to legal personality is that the philosophical notion of a person as an actual, or perhaps potential, rational individual is to be utterly disregarded, since it can only be misleading ... In a sense then the concept of legal personality is wholly formal. It is an empty slot that can be filled by anything that can have rights or duties.[19]

Law as a Closed System

Notwithstanding the dramatic political history of legal personality, jurists of the strict school, the strict Legalists, promote a definition of law's person that seems to empty it of any human or metaphysical content, and when asked for a definition of the person, this is typically what any lawyer will endeavour to achieve (though often with imperfect success). She will try to give the term its most formal Legalistic sense. Thus, she is likely to say that the legal person is a legal term of art, a legal device, and that, strictly conceived, the term refers only to a legal construct characterised purely by an ability to act in law. She is likely to add that this legal abstraction does not have to assume a human form: it is axiomatic that corporations are legal persons. She will also point out that states have personality, which enables them to be legal actors. Ships and idols have also, famously, been accorded the status of legal persons.[20] And it would be perfectly possible to confer legal personality on autonomous electronic devices.[21]

In this strict account, legal personality is taken to be purely the ability to participate in legal relations. That which is recognised to possess this capacity is a legal person. 'Legal person', therefore, is not a moral term invoked by philosophers with its connotations of agency or moral status. Nor is it the term used in ordinary language to connote a human being. Rather, legal personality exists essentially as an abstract capacity to function in law, a capacity which is endowed by law because it is convenient for law to have such a creation. The construct of the legal person and its legal personality is purely a matter of legal expedience. The legal person has no moral or empirical content, thus defined. It relies on neither biological nor psychological predicates; nor does it refer back to any particular social or moral idea of a person and it is to be completely distinguished from those

[19] Richard Tur, 'The "Person" in Law' in Arthur Peacocke and Grant Gillett (eds), *Persons and Personality: a Contemporary Inquiry* (Oxford, Basil Blackwell, 1987) 121.

[20] *Pramatha Nath Mullick v Pradyamna Kumar Mullick* (1925) L Rep 5.

[21] For an extensive discussion of this possibility see Emily M Weitzenboeck, 'Electronic Agents and the Formation of Contracts' (2001) 9(3) *International Journal of Law and Information Technology* 204, 211.

philosophical conceptions of the person which emphasise the importance of reason or intrinsic human value.

In this account, the legal person is a purely formal legal concept—a fiction, a device, a construct, an invention—and legal personality comprises the variable legal rights and duties which are, or can be, exercised within purely legal relations. This view is nicely expressed by Bryant Smith who asserts that 'without the relations . . . there is no more left than the smile of the Cheshire Cat after the cat had disappeared';[22] or, according to Kocourek:

> [l]egal personality is the sum total of the legal relations of a person. A person, therefore, in the law is a mere ideal or conceptual point of reference . . . The person . . . is an irreducible juristic subsistent. It comes into existence and goes out of existence. During existence it has only one quality—the capacity of attracting legal relations . . . In a word, a person has a capacity for rights and ligations. The legal relations which the person attracts are the person's personality.[23]

From this it follows that there is no essence to the legal person. Consequently, legal capacities possessed and exercised within legal relations depend on specific legal purposes which vary according to the particular, specifically legal, concerns of the parties and their particular circumstances. They are not determined by the intrinsic character of antecedent subjects, subjects who precede law, whose character is formed before they come to law. Rather, the legal person is fully a creature of law and, within law, legal capacities vary according to legal relation.

Jurists who hold this stringent Legalist view of the person tend to assert the complete separation of legal persons from other senses of the person. They say that the legal person is pure legal abstraction and implicitly nothing to do with Religious, Rationalist or Naturalist views of the person. As David Derham, for example, has expressed this abstract quality of persons:

> Just as the concept 'one' in arithmetic is essential to the logical system developed and yet is not one something (eg apple or orange, etc), so a legal system (or any system perhaps) must be provided with a basic unit before legal relationships can be devised . . . The legal person is the unit or entity adopted. For the logic of the system it is just as much a pure 'concept' as 'one' in arithmetic. It is just as independent from a human being as one is from an 'apple'.[24]

Law is a self-enclosed system, in this view, which does not look elsewhere for its meaning. And as Lawson suggests:

> We must first note and emphasize the separateness and completeness of what we may call the legal plane . . . the instruments with which the business lawyer works do not belong to the world of fact . . . Legal personality, estates and contracts are

[22] Smith, above n 1, at 294.
[23] A Kocourek, *Jural Relations* (2nd edn, Indianapolis, Bobbs-Merrill Company, 1928) 292.
[24] DP Derham, 'Theories of Legal Personality' in Leicester Webb (ed), *Legal Personality and Political Pluralism* (Melbourne, Melbourne University Press, 1958) 1, 5.

> parts of a world of their own, which is in some way related to the world of fact but is separate from them. It is an artificial world whose members are to some extent arbitrarily, though not irrationally, created to serve certain purposes. Thus they can be defined with fair exactness, much more satisfactorily than the facts of everyday life.[25]

Because legal artifice generates the legal person, it is wrong to characterise the corporation as an artificial person and the human being as a natural person. As Bryant Smith maintains:

> The legal personality of a corporation is just as real and no more real than the legal personality of a normal human being. In either case it is an abstraction.[26]

Consequently:

> it is as correct to speak of the legal personateness of a human being as artificial, fictional, conceded by law, etc, as it is so to describe the legal personateness of a fund, a purpose, a corporation, or an idol.[27]

We are dealing with something which exists 'only in contemplation of law'.[28]

There is no moral essence to the legal person, in this view, and those who have sought to find one are misguided. To Derham, 'the seeds of difficulty in most of the great arguments of the past' lie here:

> in the failure to distinguish, on the one hand, between the roles played by certain legal terms with the consequent search for the 'essence' of a non-existent 'thing' for which some terms were wrongly assumed to stand, and, on the other, between the function of the term 'legal person' in the logic of the law and the 'things' to which the term is validly applied.[29]

Thus, it is futile to search for something apart from, and in addition to, the legal entity, which as it were becomes the legal entity, by law's edict, or which has this status ascribed to it. There is nothing or no one which bears the rights and duties which constitute someone or something as a person in law. There is no separate moral subject of rights, even though this is often how we talk of legal persons. Legal personality is therefore not a quality or attribute of a separate free-standing subject: 'This substance [this subject]', as Kelsen explains, 'is not an additional entity'.[30]

We are, in other words, tricked by a grammar of subject and predicates into thinking that the legal person is something other than a pure idea of law. To return to Kelsen: 'The person exists only insofar as he "has" duties

[25] Lawson, above n 3, at 913.
[26] Smith, above n 1, at 293.
[27] Derham, above n 24, at 6.
[28] Lawson, above n 3, at 914.
[29] Derham, above n 24, at 7–8.
[30] Hans Kelsen, *General Theory of Law and State* (New York, Russell and Russell, 1945) 93.

and rights; apart from them the person has no existence whatsoever'.[31] For Kelsen, persons are only the rights and duties: there is no one who possesses them; or as Richard Tur has expressed the strict idea of the person: the concept, thus understood, is 'wholly formal . . . an empty slot'.[32] More recently, Peter Cane has likewise affirmed that:

> legal personality is not a matter of physical and mental attributes. Human beings are not legal persons by virtue of their physical and mental characteristics, but by virtue of meeting the formal criteria for personhood laid down by the law . . . it is the law, not nature, that tells us what entities are subject to law.[33]

Construed thus, in their strict sense, we might say that legal persons are reduced to 'mathematical equations devised for the purpose of simplifying legal calculations'.[34]

The Legal Person as Legal Language Use

In his inaugural lecture at Oxford, HLA Hart analysed legal concepts in a slightly different way, though one that also emphasised the difference between the legal and the non-legal spheres of meaning. He observed that legal words:

> like 'corporation' 'right' or 'duty'. . . do not have the straightforward connection with counterparts in the world of fact which most ordinary words have and to which we appeal in our definition of ordinary words. There is nothing which simply 'corresponds' to these legal words and when we try to define them we find that the expressions we tender in our definition specifying kinds of persons, things, qualities, events . . . are never precisely the equivalent of these legal words though often connected with them in some way.[35]

Hart's concern, therefore, was not to declare a separation between legal and everyday meanings of words, for he acknowledged that there is indeed a connection between the two. Rather, his intention was to capture the specifically legal dimensions of the legal terms which do not have a counterpart in the world of fact. Hart referred to 'the great anomaly of legal language—our inability to define its crucial words in terms of ordinary factual counterparts'.[36]

Legal language, for Hart, had 'distinctive characteristics' which demanded 'a special method of elucidation'.[37] He endorsed Bentham in

[31] Hans Kelsen, *General Theory of Law and State* (New York, Russell and Russell, 1945) 94.

[32] Tur, above n 19, at 121.

[33] Peter Cane, *Responsibility in Law and Morality* (Oxford, Hart Publishing, 2002) 2.1.4.

[34] Lawson, above n 3, at 915.

[35] Hart, above n 2, at 5.

[36] *Ibid* 7–8.

[37] *Ibid* 8.

his view that 'we must never take [legal] words alone, but consider whole sentences in which they play their characteristic role'.[38] We should not 'hammer away at single words'.[39] It followed that such a fundamental term as 'person' in law was not to be understood by a concerted effort to glean the meaning of the term on its own: it was only to be made sense of within the context of utterances in which it is doing its legal work.

For Hart, the fundamental point is that words such as 'right', 'duty' or 'corporation' (ie corporate person) do not 'stand for or describe anything but a distinct function' and thus it is senseless to abstract them from the context in which they are performing that function.[40] He explicitly rejects the dictionary-style definition of terms, which entails a use of synonyms. Instead, he advocates taking a sentence in which our puzzling legal term, such as 'corporate person', 'plays its characteristic role' and working out 'how it is used' and the conditions which make the entire legal utterance or sentence in which our term is placed true.[41] It follows that a term such as 'person' cannot be understood alone: its meaning derives from *legal* use within *legal* context. Thus, the meaning of 'Smith & Co Ltd', a notional corporate person, is to be found in 'a description of how, and under what conditions, the names of corporate bodies are used in practice'.[42] It is not to be derived from 'the search for what it is that the name taken alone describes, for what *it* stands for, for what *it* means'.[43]

The very idea that there must be some essence to the personality of the corporation, to Hart, is an artefact of asking the wrong question. It derives from the common but false assumption that there is and must be something for which it (corporate personality) stands. When we study group or even individual personality in context, and in use, however, we discover 'that there are many varieties of widely different conditions . . . under which we talk in this unifying personal way'.[44] The 'cardinal principle' for Hart is 'that legal words can only be elucidated by considering the conditions under which statements in which they have their characteristic use are true'.[45]

Hart and Wittgenstein

Hart was writing very much in the tradition of the ordinary-language philosopher Wittgenstein, who also advocated the study of concepts by examining the work they did in real, everyday, social and linguistic settings.

38 *Ibid.*
39 *Ibid.*
40 *Ibid* 12–13.
41 *Ibid.*
42 *Ibid* 18.
43 *Ibid.*
44 *Ibid* 24.
45 *Ibid* 28.

Wittgenstein explicitly rejected the notion (which he had put forward himself in his earlier work) that concepts name reality: that they paint a picture, through words, of what is 'out there' in the non-linguistic world. He rejected the idea that terms or propositions are more or less accurate pictures of the world (his picture theory of reality developed in *The Tractatus*).[46] Rather, he argued that any term, such as 'person', could only be understood within the settings in which it was used and when all of its usages were considered together we had the full meaning of that term, or at least all that we could ever know of it. To think that there was more to a term than its use was to become philosophically confused.

Conceiving of language as a type of game, with rules and conventions, Wittgenstein said that we must consider the various uses of any given word in all the contexts in which it is actually put to work; in all the games it is played. 'Here the term "language-game"', as he elucidated, 'is meant to bring into prominence the fact that the speaking of language is part of an activity, or of a form of life'.[47] The meaning of a term resides in its actual applications in real social contexts—in the real conversations of real people. In different social contexts, within different language games, the same term might perform a different function; it might carry different connotations or seem quite dramatically different. And these differences should be attended to if we were to understand the richness of the term. However, the different usages would bear a 'family resemblance', and these commonalities of meaning were also a part of the term.[48]

As Wittgenstein famously declared, when words are taken out of the situation in which they have a job to do, 'language goes on holiday'.[49] By this he meant that language ceases to make meaning if it is taken out of its operational setting. It idles, stalls and may even stop altogether.[50]

[46] He came to reject the sense we might have that '[t]hought, language, now appear to us as the unique correlate, picture, of the world. These concepts: proposition, language, thought, world, stand in line one behind the other, each equivalent to each'. *Philosophical Investigations* (GEM Anscombe (tr), Oxford, Blackwell, 1953) para 96.

[47] *Ibid* para 23.

[48] Wittgenstein explained that 'family resemblances' entail 'a complicated network of similarities overlapping and criss-crossing: sometimes overall similarities, sometimes similarities of detail'. *Ibid* paras 66–67. He urged us to ask ourselves 'How did we learn the meaning of this word ("good" for instance)? From what sort of examples? In what language games? Then it will be easier for you to see that the word must have a family of meanings'. *Ibid* para 77.

[49] As Wittgenstein expressed it, 'philosophical problems arise when language goes on holiday. And here we may indeed fancy naming to be some remarkable act of mind, as it were a baptism of an object'. *Ibid* para 38.

[50] 'Naming', said Wittgenstein, 'appears as a queer connection of a word with an object. And you really get such a queer connexion when the philosopher tries to bring out the relation between name and thing by staring at an object in front of him and repeating a name or even the word "this" innumerable times.' (*ibid*); a simple exercise, which Wittgenstein suggested that we try for ourselves, and which demonstrates the point nicely, is the repetition of a familiar word. Soon it seems strange and unfamiliar and the meaning begins to disappear.

In his inaugural lecture, HLA Hart was recommending an approach to the interpretation of legal terms which is remarkably similar to that proposed by Wittgenstein.[51] Hart suggested, like Wittgenstein, that we should only look at any given legal term within legal utterances, or at least consider whole sentences in which the term is characteristically placed. We must then work out the legal conditions which make that sentence true in law. Also like Wittgenstein, Hart said that jurists should not 'hammer away at single words'.[52] However, in Legalistic fashion, Hart steers us towards the distinctively legal rules and conventions which give legal terms their meaning and, in effect, away from the larger social settings of those terms.

Hart was critical of those who sought to make legal terms correspond to some eternal truth (about a given term) which is thought to reside outside of law. Lawyers should not seek to find some counterpart to their terms in the world of fact, the world outside of law. Instead, they should concentrate on the peculiarly legal conventions which give sense to legal terms in their legal setting. Implicitly, Hart was trying to free law and its terms from what Dewey described as the great mass of non-legal considerations which can feed into legal meaning. Lawyers, according to Hart, should stick to their legal language games.

Hart was therefore pressing both for the artificial legal nature of the concept of the (corporate) person and also insisting that if lawyers were to understand this legal nature of the person (in its corporate form), they had to consider all the various uses to which it was put within the law. Implicitly, he advocated a study of legal language games in which the term 'corporate person' played a part. He appreciated that as a formal legal device, law's person serves many legal ends in many different legal contexts. It creates different legal endowments for different legal purposes.

Hart's (and Wittgenstein's) advice to us to attend to the actual uses of our concepts, as we lawyers use them, and not to search for some deep underlying metaphysical meaning, some essence which does not reside in use, does seem to entail a fairly robust form of Legalism. After all, we are being asked to attend to what lawyers do and to lawyer's conditions of meaning, and once we have examined legal uses, then it seems we should be satisfied that that is all there is. In the case of the legal person, there is no true natural or supernatural person, lurking in the background, giving a lie to our uses. This 'incubus of theory' should not drive our analysis. This seems to be Hart's message.

But if metaphysical meanings of the person, be they Rationalist, Religionist, Naturalist, have already entered the legal lexicon, as I will suggest

The meaning of the word resides in the work it does, not in the term itself as a series of letters or a sound or as the perfect match with some non-linguistic thing or idea.

[51] Though Hart makes no reference to Wittgenstein, the influence is clearly there.

[52] Hart, above n 2, at 8.

they have, then such metaphysical uses *are* legal uses. If, for example, judges invoke human sanctity (as they commonly do) when they are considering whether to endow any given human being or entity with rights, then Religious meanings of the person have already found their way into law. The Religious person is already conditioning the meaning of the Legalist's person and it is poor scholarship, especially according to the lights of Hart, not to consider this Religious manifestation of the person within law. For the Religious meaning is not just tempering Legal meaning; it *is* legal meaning; or, rather, it is one of a rich variety of legal meanings. To press the point home: if we neglect this spiritual being (or Naturalist or Rationalist being for that matter), we are not attending to legal use. We are neglecting significant legal manifestations of the person.

Keeping the Legal Legal

In all these analyses of the legal person, we have seen a concerted endeavour to keep the legal legal, to retain the essentially legal character of law's person, and thus to assert the intellectual and conceptual autonomy of law. One can understand this, perhaps. After all, if lawyers are not in charge of their most basic term, then where is the independence and authority of law to be found?

The declaration of legal autonomy has been asserted repeatedly and over a number of years. The idea that law coins its own terms, and most importantly, gives its own particular legal meaning to its legal subject, remains the currency among most technically-inclined lawyers. And as Richard Tur asserts, it is the standard fare given to the law student.[53] It is no doubt intended to impress the student with the 'Alice in Wonderland' quality of law and its concepts. (Hey Presto: law can deem into being whatever it likes. It is not constrained by Naturalism.) But at the same time, this concerted Legalism seems to reduce law's person to a dry, sterile and artificial character: all law and no life.

But if we think carefully about the Legalistic message of Hart, a man who had little time for metaphysical speculation, then even the more technically-inclined lawyer is bound to recognise the richness and variability of meaning of her legal subject which necessarily derives from extra-legal sources. Our Legalist is failing to draw out of the concept of the person some of its most interestingly creative and vital qualities if she refuses to acknowledge all the relevant influences on its operations. By denying the moral, the natural, the spiritual, even the rational dimensions of her subject, she also effectively depopulates law. She takes out the real people and replaces them with cardboard cut-outs (boring the student of jurisprudence witless in the

[53] Tur, above n 19.

mean time). She also fails to take advantage of the strategic alliances which might be made between law and the other disciplines.

By this I mean that the agnosticism of Legalists about all metaphysical positions need not stop them from invoking such positions when they are thought to be well suited to legal purpose and may help to achieve a just result. Such alliances, I suggest, are in fact already in place, as will be seen in the later chapters on Rationalism, Religionism and Naturalism. We might also say that the legal concept is already contaminated and so it is incumbent on the good technical lawyer to take account of these points of contamination (as they might see them) and to know them well and to use them well.

As I plan to show in the next chapter, things need not be like this; there need not be this Legalistic antipathy to all things metaphysical. It is not particularly helpful to retain a dogmatic position of legal isolationism, thereby neglecting important features of the concept of the person. And indeed, there is a serious problem of intellectual and moral myopia when it is so confidently asserted that law can retain its independence from extra-legal conceptions of the person.

4
Loosening the Strictures

No picture should be allowed to become an imaginative monoculture.

Mary Midgley[1]

The promise offered by Legalism is considerable. It resides partly in the claim that legal persons can be whatever and whoever law is willing to let them be. There is room for immense legal creativity: for a proliferation of personality. Within law, it would seem, we are permitted to assume a wide variety of personae. The artificiality of law's device of the person permits this legal invention.

To put this as plainly as possible, and this is what a Legalist would say, there is no formal legal reason why for some legal purposes I might not be a legal man and for others a legal woman. There is no legal reason why for some legal purposes my kidney might not be regarded as a piece of tradeable property (so that I can sell it to someone who needs it) and for other legal purposes as an intrinsic part of me, of my person, and hence protected by the offences against the person, such as assault and murder. There is no legal reason why a foetus might not be regarded as a person for the purposes of homicide law but as a part of the person of the pregnant woman for the purposes of protecting *her* from a serious assault (in some places it is already); that is, the injury to the foetus can legally be regarded as injury to the woman for the purposes of one law, but as injury to the foetus itself for the purposes of another. All this is possible.

But clearly the willingness of law-makers to countenance such mutability of personality, to permit such fluidity of legal being, will depend on what *they* think legal persons are and should be, and this is where philosophy or religion or views of nature necessarily intrude. Law-makers do not, nor cannot, simply content themselves with the Legalistic assertion that the legal person is a legal device which can have any content and then proceed to personify it with complete licence. Always there is a decision to be made about who and what is to count for any particular legal purpose and this is a normative, not just a factual decision. So my point, which will be developed over the course of this book, is that Rationalism, Religionism and Naturalism necessarily inform legal decisions about legal personality—about who can be what and when and why—because they are such powerful ways

[1] Mary Midgley, *Science and Poetry* (London and New York, Routledge, 2001) xi.

of thinking about moral and legal existence, and they supply the rationale for making 'x' count in law, but not 'y'.

For example, to give content to laws about pregnant women or foetuses or animals or organs, law-makers and interpreters necessarily draw on these other ideas about the nature of humanity. Laws criminalising abortion make little sense unless we recognise that late-term foetuses are sometimes regarded as intrinsically valuable: as possessing a perceived value which typically derives from a religious idea of human sanctity. And laws which treat animals as property make little sense unless we recognise the powerful cultural ideas which countenance this approach to the animal world; especially Religionism, but also Rationalism (animals are not thought to be intelligent enough to be considered persons).

In this chapter, I will consider further the creative conceptual possibilities of the Legalist's person: why and how the technical concept itself permits such flexibility of legal being. I will consider also why and how the concept necessarily remains open to outside influences, despite the protestations of the strict Legalists. I will examine some case law which demonstrates the efforts of Legalist judges both to exploit these creative possibilities and to oust what they see as a constraining metaphysics or naturalism from their concept of the person, as well as their constant mindfulness of their presence. These cases show well how the non-legal necessarily keeps intruding on the legal. Finally, I will begin to consider some of the ways in which certain metaphysical understandings of the person have tied and limited the concept of the person, often in highly illiberal ways. In the making of real empirical legal persons, strong metaphysical understandings of the person, often of a religious nature, have ensured the endowment of some beings with moral and social status, and so with the ability to act in law, and the positive denial of status to others.

The Legal Person as Cluster Concept

An important reason why the legal person can be said to have a highly variable and flexible character (indeed, why it is a highly creative term) is because it is a cluster concept. By this I mean that legal personality is made up of a cluster of things: specifically, it comprises single or multiple clusters of rights and/or duties, depending on the nature and purpose of the particular legal relation. Rights and duties, which effectively make the person, can come in thick and thin bundles, in larger and smaller clusters, which means that we are actually different legal persons in different legal contexts.

It follows that personality can be analysed in much the same way as the concept of property, from which it is typically distinguished.[2] Bundles or

[2] It is often said that that which is person is not property and the converse is also said to apply, though the corporation puts pay to this stark distinction.

clusters of rights and duties are said to make up the idea of property;[3] so too bundles or clusters of rights and duties make up the idea of the legal person.[4] Both personality and property may therefore be viewed as cluster concepts. They entail the possession of transient clusters of rights and duties arising in shifting legal relations. As Richard Tur observes, '[t]he law will ascribe legal personality to two entities even where they bear different clusters of rights and duties'.[5] And indeed, 'it is conceivable that two entities, both of which are legal persons, might have no rights or duties in common at all'.[6]

Personality and property are therefore not to be confused with a fixed, solid entity consisting of stable matter, which often bears the same term, be it a thing, such as a book, in the case of property or a human being in the case of personality. Both property and personality can be disaggregated into their constituting rights and duties, thus undermining the idea that property is something solid you have and hold and that a person is a unified, singular, human, corporeal being. Both property and personality thus can be viewed in this creative, conceptual manner: as an assemblage of changing rights and duties within a host of legal relations.

Sometimes we are endowed with a rich and robust legal personality; other times we are hardly there at all. Thus, there are thin and thick versions of the concept. The rational, adult actor possesses the biggest bundle of rights and also the greatest bundle of duties, producing a richness of legal personality. By contrast the personality of the foetus is thin; some would say non-existent. So too the owner of property can be said to possess the biggest bundle of property rights and so the best set of property interests: to have a richness of property.

Moreover, there can be a blending of the two concepts of personality and property; and a continuum may even be observed, from one to the other. Corporations, of course, provide a prominent example of an entity of hybrid status in that they are formally both property and persons.

Division Between Persons and Property

A dimension of legal personality which has been only weakly explored by jurists is its relationship to its conceptual opposite, property. And yet it is

[3] For a classic statement of the various rights and duties (the sticks in the bundle) that constitute property, see AM Honore, 'Ownership' in AG Guest (ed), *Oxford Essays in Jurisprudence* (Oxford, Oxford University Press, 1961).

[4] For a recent discussion of the bundle theory of property, see Margaret Davies and Ngaire Naffine, *Are Persons Property? Legal Debates about Property and Personality* (Aldershot, Ashgate 2001).

[5] Richard Tur, 'The "Person" in Law' in Arthur Peacocke and Grant Gillett (eds), *Persons and Personality: a Contemporary Inquiry* (Oxford, Basil Blackwell, 1987) 121, 122.

[6] *Ibid.*

difficult to make sense of the concept of the legal person without regard to this other great legal concept, and certainly we cannot make sense of the status of animals without knowing a little about property.

The distinction between 'personality' and 'property' is perhaps the most fundamental division of legal matter, for these are the two major concepts employed by law to classify the world. The distinction is conventionally traced back to ancient Rome. It is in the Roman codification of law that we first find elaborated the concept of the person as a legal category and we also find the concept of the person distinguished from other legal categories, especially the concept of property.

The Romans drew a basic distinction between *ius publicum* and *ius privatum*. Public law pertained to the relationship between the individual and the state and included what we now call criminal law, constitutional law, ecclesiastical law and administrative law. Private law pertained to the relationship between individuals and included family law, the law of obligations, succession and property. The law of persons fell within private law. Within their private law, the Romans (under Justinian and his predecessor Gaius) created a tripartite division of law into persons, things and actions. As Thomas has expressed it, the law considered 'the persons involved, the subject matters in issue and the remedies available'.[7] The law of persons was:

> a catalogue of the classes of person capable of being affected by Roman Law and how they enter and leave their categories; the law of things [was] a list of rights and duties that such persons may have, their creation and extinction; and the law of actions [was] the various legal processes and where they apply.[8]

It is often said that the concepts of the person and of property are now mutually exclusive; that there is a neat cleavage of the legal world into two mutually exclusive categories: person and property; being and thing.[9] It is thought that a person, of her very nature, is not property, because persons can never be owned, and that if something is property, it is not a person. But this proposition requires significant qualification. Corporations are created as both persons and property and so have a dual status. Thus, they can both trade as persons and be traded as property. But humans too can possess an ambiguous legal status, especially at the margins of life.

As we will also discover, the legal rights and duties that make someone count as a person and something count as property are shifting and variable. Persons can sometimes bear some of the features of property (this has been said both of foetuses and pregnant women) and certain types of property (notably animals) are in some very limited respects protected in the manner of persons. Though it is often said that that which is a person

[7] JAC Thomas, *Textbook of Roman Law* (Amsterdam, North Holland, 1976) 66.
[8] *Ibid.*
[9] This is a view which is specifically disputed in Davies and Naffine, above n 4.

cannot be property and that which is property is mere thing,[10] it is not unusual for elements of personality to find their way into property and also, reciprocally, for persons to assume some of the characteristics of property. In fact, it is possible to count as a person in some legal contexts, but to be treated as something akin to property in others, or simply not to exist in law at all. As Margaret Davies has observed, 'the distinction between persons and property . . . is not a bright line, but is rather contextual and flexible'.[11]

Chameleon Nature of Personality Strictly Conceived

The legal person, understood as a cluster concept, is really quite remarkable. The beauty of this Legalistic account of personality is that it is flexible and instrumental. It is not, of necessity, tied to any one idea of a person. The concept can be put to different ends; indeed, identity can be multiple: the one individual can be a different person (a different bundle of rights and duties to be more precise) in different relations. For some legal purposes, they may barely exist. For others, they may be in the full flush of personality.

Thus, legal persons can, in theory, conceptually include animals, foetuses, the dead, the environment, corporations, states, indeed whatever law finds convenient to include in its community of persons. As one Legalist claimed, with glee:

> All that is necessary for the existence of the person is that the lawmaker . . . should decide to treat it as a subject of rights or other legal relations. Once this point has been reached, a vista of unrestricted liberty opens up before the jurist, unrestricted, that is, by the need to make a person resemble a man or collection of men.[12]

I am not convinced that the liberty is as unrestricted as Lawson seems to suggest. Indeed, the point of this book is to show the ties between legal persons and other people's persons. But, still, there is no denying the remarkable freedom which resides within the structure of the concept of the person, potentially.

Strictly speaking, there is no reason why animals cannot be persons in this formal sense. The endowment of even one right or duty would entail recognition of their ability to enter into legal relations and so be persons, even though a human would necessarily be required to enforce any right.[13] But

[10] Corporations, of course, provide a prominent exception to this rule as they are formally both property and persons.

[11] Margaret Davies, *Property: Meanings, Histories, Theories* (Abingdon, Routledge-Cavendish, 2008) 80.

[12] FH Lawson, 'The Creative Use of Legal Concepts' (1957) 32 *New York University Law Review* 907.

[13] For the view that animals may have already acquired some of the rights we associate with persons, see Cass Sunstein, 'Standing for Animals (with Notes on Animal Rights)' (2000) 47 *UCLA Law Review* 1335. We will return to Sunstein in Chapter 8.

this is perfectly possible: babies and other human legal incompetents always rely on a competent other to enforce their rights.

The human dead may certainly already be regarded as persons in this sense: after all, testamentary succession depends on the observance of the wishes of the dead.[14] But perhaps even more indicative of the personality of the dead human is the legal insistence that consent has been obtained from the deceased (obviously while still living) before their body parts and fluids, including sperm, are removed and used.[15] Foetuses too can be regarded as persons, though their rights are generally said to crystallise at birth.[16]

What tempers all these decisions about legal status, and constrains the hand of judges, is not the formal properties of the cluster concept of the person. Rather, it is the presence within all these legal determinations of other considerations of a moral, metaphysical and even political sort. These considerations are actually a part of legal reasoning. They are part of the conditions of use, as Hart would put it. Sometimes they will be made explicit; other times they will remain silent premises. For example, if there is a deep conviction that animals are inappropriate subjects for legal rights (because they cannot reason or because they do not have souls) then that conviction will form part of the legal determination about their status; or by way of another example, if women are not considered the right sort of people to be public persons, then that conviction will form a part of the determination about their legal status.

The Legalist's Person in the Courtroom

To give a sense of the flexible operations of this cluster concept of the person in the courtroom, and also of the necessary impingement of meta-

[14] According to Richard Tur, '[w]e do not have . . . any clear idea of when a legal person . . . ceases to exist . . . Nor should we regard physical death as marking the termination of a legal life, if for no other reason than the existence of a legal will, through which the physically dead person seeks to control the disposition of his property'. See Tur, above n 5, at 123.

[15] In the case of wills, it is arguable that the living executor, trustee or beneficiary is the holder of any legal claim by the estate, not the dead person herself. However, the legislative prohibition of the removal of tissue, post-mortem examinations and anatomical examination after death, if the person objected to such procedures (obviously) while alive, is strongly suggestive of legal personality in the dead. For here the dead person's wishes *and* interests are being respected and the next of kin and beneficiaries are disabled from overriding those wishes. See, eg Human Tissue Act 1983 (NSW), s 24 which authorises removal of tissue outside of a hospital 'where the deceased person had, during that person's lifetime' consented to the removal 'for the purpose of its transplantation to the body of a living person or its use for other therapeutic purposes or for medical purposes or scientific purposes' and disallows 'a senior available next of kin' from granting such authority if 'the deceased had . . . expressed an objection' while alive.

[16] These contingent rights of the foetus were recognised in *Watt v Rama* [1972] VR 353. For a sustained discussion of the legal status of the foetus, see John Seymour, *Childbirth and the Law* (Oxford, Oxford University Press, 2000).

physical considerations, let us consider briefly a series of cases about foetal status. In these cases we have an opportunity to observe judges who are highly conscious of the moral and metaphysical and even scientific claims being made on them, but who are also keen to assert the conceptual autonomy of law: its ability to make its person its own. And as a consequence, they achieve some highly creative outcomes in their judgments.

In *Re the Estate of K*,[17] the Tasmanian Supreme Court considered whether a frozen embryo could inherit and decided that 'any philosophical or biological question of what is life' was irrelevant 'since the question relates solely to the status recognised by law and not to any moral, scientific or theological issue'.[18] And in law, the cloak of a legal fiction operating within the law of inheritance had allowed foetuses to be deemed to be born as of the date of death. Logically this rule should be extended to frozen embryos. This was a purpose-specific legal personification designed to confer a property right.

Similar reasoning was employed by the Canadian Supreme Court in *Tremblay v Daigle*.[19] The so-called 'father' of a foetus had successfully sought an injunction from the Quebec Supreme Court to restrain a pregnant woman from having an abortion. The foetus was deemed to be a human being and therefore had a right to life under the Quebec Charter. The court inferred from the Quebec Civil Code that foetuses were legal persons because they had the right to inherit. The woman unsuccessfully appealed to the Quebec Court of Appeal, and then to the Supreme Court, which allowed her appeal. The Supreme Court admitted that:

> [m]etaphysical arguments may be relevant but they are not the primary focus of inquiry. Nor are scientific arguments about the biological status of a foetus determinative in our inquiry.[20]

The legal nature of the foetus was to be determined by neither a moral nor a scientific assessment of whether it had achieved a certain human status from which rights could then be derived. The court declared that:

> [t]he task of properly classifying a foetus in law and in science are different pursuits. Ascribing personality to a foetus in law is fundamentally a normative task. It results in the recognition of rights and duties—a matter which falls outside the concerns of scientific classification.[21]

The critical legal question was whether rights and duties should be ascribed within a given set of legal relations. This did not *necessarily* entail a resort to philosophy or science to discover whether the entity in question had a particular character.

17 (1996) 5 Tas R 365.
18 *Ibid* 371.
19 (1989) 62 DLR (4th) 634, 660.
20 *Ibid.*
21 *Ibid.*

This approach was reaffirmed by the Canadian Supreme Court in *Winnipeg Child and Family Services v G.*[22] The court was asked for an order detaining a pregnant woman against her will in order to protect her foetus. McLachlin J responded that '[t]he issue is not one of biological status, nor indeed spiritual status, but of legal status'.[23] This dictated that the woman should not be so detained. Conformity to scientific or theological understandings of the foetus, in this instance, would not necessarily conduce justice.

In *Harrild v DPP*,[24] the New Zealand Court of Appeal considered whether harm to a foetus constituted harm to the pregnant woman for the purposes of no-fault accident compensation legislation. If the foetus were defined as a separate entity, and not part of the mother, the woman could not recover under this statute. In the view of Elias CJ, the governing law permitted the foetus to be treated both as part of the woman and as a separate entity. The law did not have to rely on a single status. Keith J similarly emphasised 'the critical importance of the particular legal, statutory and policy contexts'.[25] McGrath J confirmed that 'in the end it is the nature of the rights under the relevant statute that must be ascertained'.[26] And here it would be wrong to deny the right of the woman to claim compensation for her injury to herself by a finding that the foetus was not part of her. And yet the same court understood the logic of another New Zealand decision, of the same year, *Re an Unborn Child*,[27] in which the court decided that a foetus could be treated as a distinct legal person and thus appointed a guardian, as if it were a child, in order to protect it from the mother's determination to make a pornographic film of its birth. Here, the court drew assistance from the UN Convention on the Rights of the Child, which it felt had a direct bearing on their decision.

When asked to determine whether the killing of a foetus could amount to the criminal offence of grievous bodily harm to the woman, the NSW Court of Criminal Appeal, in *R v King*,[28] examined both New Zealand cases. It decided that a fatal injury to the foetus could constitute injury to the woman. The 'father' of the foetus had kicked and stomped on the woman's stomach. The court asserted that:

> there is no clear rule, applicable in all situations, as to whether the mother and foetus must be considered as one or separate. The answer will turn on the incidents of the particular legal situation under consideration, where relevant, the scope, purpose and object of a particular statutory regime.[29]

[22] [1997] 3 SCR 925.
[23] *Ibid.*
[24] [2003] 3 NZLR 289.
[25] *Ibid* 297.
[26] *Ibid* 312.
[27] [2003] 1 NZLR 115.
[28] [2003] NSWCCA 399.
[29] *Ibid* para 87.

Here, it was appropriate to treat the foetus as part of the woman because this would properly 'reflect the community's legitimate concern to control violence between persons'.[30] In other words, 'the purposes of the law are best served by acknowledging that, relevantly, the foetus is part of the mother'.[31]

Can we be Strict about Persons?

The judges in these cases about foetal status are concerned about the claims of other disciplines to their person and their ability to stifle legal freedom and so, to varying degrees, the judges claim the autonomy of law to define its own person. But they are not dogmatic. The judges are mindful of religious, metaphysical and scientific considerations and their purchase on law. As the Canadian court said in *Tremblay*: 'Metaphysical arguments *may* be relevant but they are not the *primary* focus of inquiry' (emphasis added).[32] I now want to consider, more closely, some of the reasons why 'metaphysical arguments' about the nature of law's person are necessarily at least part of the focus of legal inquiry and why sometimes they may even form the primary focus.

Hohfeld on Legal Conceptions

As Wesley Hohfeld conceded nearly a century ago, in his celebrated discourses on the nature of fundamental legal conceptions, it is not easy to separate the legal from the non-legal, even though (in his view) this is precisely what lawyers must do:

> At the very outset it seems necessary to emphasize the importance of differentiating purely legal relations from the physical and mental facts that call such relations into being. Obvious as this initial suggestion may seem to be, the arguments that one may hear in court almost any day, and likewise a considerable number of legal opinions, afford ample evidence of the inveterate and unfortunate tendency to confuse and blend the legal and the non-legal quantities in a given problem.[33]

Hohfeld gave two reasons for this confusion.

> For one thing, the association of ideas involved in the two sets of relations—the physical and the mental on the one hand, and the purely legal on the other—is in the very nature of the case, extremely close.[34]

[30] *Ibid* para 96.

[31] *Ibid* para 97.

[32] Above n 19.

[33] WN Hohfeld, *Fundamental Legal Conceptions as Applied in Judicial Reasoning* (New Haven, Yale University Press, 1934) 27.

[34] *Ibid.*

Secondly, 'the tendency to confuse or blend non-legal and legal conceptions consists in the ambiguity and looseness of legal terminology'.[35]

If we accept Hohfeld's analysis, loose usage is one cause of the confusion about persons, which inappropriately blends the legal and the non-legal, but this is obviously something we can solve with the exercise of greater care. However, can the other problem, that of contamination from the non-legal 'physical' world, because of the close association of ideas, be so easily solved? The problem of contagion, as Hohfeld sees it, arises from the fact that 'many of our words were originally applicable only to physical things; so that their use in connection with legal relations is, strictly speaking, figurative or fictional'.[36]

The problem is that lawyers make 'metaphorical use' of terms borrowed from elsewhere.[37] Hohfeld warns that 'chameleon-hued words are a peril both to clear thought and to lucid expression'.[38] So can the advocates of the strict definition of the person ensure the legal purity of their term simply with the application of greater linguistic vigilance? There are several reasons why this may not be the case.

First, the very concept of the person (defined in the strict legal sense as that which has a capacity to bear a right or duty and of course with the appellation 'person') may linguistically invoke the idea of a particular sort of moral being which naturally can act in law. In other words, the strict definition of person linguistically suggests a being endowed with its own (and not just law-given) capacity to act in law and to exercise a right. Perhaps we are therefore compelled by the strict definition of person to think of a being which is able to act in a certain rational manner: a natural rights bearer.

The double meaning of 'capacity' in law may exacerbate this perceived problem of conceptual impurity. The capacity to bear a legal right or duty is not meant to be confused with the idea of legal competence, also often called capacity, which is the ability to make one's own legal decisions, personally, rather than have them made for one. The latter sense of 'capacity' explicitly brings into issue the actual mental abilities of the particular human being. It calls for a positive inquiry into the actual cognitive abilities of the being in question (or, more typically, positively presumes their existence). By contrast, the former sense of the term capacity (our personality in the strict sense) entails a formal external endowment, by law, of a legal ability, notionally quite unrelated to the actual abilities of the being or entity so endowed.

[35] WN Hohfeld, *Fundamental Legal Conceptions as Applied in Judicial Reasoning* (New Haven, Yale University Press, 1934) 28.

[36] *Ibid* 30.

[37] *Ibid* 31.

[38] *Ibid* 35.

We might say, therefore, that capacity can either come from law (as in the capacity for participating in legal relations) or it can come from the individual human being, and then be recognised by law (as in competence). The efforts of the purists of personality are likely to be hampered by these two opposing legal meanings of capacity. The two terms, with the same name, pull in quite different directions: one towards law as a formal autonomous meaning-making institution, in control of its terms, and the other towards the individual and her extra-legal human characteristics.

Another reason why it may be difficult to retain personality as a strictly legal abstraction is that the concept has an intimate connection with two other legal concepts—rights and duties—and these concepts have been directly linked to a certain understanding of human beings. As will be seen in later chapters, there is an influential view among rights scholars that both rights and duties can only be borne by those with the ability to exercise rational choice. It is impossible, therefore, in the view of these jurists, to understand rights and duties away from the beings that are mcant to have them. The 'choice theory' of rights thus 'explains why rights are often regarded as fundamental to one's personhood, individuality, and self-determination'.[39]

The idea advanced by choice theorists, as Harel explains, is that '[b]y exercising choice one manifests one's individuality and personhood'.[40] Consequently 'choice theorists typically share a particular moral vision—a vision stressing the importance of self-determination and autonomy'.[41] Because the very idea of a right, thus understood, connotes a being with the ability personally to enforce it, there is a necessary relationship between real human beings and their attributes and the formal concept of the rights-bearing legal person. The choice theory of rights therefore forges a direct link between the legal concept of a right and a certain extra-legal understanding of a person. Thus, again, the legal is contaminated by the non-legal.

A further reason why it may be virtually impossible to maintain the legal conceptual purity of the person is that of intelligibility. Can we actually think of an abstract legal person without immediately giving it empirical content and thus losing sight of the artifice of this formal legal device?[42] Surely every application of legal personality (and after all, law is an applied discipline) engenders this problem of loss of abstraction. With each application, the legal person seems to become a real, non-abstract, person

[39] Alon Harel, 'Theories of Rights' in William Edmundson and Martin Golding (eds), *Blackwell Guide to the Philosophy of Law and Legal Theory* (Cambridge, Blackwell, 2005) 194.

[40] *Ibid.*

[41] *Ibid.*

[42] This was precisely the concern of Lon Fuller in *Legal Fictions* (Stanford, Stanford University Press, 1967) 19. He said that we see the abstraction when the person is a corporation but tend to lose sight of the abstract nature of the concept when it is applied to a human being.

participating in particular legal relations. This means that the concept may not be able to transcend its actual empirical use. As soon as it has any work to do, it seems to materialise.

Real Uses of Persons

If this is indeed the case, if the person cannot transcend her empirical uses, then a related problem confronts those who wish to secure legal conceptual purity. For if we are obliged to think of the legal person empirically, no doubt our minds will turn to the actual empirical ways in which legal capacity is (and historically has been) distributed across the actual population of potential legal beings. Indeed, Hart and Wittgenstein would surely urge us to do just this. In their view, conceptual meaning was precisely to be found in the empirical uses of the concept. The conditions of meaning resided in use.

And in the making of empirical legal persons, there have been powerful historical, political and social forces at work, shaping legal use: ensuring the endowment of some beings with moral and social status and so with the ability to act in law (notably men of property), and the denial of others (notably slaves). These social forces, according to Hohfeld and other like-minded jurists, are better kept to the periphery of law, or better still excluded altogether. After all, the point they press is that law's person is a purely legal abstraction, an empty slot, capable of being filled and refilled in any way, not in particular historical ways. Thus, Richard Tur avers that 'the empty slot' which is the legal person 'can be filled with *anything* that can have rights and duties' (emphasis added).[43] But the actual empirical ways of personifying suggest otherwise. And, with Hart, I would say that we must attend to use.

In reply, the strict Legalists would no doubt say that their 'empty slot' characterisation of the person is intended simply to convey the formal availability of the slot to anyone. And yet it can easily be read as a covert empirical claim that personality is open, ecumenical and unbiased in its application. In other words, it can be taken to mean that the 'slot' of the person does not have any particular contour and so can (and perhaps implicitly does) fit anyone. Richard Tur asserts as much when he says that 'if legal personality is the legal capacity to bear rights and duties, then . . . anything or anyone can be a legal person'.[44] Such a statement prompts one to observe that this is not how the concept of the person has been deployed as a matter of practice; it invites discussion of the actual uses of the concept.

As soon as we try to personify in ways that are profoundly at odds with prevailing conventions about who and what should count as a metaphysical

[43] Tur, above n 5, at 121–2.
[44] *Ibid.*

person, we see the patterned ways in which personification occurs. We discover that the empty slot of the person has been given certain dimensions, fitting some and not others. It eminently seems to suit the rational adult (as we will see in the next chapter) but it seems completely wrong for animals (as we will see in Chapter 8). There is absolutely no reason why animals cannot be legal persons and yet the well-accepted legal view is that they are not. It is difficult to find a single instance of a right invested in animals, and jurists have resisted the idea of ever calling them persons.

The legal resistance to the personification of animals strongly suggests that the term 'person' is not in fact a formal conceptual slot that fits anyone or anything, but rather a slot thought by many to be designed exclusively for human beings, especially of a rational nature, because they are thought to possess a certain moral status. It is conceded that animals can suffer, and even think at a primitive level, and so should be afforded certain legal protections. But they lack sufficient moral status to count as persons. It suggests that the legal person is not immune from metaphysical notions of what it is to be a person.[45]

Powerful moral conventions not only govern the species of law's person but they also govern his sex. Some of the most troubling cases of legal personality, as we have already seen, concern the foetus and the pregnant woman. Men, *qua men*, have never caused this sort of legal consternation. What this strongly suggests is that the legal person is powerfully modelled on a certain conception of an individuated moral subject, and hence has a significantly male dimension (more of this in Chapter 9).[46] (This individuation is also apparent in the treatment of the corporation as an atypical and artificial legal person.)[47] If these moral and political dimensions of personality are neglected, then Legalists are poorly equipped to say anything of a moral or political nature about their subject: to say what is right and wrong about the past and present endowment and withholding of personality (think of slaves or women or animals).

The task that lies before me is to examine both these underlying metaphysics and the formal mechanisms by which they are translated into legal personality. It is to uncover the metaphysical suppositions which inform law's person, to show that they have their own particular history and that

[45] As we saw above, the implicit humanity of the person creates problems for the corporation as well. The anthropomorphising effects of the concept on corporations have been extensively analysed and decried by corporate jurists.

[46] For a more sustained analysis of the legal individualism implicit in many applications of the concept of the legal person, see Davies and Naffine, above n 4, and Jennifer Nedelsky, 'Law, Boundaries and the Bounded Self' in Robert Post (ed), *Law and the Order of Culture* (Berkeley, University of California Press, 1991).

[47] The individualism implicit in the concept of personality and the problems it generates for the corporation as person is discussed also in Nicholas James, 'Separate Legal Personality: Legal Reality and Meaphor' (1993) 5 *Bond Law Review* 217.

they are still in flux. Our sensibilities have a history and keep changing: the significance and status of women, foetuses, the dying and animals have changed dramatically over the last century and, with them, law's conception of its person.

But more particularly, my task in the chapters that follow is to examine closely and to evaluate the arguments of those who positively favour a coming together of legal and moral or metaphysical understandings of the person: who positively approve a certain distribution of personifying rights and duties, a certain constellation or patterning of persons, because it is thought that, for one reason or another, it best reflects the nature of beings and things. In short, I will examine the scholarship (and the associated law) of those who offer direct opposition to the strict Legalists; who believe that legal persons *should* have a strong kinship to natural persons, variously conceived. I call these thinkers metaphysical realists because they seek to discern the true metaphysical nature of being and to link law to that true, real nature.

I will reflect on the thoughts of three types of metaphysical realists. The next two chapters are about those who would link legal personhood with the capacity for reason: the Rationalists. In Chapter 7, I consider those scholars who are convinced that it is human sanctity which matters: the Religionists. In Chapters 8 and 9, I examine the idea that it is as natural biological beings that persons should come into legal being and perhaps that the legal and moral species divide should even be done away with: the Naturalists.

5
Moral Agents and Responsibility

> [T]hose creatures who have received the gift of reason from Nature have also received right reason, and therefore they have also received the gift of law.
>
> Cicero[1]

> Those who can give justice are owed justice.
>
> John Rawls[2]

Law must operate with some understanding of what we are and why we matter in order to do its work of regulating society. Although strict Legalists prefer to play down this life-defining role of law, it is unavoidable. It is important, therefore, to reflect on the way particular views of our natures play out in law, how they shape and influence legal reasoning and help to determine the spread of rights and responsibilities. My suggestion is that there is a variety of competing views of our natures operating in the legal realm, and in this chapter and the next I will examine those legal thinkers who believe that it is our capacity for reason which most defines us and makes us worthy recipients of law's attention and protection. In this view, legal persons are, in essence, real flesh-and-blood human beings whose most important characteristic is their ability to reason and deliberate.

This chapter will focus on those legal thinkers who believe that it is the capacity for sophisticated, high-level reason which most defines law's person. In this highly influential legal view, we are fitting legal subjects who can assume rights and duties precisely because of our human-defining powers of deliberation which allow us to make intelligent choices and, importantly, to be held to account for those choices. Law's person, in this rendition, is not a formal legal device but rather a real intelligent human agent.

As legal-rights theorist Jeremy Waldron expresses this view of persons in law, and why they should be endowed with rights, it entails 'typically an act of faith in the agency and capacity for moral thinking of each of the individuals concerned';[3] or as philosopher Roger Scruton describes this subject of rights, it is:

[1] Cicero, *De Legibus*, vol 1, x 29, xiii 33, quoted in Lesley J Rogers and Gisela Kaplan, 'All Animals are Not Equal' in Cass Sunstein and Martha Nussbaum (eds), *Animal Rights: Current Debates and New Directions* (New York, Oxford University Press, 2004) 195.

[2] John Rawls, *A Theory of Justice* (Cambridge, Mass, Belknap Press, 1971) 510.

[3] Jeremy Waldron, *Law and Disagreement* (Oxford, Clarendon Press, 1999) 222.

> the kind of being that can settle disputes, that can exert sovereignty over its life and respect the sovereignty of others, [and] that can respond to the call of duty.[4]

Here we have an active, autonomous actor: someone who is positively able to bear legal duties and to assert legal rights in their own capacity. This person is imagined as an attentive, articulate litigant or defendant, who can appreciate the complexity of law's demands and respond directly and personally, for his own reasons.[5] This is someone who can choose to heed or reject those demands and can fairly be blamed if the choice is made to refuse the dictates of law.

It is not difficult to see the importance to legal legitimacy of such a being. For this is the person whom laws are supposed to be designed for and addressed to: the one who is meant to be listening and heeding the counsel of law. It is the person supposedly engaged in rational dialogue or conversation with law's representatives and who can therefore justly be made accountable for his harmful actions; whose will can thus be constrained by state power. If we imagine this person in a criminal court of law (as many legal thinkers do), he is listening attentively to the charge against him and all the supporting evidence; he is deciding whether to take advantage of a full criminal trial: to invoke the presumption of innocence and perhaps the right to remain silent. He is actively testing the case against him; he is positively instructing his lawyer at all times. This is an intellectually vigorous, assertive and engaged individual.

Other Rationalists demand less of their legal person, because theirs is a rather different legal and human concern. Such legal thinkers are not endeavouring to describe the robust, autonomous, legal individual who 'can respond to the call of duty', who can fully appreciate the complex demands of law, who can assume complex legal obligations and so be held to account. Rather, their interest is in the vulnerable among us: those of more modest intellect or those whose weakened physical condition (be it temporary or permanent) exposes them to exploitation and abuse. In the next chapter I will consider those thinkers who concentrate on the mentally and physically infirm (individuals often pictured in the doctor's clinic or the hospital ward), and also on children. These theorists seek to define and assert the minimal cognitive abilities needed for self-management and self-determination, and especially for the legal right to say 'no' to the intervention of others. But in this current chapter, my concern is with the highly influential legal conception of the robust and sophisticated reasoner as the bearer of legal rights and duties.

[4] Roger Scruton, *Animal Rights and Wrongs* (3rd edn, London, Metro Books, 2000) 55.

[5] This understanding of the defendant is especially evident in the writings of Anthony Duff on the nature of the trial. See, eg RA Duff, *Trials and Punishments* (Cambridge, Cambridge University Press, 1986).

Creation Story

Typically, legal Rationalists who invoke a sophisticated reasoner (not the impaired person) draw upon the liberal political creation story of contract and of the emergence of the modern autonomous individual. This is the story of the rise of modern Anglo-American law, often rendered as a political tale of liberation and enlightenment, of coming to see the world in the light of human reason and so prevailing over the darker forces of nature. It is an account of human progress, of a loosening of the constraining ties of custom and the embrace of efficient and productive human relations of choice. It describes a movement away from inegalitarian natural relations to social relations formed freely through the mechanism of contract. The legal being that emerges from this process of modernisation is often depicted as rational and autonomous.

In this imaginary account of the formation of modern political society, people come together not by custom or tradition or nature but by free rational agreement or contract to form a society under government. In the story of the social contract, the person enters into (modern) social and legal relations only by an act of free and essentially self-interested choice. This individual decides to contract with others to surrender some of his freedoms to the state which will then regulate his relations with others and preserve him from unwanted interference. Contract, based on free choice, provides the model for all of this person's relations. In this liberal account of social life, as Ignatieff explains, 'freedom is a problem of external constraints: give everyone ... sufficient rights and they will be free to act according to their choices'.[6] Freedom is not thought to be a matter of being positively enabled to act by others.

The master teller of the creation story of our modern contractual society and of modern law is Sir Henry Maine.[7] Taking a broad historical sweep, from the medieval to the modern period, he described a shift from a hierarchical or vertical society, based on customary status, to an equal or horizontal society, based on personally-chosen contracts.[8] This was a movement distinguished by the loosening of family ties and the gradual emergence of the autonomous modern individual, unencumbered by domestic and community obligations. In the medieval world, persons in law were assumed to be interdependent. Each person took their nature and their social role from a place they were assigned by custom, not by choice. Within the medieval household, as Gray and Symes observe, human relations were

[6] Michael Ignatieff, *The Needs of Strangers* (New York, Viking, 1984) 63.

[7] On the strong contemporary influence of Maine on our understanding of modern Anglian law and the modern legal actor, see Brian Tamanah, *A General Jurisprudence of Law and Society* (Oxford and New York, Oxford University Press, 2001).

[8] Henry Maine, *Ancient Law* (London, John Murray, 1930).

'mediated by principles of love and duty . . . It was a family-oriented, status-dependent form of association'.[9] With the shift to contract '[t]he individual [was] steadily substituted for the Family, as the unit of which civil laws take account'.[10]

Major social theorists have also depicted this change. Max Weber saw it as the shift from a society characterised by fraternal bonds to relations defined by purposive contracts.[11] Ferdinand Tonnies interpreted the move as one from social relations of *Gemeinschaft* (community) to relations of *Gesellschaft* (association).[12] The shift to contract meant an extraction of the individual from obligatory customary social roles, determined at birth, and thought to arise from nature. Human relations were now to be established by rational choice and were to assume a contractual form.

William Blackstone is the jurist responsible for the boldest and starkest legal evocation of this autonomous being in the state of nature, deciding what he wants for himself before he enters the social world. Blackstone drew up the great legal document of the eighteenth century, which captured much of this liberal spirit of individualism. In his *Commentaries on the Laws of England*, Blackstone wrote of 'the natural liberty of mankind' which 'consists properly in the power of acting, as one thinks fit, without any restraint or control, unless by the law of nature'.[13] To Blackstone 'every man, when he enters into society, gives up part of his natural liberty ... in consideration of receiving the advantages of mutual commerce'.[14] This being does not take his nature from his connection with others, but is self-defining. He is already whole and sufficient unto himself. He enters the social and legal community on his own terms, autonomous, rational, self-governing.

The curiously mythological or fictitious nature of this story is not difficult to discern and indeed it is broadly accepted that the story of contract is an heuristic device (of liberal political theory) rather than a factual account of the formation of modern society. Nevertheless, it has had a considerable effect on legal thinking about law's subject, permitting a concentrated focus on the rational mature adult. Most conspicuously, this story of the genesis of our legal person is silent about his actual biological birth and his long period of dependency. This omission is important for the integrity of the story of contract, which is about entry into society by rational decision.

[9] K Gray and P Symes, *Real Property and Real People: Principles of Land Law* (London, Butterworths, 1981) 15.

[10] Maine, above n 8, at 168.

[11] Max Weber, *Economy and Society: an Outline of Interpretive Sociology* (New York, Bedminster, 1968) 673.

[12] Ferdinand Tonnies, *Community and Association* (London, Routledge and Kegan Paul, 1955).

[13] William Blackstone, *Commentaries on the Laws of England* (17th edn, London, Sweet and Maxwell, 1830) vol 1, 121.

[14] *Ibid.*

The Legal and the Philosophical Person

The sophisticated reasoner who contracts his way into civil and legal society is imagined at a fairly high level of abstraction and so it is perhaps not surprising that his character owes more to political and philosophical speculation about the nature of 'persons' than to empirical sociology. He is more the product of high-level philosophical theory than close empirical study of particular defendants or litigants in real courts of law. According to orthodox philosophical thinking, a person is 'a mental being . . . [who] possesses a mind'[15] and not just any sort of mind will do. As philosopher Brian Garrett explains, '[p]ersons possess a range of particularly sophisticated mental states, including—most crucially—self-reflective mental states'.[16] This characterisation of the person as an intelligent agent can be traced directly to John Locke (the great theorist of the social contract) who provides the most quoted and influential philosophical definition of the person. Locke conceived of the person as:

> a thinking, intelligent being, that has reason and reflection, and can consider itself the same thinking thing, in different times and places.[17]

Locke explicitly connected the philosopher's and the lawyer's person, conceding that the term 'person' was essentially 'forensic' in nature in that it appropriated 'actions and their merits and so belongs only to intelligent agents, capable of a law, and happiness and misery'.[18] Locke therefore demanded a good deal from his person, notably the capacity to act under law and the ability to reason; or as philosopher Elizabeth Wolgast conceives of this autonomous kind of intellectual being, this philosophical person, he is 'an individual who first decides and then executes actions, does both himself'.[19] This person 'commands herself to act and acts under her own direction'.[20]

Criminal law theorist Ashworth rings the changes on this view of the person as intelligent decision-maker and as legal subject. He declares that:

> individuals should be respected and treated as agents capable of choosing their actions and omissions, and ... without recognising individuals as capable of independent agency [we] could hardly be regarded as moral persons.[21]

15 Brian Garrett, *Personal Identity and Self-Consciousness* (London, Routledge, 1998) 4.

16 *Ibid.*

17 John Locke, *An Essay Concerning Human Understanding* (John W Yolton (ed), London, Everyman and J M Dent, 1993) bk 2, ch xxvii, 180.

18 *Ibid.*

19 Elizabeth Wolgast, *Ethics of an Artificial Person: Lost Responsibility in Professions and Organizations* (Stanford, Stanford University Press, 1992) 65.

20 *Ibid.*

21 Andrew Ashworth, *Principles of Criminal Law* (4th edn, Oxford and New York, Oxford University Press, 2003) 29.

Thus, he emphasises the close connection between legal and moral personhood and between legal and moral responsibility. Roger Scruton also maintains that the very concept of the person:

> denotes potential members of a free community . . . [who] live by negotiation and, through rational dialogue, create the space which their projects require . . . Both parties to the dialogue must be rational—that is, able to give and receive reasons for action and to recognise the distinction between good and bad reasons, between valid and invalid arguments, between justifications and excuses . . . Each party must understand and accept obligations.[22]

Influence of Kant

A further powerful philosophical influence on legal thinking about the person conceived as a rational choosing agent is the Rationalist philosopher Immanuel Kant. Perhaps more than any other philosopher, Kant has shaped legal thinking about the nature and legal significance of human intelligence. He has influenced jurists in such a way that the legal actor tends to be thought of, in the first instance, as an adult rational rights holder, a moral individual, asserting his authority in a world of similar rational beings. This view orients the law (or it least its Rationalist interpreters) around the capable, the rational, indeed the educated, rather than the inarticulate, the dependent, the weak. It tends to overlook the real, more mixed, abilities of those who actually come before the law. (Typically, criminal defendants, for example, are characterised by educational and social and economic disadvantage.)

Kant himself saw no need to turn to the study of society or anthropology or to any of the empirical sciences for his account of the nature of reason, properly understood, because 'moral philosophy rests entirely on its pure part'; it is based on naturally existing and eternal laws.[23] Kant's moral philosophy involved the study of 'man' as a naturally rational and as a moral being; he believed that one necessarily entailed the other. The 'highest practical function of reason', for Kant, was 'the establishment of a good will'.[24]

Reason defined 'man', but it did not properly dignify him and others until it was applied to the will in the right, indeed naturally ordained, manner. A good will was one in which man (naturally) reasoned—worked out for himself—that he must treat himself and other rational beings as ends in themselves. Man's capacity for reason, an innate capacity, enabled him to divine this universal truth, this universal law: that he must treat other rational beings not as instruments of his own ends but as beings with their own ends, with their own goals, as moral agents. Reason commanded that he treat

[22] Scruton, above n 4, at 28–29.

[23] Immanual Kant, *Grounding for the Metaphysics of Morals* (James W Ellington (tr), Indianapolis, Hackett Publishing Company, 1981) 3.

[24] *Ibid* 9.

others as autonomous beings, with their own life plans, because 'rational nature exists as an end in itself'.[25] Kant insisted that:

> all rational beings stand under the law that each of them should treat himself and all others never merely as means but always at the same time as an end in himself.[26]

Kant conceded that 'these [moral] laws require ... a power of judgment sharpened by experience'.[27] Thus, man is 'capable of the idea of pure practical reason' but often needs practical experience to put it into effect.[28] Kant thus declared autonomy to be 'the ground of the dignity of human nature and of every rational being'.[29] For Kant:

> A rational being belongs to the kingdom of ends [is an end in itself] as a member when he legislates in it universal laws while also being himself subject to these laws. He belongs to it as sovereign, when as legislator he is himself subject to the will of no other.[30]

Reason demands and indeed commands (in a legislative fashion) the autonomy of one's own will and the autonomy of the will of others.

For Kant, the being who could not exercise his will, who was reduced to a state of heteronomy (the antithesis of autonomy), was not truly a person. Certainly they were shorn of dignity. Thus, Kant recognised the higher nature of rational man, who must be spoken to and reasoned with, and the lower nature of irrational man, and of man who failed to adapt his innately rational nature to the moral law.[31]

Gray on Legal Persons and the Rational Will

The classic work on legal persons which is wedded to the idea that the legal subject is essentially a rational will-driven creature is *The Nature and Sources of the Law* by John Chipman Gray, first published at the beginning of the twentieth century. Here, Gray contended that the will is the defining characteristic of the natural person and that the will finds its direct expression in law in the idea of the legal person. For Gray:

> in order that a legal right be exercised a will is necessary, and, therefore, so far as the exercise of legal rights is concerned, a person must have a will.[32]

[25] *Ibid* 36.
[26] *Ibid* 39.
[27] *Ibid.*
[28] *Ibid* 3.
[29] *Ibid* 41.
[30] *Ibid* 40.
[31] For a discussion of these implications of the Kantian view of the person, see Mary Ann Warren, *Moral Status* (Oxford and New York, Oxford University Press, 2000).
[32] John Chipman Gray, *The Nature and Sources of the Law* (2nd edn, New York, Macmillan, 1921) 27.

The paradigmatic legal person for Gray was the so-called 'normal' person: the adult of sound mind who possessed a 'natural will' and so could personally assert his legal rights without recourse to a next friend or guardian.[33] In his view of the person, the expression of the rational will was the essence of being human and also the essence of being a legal person. When this normal human being was asserting his legal rights as a legal person there was no legal fiction involved in his legal personality. It was only when a will was attributed artificially to a child or 'idiot' for legal purposes that legal personality entailed a fiction.[34]

For Gray, then, the true natural legal person was the sane rational adult who was able to exercise his will in the assertion of his rights. Children and 'idiots' were not properly to be regarded as persons; they were fictitious or ersatz legal persons. Gray thus made an important distinction between the normal and the implicitly abnormal, the intelligent and the unintelligent, which has maintained a hold on Rationalist legal thinking, though it now tends to be expressed in a more muted and politic fashion. Rationalist thinkers continue to rely on a distinction between different types of people, one which is not always made explicit in their work, but which serves well to partition law's community. This is the distinction between those whom law addresses, adult to adult, those to whom it speaks (Gray would have called them the 'normal') and those who are intended to receive the benefits of law because they are perceived to have particular needs and interests, that is law's beneficiaries, but who are not necessarily parties to law's adult discourse.[35]

Law is addressed to sane rational adults, intelligent agents, who because of their capacity for reason can assume moral as well as legal rights and responsibilities. Only 'normal' practical reasoners (persons who act for reasons) are people to whom law appropriately communicates its norms, endows with power and upon whom it imposes its obligations. Such intelligent agents are precisely the target of law; they are the type of being law has in mind. Law speaks to rational adults, as litigants or defendants. And rational adults are supposed to be responsive to law and its norms, precisely because of their powers of reason.

Such intelligent individuals are often conceived within the courtroom, responding to law's dictates, explaining their actions, or vigorously enforcing directly and personally their rights. To Richard Tur, for example, the being with 'full legal personality' is one who can 'initiate actions in the courts, to "sue or be sued"'.[36] To Matthew Kramer, the rational human

[33] John Chipman Gray, *The Nature and Sources of the Law* (2nd edn, New York, Macmillan, 1921) 28.

[34] *Ibid* 30.

[35] I thank John Gardner for drawing my attention to this distinction.

[36] Richard Tur, 'The "Person" in Law' in Arthur Peacocke and Grant Gillett (eds), *Persons and Personality: a Contemporary Inquiry* (Oxford, Basil Blackwell, 1987) 119. But note that Tur

adult is 'the paradigmatic rights holder'.[37] He has also been described as the 'typical subject' of rights and duties, the 'normal human being' who acts 'in a single capacity' and in his or her own right.[38] He (or she) possesses the best set of legal rights and responsibilities, and is thus the ideal legal actor. Less than ideal persons are those of diminished reason, or even of no reason at all.

Will Theory of the Person

To robust Kantian Rationalists, there is some doubt about whether humans of impaired or limited reason are even persons: for to be able to bear a right (and so become a person), it is thought that you need to be able to enforce that right, personally and individually, through the exercise of the will. Not surprisingly, this rather unforgiving view of rights has been called the 'will theory' and also the 'choice theory' as it is based on an agent's positively-willed choices. According to this theory, those who lack a rational will cannot meaningfully exercise any rights and so cannot be said to have them;[39] or, as Kramer explains:

> The basic idea underlying the Will Theory is that every right is a vehicle for some aspect of an individual's self-determination or initiative.[40]

It follows that the right holder must be 'competent and authorised to demand or waive the enforcement of the right'.[41] As Kramer also makes plain:

> One of the most arresting theses to which the Will Theory commits its upholders is the verdict that children and mentally incapacitated people have no rights. Because [they] are both factually and legally incompetent to choose between

acknowledges that this is a 'high threshold of personality' which is adopted by some writers but 'is not of any relevance to practical problems' given that it does not cover the case of minors or foetuses (at 119).

[37] MH Kramer, 'Do Animals and Dead People Have Legal Rights?' (2001) 15(1) *Canadian Journal of Law and Jurisprudence* 29, 36.

[38] Bryant Smith, 'Legal Personality' (1928) 37 *Yale Law Journal* 283, 287.

[39] The will theory is to be contrasted with the interest theory of rights in which 'a right is an interest which protected the imposition of a duty on another person'. In this competing theory, rights arise out of interests or needs, not from the ability personally to assert one's own claims. Thus, 'the Interest Theory can readily ascribe rights to children and to mentally incapacitated people (and indeed to animals, if a theorist wishes) . . . it maintains that any genuine right does not have to be waivable and enforceable by the right-holder'. Matthew H Kramer, 'Rights Without Trimmings' in Matthew H Kramer, NE Simmonds and Hillel Steiner, *A Debate Over Rights: Philosophical Enquiries* (Oxford, Clarendon Press, 1998) 7, 78. 'The basic idea underlying the Interest Theory is that every right protects some aspect of a person's welfare' (at 61). According to this theory, a right preserves x's interests but x does not have to be competent or authorised 'to demand or waive the enforcement of a right' (at 62).

[40] *Ibid* 62.

[41] *Ibid.*

> enforcing and waiving their claims against others and [are] . . . incompetent . . . to engage in enforcement . . . decisions, they hold no powers to make such decisions . . . the young and the mad do not have rights.[42]

This interpretation is confirmed by Alon Harel who explains that '[t]he choice theory . . . cannot assign rights to entities that are not agents, that is, those incapable of exercising choice'.[43] And as a consequence, '[i]nfants, senile people, and comatose people are, thus, under the choice theory, incapable of being right-holders'.[44] It would seem to follow that they are not legal persons, for they have neither rights that they can personally enforce, nor responsibilities.

Respect for Persons and Responsibility

There is an important dignifying dimension to this characterisation of law's person, one that is deeply political. According to the Rationalist jurist, law's persons must be accorded respect because they are intelligent agents. They are rational decision-makers who are therefore in charge of their own lives. Human dignity resides in human reason and in the freedom to put it to use. But because the capacity to reason also entails the power to make choices, it brings with it responsibility for those choices. Agents must be respected, but then they must also be assumed to know what they are doing, to make life decisions of their own free will, and quite appropriately to be held to account for those decisions.

Thus, with the personifying capacity for reason and moral agency comes responsibility. Law must treat rational adults as just that: as persons who can be addressed as mature reasoners, adult to adult. But then, if such individuals choose not to adhere to legal norms, they can quite legitimately be called to account. After all, they are free intelligent agents who brought it on their own heads; or as Tony Honore expresses it, with the 'the gift of personal identity' comes the assumption of responsibility.[45]

Indeed, respect for persons may be thought to reside in holding agents responsible for what they choose to do. For persons are, by definition, accountable. Again, as Tony Honore has described this intimate connection between being a person and being responsible:

> Outcome responsibility is . . . inescapable because it is the counterpart and at the same time a constituent of our personal identity and character. We could not dispense with . . . responsibility without ceasing to be persons.[46]

[42] *Ibid* 69.

[43] Alon Harel, 'Theories of Rights' in William Edmundson and Martin Golding (eds), *Blackwell Guide to the Philosophy of Law and Legal Theory* (Cambridge, Blackwell, 2005) 94.

[44] *Ibid.*

[45] Tony Honore, *Responsibility and Fault* (Oxford and Portland, Hart Publishing, 1999) 29.

[46] *Ibid* 15.

We are taken seriously as persons when we are asked to explain and defend our decisions. It is this assignment of responsibility which constitutes us as persons. Honore is categorical about this. He declares that 'to be responsible is part of what it means to be a person and hence to have interests'.[47]

There is, of course, a converse implication of this view of persons for those who lack intelligent agency (an implication which will be explored more fully in the next chapter). Those of reduced reason are either diminished persons or not persons at all. To most Rationalists, the very young and the intellectually disabled and diseased do and should receive law's full protection, but they do not count as authentic legal persons. American criminal law theorist Michael Moore puts this view uncompromisingly:

> One cannot judge [what he terms the mentally retarded and the young] in comparison to what the average responsible person would do because they do not have the capacities to be the kind of being on whom the law is based; they are not fully persons who reason practically.[48]

Cognitively-impaired or cognitively-limited persons, be they infants or adults of diminished or disorganised intellect, clearly pose a problem for Rationalists. Given that these individuals are lacking in the one essential requirement of personhood, the capacity for reason, how can they be said to be persons at all? Rationalists supply different answers to this question, depending on the stringency of their thinking. For the moment, we will stay with the sophisticated reasoner, the central character of Rationalism. We will return to the moral and legal problems posed by naïve and non-reasoners in the next chapter.

The Legal Subject of Criminal Law

It is among criminal lawyers that we find most clearly articulated the view that law's person is, in essence, a highly rational agent.[49] This is not surprising, given the central concerns of criminal law and its associated theory. Criminal law has been defined by one of the United States' leading theorists of the subject as 'a species of moral and political philosophy [whose] central question is justifying the use of the state's coercive power against free and autonomous persons'.[50] Influential Australian interpreters of the criminal law confirm that:

[47] *Ibid* 29–30.

[48] Michael Moore, *Law and Psychiatry: Rethinking the Relationship* (Cambridge, Cambridge University Press, 1984) 84.

[49] Peter Cane says this in his book on responsibility: *Responsibility in Law and Morality* (Oxford, Hart Publishing, 2002). So does Meir Dan-Cohen, below n 52.

[50] George Fletcher, *Rethinking Criminal Law* (Boston, Little Brown & Co, 1978) xix.

> almost the whole of our system of substantive criminal law is based upon the view that a human being is a rational creature, free to choose how to act, and deserving of punishment if she or he chooses to act immorally or wickedly.[51]

And according to Meir Dan-Cohen:

> Blaming—that is ascribing moral responsibility . . . has come to be understood in terms of . . . the free will paradigm . . . responsibility is grounded in the agent's capacity to choose her actions freely. This understanding of responsibility arises most prominently in criminal law.[52]

To Herbert Fingarette:

> It is plain that our criminal law, in its fundamental orientation, reflects and embodies certain fundamental values of our society. In particular it embodies a fundamental and characteristic resolution of the community that normally the state shall deal with all members of the community as responsible persons under law.[53]

Nicola Lacey identifies in modern criminal law theory:

> a fundamentally shared idea of where the conditions of responsibility are to be sought. They reside, in short, in fundamental aspects of human agency: in capacities for knowledge, awareness, reflection, deliberation, and choice, which justify holding people responsible for their conduct.[54]

Much of the work of criminal law scholars in the Anglo-American tradition has been about the conditions under which it is fair and appropriate to hold such free rational agents responsible for their wrongdoing. It is about the proper conditions for blaming rational beings for criminal harms. The rational agent thus tends to be the starting point of such jurisprudence, and the *sine qua non* of much criminal law theory. This does not mean that the precise criteria of rational agency or of freedom of the will are necessarily spelled out in any detail or heavily theorised. Typically, the capacity for reason, pitched at a fairly high level, is simply taken as a given and presented as the natural basis of criminal responsibility. Often conjured in criminal law

[51] L Waller and CR Williams, *Criminal Law Text and Cases* (9th edn, Chatswood, NSW, Butterworths, 2001) 258.

[52] Meir Dan-Cohen, *Harmful Thoughts: Essays on Law, Self and Morality* (University of Chicago Press, 2003) 199.

[53] Herbert Fingarette, *The Meaning of Criminal Insanity* (Berkley, University of California Press, 1972) 56–7.

[54] According to Nicola Lacey, '[a]t the start of the twenty-first century, it is generally agreed among theorists of criminal responsibility in England (as indeed in other common law systems) that responsibility for crime is founded in a certain set of capacities. These capacities have both cognitive and volitional dimensions: it is argued that the responsible subject is an individual who was in possession of, or at least capable of being in possession of, the relevant knowledge or beliefs about the context in which they acted or omitted to act, and who had a fair opportunity to act otherwise than they did'. 'Responsibility and Modernity in Criminal Law' (2001) 9 *Journal of Political Philosophy* 249, 255.

writing is a highly articulate defendant, frequently pictured in a courtroom, giving eloquent explanations of his wrongful actions, offering reasoned justifications and excuses.

For these theorists of the criminal law, there exists a fundamental and noble metaphysical truth about what we are. By nature we are rational beings; it is reason that endows us with value; and (criminal) law does and should reflect our inherently valuable rational human nature by formally recognising it and giving it important legal work to do. Criminal law shows its respects for us, as rational agents, as autonomous beings, by holding us responsible for what we do. When we wrong another, we can be taken to have chosen our actions; we can be blamed and made accountable. Indeed, it is vital for law's respect for us as rational persons that we be blamed and punished for our criminal wrongs. In this view, criminal legal norms are essentially designed for rational actors who must be reasoned with, not simply told what to do, who must be pressed to accept responsibility for their actions, but who must be given a proper right of reply when accused of wrongs.

There are factual and normative dimensions to this noble truth about us. It is considered factually to be so that we *are* by nature rational subjects. And it is considered, normatively, that we *should* be treated as if we were like this. It is therefore vital for our dignity as persons that we be treated as reasoners. One slightly paradoxical way of putting this view is to declare that it is good for us to be punished if we do wrong because it holds us to account. It obliges us to justify ourselves and to give our excuses; in short to be responsible. It recognises us for the moral subjects that we are.

There is an important political intention behind this becoming view of the criminal legal actor. Criminal law represents a significant incursion into our freedoms to decide how best to live. It tells us that we cannot harm others. But then it goes a great deal further, and regulates and limits our lives in increasingly diverse, complex and intrusive ways.[55] Such intervention in our lives in a liberal democracy requires strong political legitimation. This can be derived, at least in part, from the assertion that criminal law entails a reasoned communication between the state and its citizens, as free legal actors, about the limits of acceptable action.

The central organising idea, which is accepted by leading criminal law theorists, is that criminal law communicates its freedom-limiting norms directly to us, as rational agents. It assumes that we have the capacity to control our actions and so to direct our lives; that we can hold coherent beliefs and form rational intentions and make choices for reasons. Thus, we can legitimately be held accountable. Criminal law is meant to give us fair

[55] Notably, criminal laws associated with terrorism are expanding the scope of criminal jurisprudence, criminalising human associations and speech and even the possession of certain knowledge.

opportunity, as rational agents, to avoid criminal actions;[56] and then it is meant to offer us reasoned justifications and excuses, if we end up engaging in criminal activity. We should not simply be ordered around, treated like children, with no reasons given on either side. Criminal law derives much of its authority in a liberal democracy from its claims to reason with us as free responsible subjects, and not just impose itself upon us without warning and without explanation.

Criminal law theory, as we will see, tends to pitch the reason of the defendant at a fairly high level. To many, he appears as a sophisticated reasoner: someone offering reasoned justifications for his actions, almost a Rumpole-style character. A natural corollary of this dignifying legal view of us, as rational agents, is that young children and the intellectually disabled are neither responsible criminal legal subjects nor are they the addressees of criminal legal norms. They are incapable of law, to borrow from Locke. To some, they cannot even be said to possess the sort of rights with which the criminal defendant is legally endowed.

Two Criminal Legal Thinkers

An eminent and influential group of criminal law theorists, from both sides of the Atlantic, has described this highly rational character: the one brought before the criminal courts. To these theorists, criminal law rightly makes strong metaphysical claims about what we are when it makes us responsible for crimes. In this view, we are, constitutionally, rational beings and it is reason which endows us with value and dignity. We are creatures of intention, belief and choice and how we see ourselves and our lives matters. We must be accorded the right to make our own decisions about how we are to live, but we can be and should be given reasons to behave well and persuaded to comply with law's norms. Ultimately the decision is ours: so that when we choose to offend, for our own reasons, we can and should be blamed and held accountable, supposing there are no excusing reasons. This criminal-legal commitment to our reason has been expressed in various ways.

The Uncompromising Michael Moore

Michael Moore is the criminal law theorist who has presented the starkest portrayal of the legal subject as a rational being. To Moore, the law takes a view of 'man' which permits us 'to view his behaviour as the rational product of his autonomous choices'.[57] He maintains that:

[56] This understanding of the nature of a good criminal law is particularly associated with the work of HLA Hart.

[57] Michael Moore, 'The Relevance of Philosophy to Law and Psychiatry' (1984) 6 *International Journal of Law and Psychiatry* 177, 179.

> the legal and moral concepts in terms of which rights and responsibilities are assigned—concepts such as action, intention, rationality, and justification or excuse—presuppose the concept of persons as practical reasoners.[58]

It follows that someone whose reason is undeveloped or damaged may not be 'enough of a person to be held responsible'.[59]

But Moore is saying more than that the ascription of responsibility logically presupposes the presence of someone who, as a practical matter, is capable of assuming that responsibility. He is also positively equating legal persons with moral persons, with rational agents. He asserts that, morally and legally, someone is a criminal legal subject, a legal person, *only* if he is a practical reasoner, that is, if he is a rational moral agent. Thus, 'the legal concept of a person does not differ from the moral concept of a person',[60] which means, to him, that legal persons must be 'practical reasoners':[61] 'that is, they act for reasons'.[62]

To Moore, '[a] person is a rational being, a being who acts for intelligible ends in light of rational beliefs'.[63] He does not resile from the consequences of his own logic: those who 'are not yet sufficiently rational that they can reason about moral or legal norms and adjust their behavior to them' simply are not persons.[64] And thus:

> very crazy human beings are not enough like us in one of our essential attributes, rationality, to be considered persons to whom moral and legal norms are addressed.[65]

The intellectually disabled and the very young simply 'do not have the capacities to be the kind of being on whom the law is based; they are not fully persons who reason practically'.[66] To be absolutely clear, they are the wrong 'kind of being' for law.

The term 'person', for Moore, carries considerable moral freight. To be a person is to be a moral agent who can therefore assume moral and legal responsibility. One cannot be legally liable without moral agency and moral responsibility: 'legal rights are seen to depend on moral rights'.[67] Beings are only moral agents if 'they are "practical reasoners'.[68] 'Young infants, the

[58] *Ibid.*

[59] Michael Moore, *Placing Blame: a General Theory of the Criminal Law* (Oxford, Clarendon Press, 1997) 61.

[60] Moore, above n 48, at 48.

[61] *Ibid* 49.

[62] *Ibid* 3.

[63] *Ibid* 66.

[64] *Ibid* 65.

[65] *Ibid.*

[66] *Ibid* 84.

[67] *Ibid* 2–3.

[68] *Ibid.*

very seriously insane, and animals' are not accountable; they are not moral agents.[69]

Moore is quite explicit that law has a natural subject, a natural person, who is an intelligent agent. He therefore offers the most direct opposition to the strict Legalists of the last chapter for whom the legal person is a legal abstraction: a pure device of law.

John Gardner: the English Rationalist

John Gardner has more recently advanced a similar thesis, with perhaps an even more idealised view of the rational defendant in mind, but without the accompanying assertions that those without reason are not persons. Gardner declares that we are by nature rational beings, with a powerful positive interest in presenting ourselves to the world as such and thus giving an adequate account of ourselves when we are accused of criminal wrongs. We want to justify or, at the very least, excuse ourselves, and not just with a view to getting ourselves out of trouble, which is the conventional understanding of why we give excuses. We also want to be able to demonstrate the kind of creatures that we are: creatures who act for reasons. In Gardner's words, 'explanation in terms of reasons is what a rational being aspires to'.[70]

Gardner's modest linguistic point is that rational beings cannot, by definition, question their desire to act for reasons for as soon as they do so, they must offer a reason, thereby demonstrating both their reason and their desire to act for reasons. But his larger metaphysical point, the one that matters here, is that human beings are indeed creatures of this sort; that we are rational by nature and this is what is most important about us. And this is why we, as rational creatures, would positively want to avoid pleas of diminished responsibility. We do not want our reason to be regarded as legally diminished; rather we want our actions to be understood and made comprehensible. To Gardner, we are rational beings who:

> cannot but want our wrongs and mistakes to have been justified or, failing that, at least to have been excused. This makes it part of our nature (in Aristotle's sense of *ergon*, purpose, destiny) to hunt for justifications and excuses as soon as we spot that we have done something wrong or mistaken—never mind what unpleasant moral or legal consequences we can or can't avoid thereby.[71]

Moreover, we aspire to 'excellence in rationality'[72] and to communicate our rationality to others.[73] Gardner thus invokes a high degree of reason in his

[69] *Ibid* 51.

[70] John Gardner, 'The Mark of Responsibility' (2003) 23(2) *Oxford Journal of Legal Studies* 157.

[71] *Ibid* 159.

[72] *Ibid* 158.

[73] Though Gardner relies here on the rationalism of Aristotle, elsewhere he has invoked and endorsed the rationalism of Kant. See especially John Gardner and Stephen Shute, 'The

legal person, 'a developed ability to use reasons',[74] not just ordinary common sense. A court of law is said to provide us with this opportunity to demonstrate our responsibility:

> which is a compound ... of our ability to use reasons in acting, thinking, choosing, wanting etc and our ability to use those reasons again in giving an account of whatever it was we did, thought, chose, wanted etc and in that sense as rational beings giving an account of ourselves.[75]

In the trial, people are rightly pressured 'to give decent public accounts of themselves'.[76]

Moore, too, suggests a sophisticated reasoner in his rendition of the rational responsible person, to whom law addresses its norms. Law speaks to someone who has:

> the ability to form and act on valid practical syllogisms that proceed from intelligible desires and from rational beliefs and which not self-defeatingly conflict with other desires and beliefs held by the agent.[77]

Conjured here is a highly rational and articulate legal actor, providing an eloquent account of his behaviour, someone who offers compelling explanations for alleged criminal wrongdoing in the public forum of a criminal court of law.[78]

Wrongness of Rape' in J Horder (ed), *Oxford Essays in Jurisprudence* (Oxford, Oxford University Press, 2000) 214.

[74] Gardner, above n 70, at 164.

[75] *Ibid.*

[76] *Ibid*, at 168.

[77] Moore, above n 59, at 62.

[78] The defence of insanity is often invoked to support the Rationalist argument that we are quintessentially creatures defined by our reason that law should recognise as such. Moore remarks that 'the insanity defence is a theorist's royal road into the criminal law's presuppositions of what persons must be like' (Moore, above n 59, at 62). For Herbert Fingarette, the availability of the plea 'expresses, even if only in a symbolic way, the concern of the law with citizens as rational beings and not as mere creatures. For it expresses . . . the principle that one who has lost his reason may not be criminally condemned, that the criminal law is a law for those who can be held responsible for what they do' (Fingarette, above n 53, at 7). The defence has been described as 'a manifestation of the basic principle of criminal responsibility which regards individuals as responsible agents who should be punished for choosing to engage in criminally proscribed conduct'. Editorial, Crim L J, October 2002, 257. The defence, it is said, 'purports to draw a line between those who are morally responsible and those who are not, those who are blameworthy and those who are not, those who have free will and those who do not, those who should be punished and those who should not'. A Stone, *Mental Health and Law: a System in Transition* (Rockville, Md, National Institute of Mental Health, 1975) 218, quoted in JA Lymburner and R Roesch (eds), 'The Insanity Defense: Five Years of Research (1993–1997)' (1999) 22 *International Journal of Law and Psychiatry* 213. Thus, the insanity defence is invested with great symbolic importance: it divides the rational from the irrational. It is the legal norm which best exemplifies law's commitment to us as persons of reason.

Are We Really So Rational?

The idea that we are, in essence, intelligent agents, that our powers of reason most define and dignify us, and that this is how best to think of persons generally and law's persons specifically, has met with a good deal of opposition. Perhaps the most powerful objection to this theory of the intelligent, autonomous, choosing agent as legal actor is that he is portrayed as a universal character, but in truth he is quite culturally specific. He represents a modern Western idea of a person which has found its way into Western legal thinking and has then been presented as worldwide and timeless, rather than as specific to a certain time and place. As Rita Carter expresses this simple and important anthropological point:

> The modern Western world is highly individuated and the selves within it generally regard themselves as discrete 'atoms' of consciousness, constantly interacting with one another, but essentially separate. In some cultures, however the self, including its boundaries, is primarily defined in terms of its relationship to others. The Polynesian islanders, for example, speak of themselves almost entirely in terms of social interactions. Asked, for example, to describe an emotion like sadness, the response will be to describe a sad social situation—like a neighbour leaving the island—rather than an inner feeling.[79]

Further, '[t]raditional, close-knit societies which give high importance to kinship and family encourage this extension of self and the downgrading of individual intention'.[80] Such societies tend to be dismissed as primitive by modern Western legal scholars.[81] Maine's story of the move from status to contract is one of progress and enlightenment away from such interdependent forms of association.

There is the related objection that even real Western people are simply not as Rationalists describe them. The intelligent agent tends to be depicted as a curiously static being: a permanent, autonomous, rational adult, unaffected and undiminished by time and circumstance.[82] When Locke considers 'what person stands for', he settles on 'a thinking intelligent being that has reason and reflection and can consider itself as itself, *the same thinking thing in different times and places*' (emphasis added).[83] The nature of his being comes from himself not from others: it derives from his own powers of reason and his ability to tell a continuous rational story about his own life. His social relations are inessential. Implicitly, he is a rational self-determining person well before he engages with and contracts into society.

[79] Rita Carter, *Consciousness* (London, Weidenfeld & Nicolson, 2002) 220.

[80] *Ibid.*

[81] It is implicit in the writing of Hart, for example.

[82] Admittedly, Dworkin was sensitive to the problem of change and asserted that the rational person should trump their irrational self.

[83] Locke, above n 17, at 162.

He is untroubled by the long periods of dependence which comprise the lives of all of us.

This so-called 'man of reason', the autonomous sophisticated reasoner, has been the object of a good deal of feminist and other critical legal analysis.[84] He has been described as an undesirable caricature of human being: impossibly self-possessed and self-reliant, will-driven and individualistic. He is never dependent on others. (I will return to this set of criticisms in Chapter 9.)

It is vital for the story of the social contract that our legal human comes into society only by an act of will and with his own interests in mind and he must therefore implicitly already be a competent adult for this purpose. By nature, this person is therefore self-defined and produced, not socially defined or biologically produced. Omitted from the story of contract is any reference to the mortality of our protagonist. Not only is he without a birth, but he is without a death. Physical decline and cessation are not parts of the story. He is a perpetual mature adult, possessed of an enduring, abstract, autonomous will.

And even as an adult actor, the idea of the sophisticated reasoner does not accord with what we know about those who actually engage with the law, especially with the criminal law. Gardner himself alludes to the less appealing realities of the criminal courts and the real defendants who inhabit them. Here, guilty pleas are the norm rather than the exception. Here, real defendants do not typically engage in sophisticated discourse about their thoughts and their actions as between equals.

In the arena of criminal law, where the liberties of the accused are most at risk, those of very modest intellectual abilities are simply assumed to be fully responsible for their actions. Legal competence is presumed and typically there is no inquiry into the defendant's actual powers of reason. We might say that the arguments of the criminal legal thinkers are largely aspirational in that persons brought before the criminal courts tend to be characterised by social, economic and educational disadvantage.

A further objection to the Rationalists' legal person is that it greatly exaggerates the rational powers of us all. Recently, John Gray has advanced a far less flattering oppositional view of ourselves, insisting that we are not in essence intelligent agents but rather creatures who tend to act unthinkingly, reactively and barely know our own minds.[85] We gull ourselves into thinking that our actions are guided by rational thoughts. But in truth we are not

[84] There is a vast feminist literature on the legal subject; in fact he has been a central preoccupation of legal feminism. A fairly representative collection of essays on this topic is Susan James and Stephanie Palmer (eds), *Visible Women: Essays on Feminist Legal Theory and Political Philosophy* (Oxford and Portland, Hart Publishing, 2002). For a recent overview of the literature, see Ngaire Naffine, 'In Praise of Legal Feminism' (2002) 22(1) *Legal Studies* 71.

[85] John Gray, *Straw Dogs: Thoughts on Humans and Other Animals*(London, Granta Books, 2002).

the authors of our own lives. Rather, our lives are written for us by our circumstances: by our place, our time, our culture, by the accident of our birth.

Gray disputes the very idea of 'the person' which has been so vital to philosophical and legal thinking. 'A person', to Gray, 'is someone who believes that she authors her own life through her choices'.[86] But this is not the way we really are and '[t]hat is not the way most humans have ever lived'.[87] The concept of the person, he says, is a relatively recent European invention. In direct reply to the Rationalists, Gray insists that our actions are not the products of our conscious decisions, of our free will. We are not really rational beings who know our own minds, whose thoughts control our actions.

In support of this less sanguine view of ourselves, Gray cites the work of Benjamim Libet on the 'half-second delay'. Libet's now famous neurological experiment demonstrated 'that the electrical impulse that initiates actions occurs half a second before we take the conscious decision to act'.[88] We may think that thought precedes and guides action and indeed this supposition is at the heart of Rationalist thinking. But:

> [i]n fact in nearly the whole of our lives, our actions are initiated unconsciously: the brain makes us ready for action, *then* we have the experience of acting.[89]

The view that unconscious processes more typically guide our actions, rather than the deliberate and conscious rational will, is indeed one increasingly supported by neuroscience.

We may believe that our powers of choice are critical to our lives; that the well-lived life is the deliberated and chosen life; that as we mature, our choices refine; that we reflect on our choices; that we come to know our own minds; that we cease being reactive animals and become intelligent creatures in command of our destinies. But to Gray this way of viewing ourselves is a recent historical invention and also false. 'For the pre-Socratic Greeks', for example, 'the fact that our lives are framed by limits was what makes us human'.[90] Gray argues that the central 'features of our lives are given to us, they cannot be chosen'[91] and thus he directly disputes the Rationalist and dignifying view of ourselves that we are agents who write our own life stories. According to Gray:

> We are not authors of our lives, we are not even part-authors of the events that mark us most deeply. Nearly everything that is most important in our lives is unchosen.[92]

[86] *Ibid* 58.
[87] *Ibid.*
[88] *Ibid* 66.
[89] *Ibid.*
[90] *Ibid* 109.
[91] *Ibid.*
[92] *Ibid.*

Poetically, he asserts that '[i]t is the casual drift of things that shapes our most fateful relationships. The life of each of us is a chapter of accidents'.[93] Our lives are not a sequence of reasoned decisions. Instead, '[w]e simply deal with whatever is at hand'.[94] As we will see in a later chapter, which considers our animal status, there is still another competing understanding of the person, even in the modern Western tradition, one which starts with dependence rather than with autonomy and separation.

One final concern about Rationalism, and its view of us as responsible and accountable subjects, is that it serves the state well and so should be treated with caution. It is politically expedient for the state to cast us as self-responsible subjects who can then be held accountable for our actions when they are considered harmful to others. The very legitimacy of criminal justice rests on the principle that it is fair to punish us for our wrongs to others because they are our own deliberate choices, the product of our will: we know what we are doing; we supposedly intend our actions; we can be blamed for them. The institutions of the criminal law could not practically function without this presupposition of responsibility and reason. We might therefore regard with some scepticism a theory of ourselves which is so advantageous to the state and which calls for so little supporting evidence—which rests almost entirely on an edifice of high theory.

[93] *Ibid* 109–10.

[94] *Ibid* 112.

6
Persons of Limited Reason

> There are unfortunate human beings who for one reason or another cannot [be normal] and they must live among us in a reduced status, rather like pets, at best, cared for and respected, restrained if necessary, loved and loving in their own limited ways, but not fully participants in the human social world, and, of course lacking morally significant free will.
>
> Daniel Dennett[1]

> [P]lants, stones, ships, earthworms, dogs . . . robots, corpses, corporations, infants and very crazy human beings . . . are either not persons at all, or at least entities whose personhood is in question.
>
> Michael Moore[2]

Of course, we do not begin our lives as sophisticated reasoners and many of us who now reason well will one day lose this ability, or find that it just slowly wanes. Dementia afflicts a significant minority of the population, and increasingly so as those in the affluent West live longer. Law is bound to regulate these mixed populations: the rational and those of impaired or diminishing or even absent reason. And Rationalist legal thinkers must make sense of these cognitively less able people, for they are all about us.

With their orientation towards mature reasoning adults, Rationalists have tended to pass over these basic facts of the human condition. The sophisticated reasoner remains their central moral and political interest and their paradigm legal person; or as moral philosopher Alasdaire MacIntyre encapsulates this approach within his own discipline, it adopts 'the standpoint of those who have taken themselves to be self-sufficiently superior'.[3] But Rationalists have not entirely neglected the irrational and those of modest reason. In particular, Rationalists have explored some of the implications for personhood of the dramatically changing capacities for reason over the human life-cycle. As we will see, Ronald Dworkin, a committed liberal Rationalist, has dilated on the plight of sophisticated reasoners who are losing their reason and demanded that law cordon off and protect the able

[1] Daniel Dennett, *Freedom Evolves* (New York, Viking, 2003) 169.

[2] Michael Moore, *Law and Psychiatry: Rethinking the Relationship* (Cambridge, Cambridge University Press, 1984) 62.

[3] Alasdaire MacIntyre, *Dependant Rational Animals: Why Human Beings Need the Virtues* (Chicago, Open Court Publishing Company, 1991) 7.

reasoner from her demented future self. In Dworkin's view, the past (rational) person should prevail when it comes to making critical personal legal decisions.[4] Other Rationalists have turned their attention to babies and infants. Regarding them as future reasoners, as persons in waiting, they have argued for the careful preservation of the full intellectual potential of these future persons. Still other Rationalists have considered the legal condition of children who possess modest reason but who cannot yet think as mature adults. Such Rationalists have insisted that reasoning children must be permitted to exercise their modest capacities as legal actors, for they are persons in training. As for those with virtually no capacity to reason, those whose brains are profoundly impaired by injury or disease or congenital disability, strict Rationalists maintain that there is no person here at all.

Lawyers who demand intelligent agency and a rational will from their subjects draw a confined circle around the moral and legal community. Only the rational are law's true legal persons: beings who can enter into legal relations on their own account, without a helper (a legal guardian), who can personally assume legal obligations and be held legally responsible. Our law does not engage with 'impaired' individuals directly as legal subjects. Law does not speak to them; it speaks only about them. To count as a genuine legal actor or agent, as a legal person, one must be able to assert one's legal rights, directly, without the aid of another; one must be able to assume and be held to obligations largely of one's own choosing and one must also be able to assume personal responsibility for one's civil and criminal wrongs to others. It follows also that those who cannot reason at all are not strictly speaking persons.

Each of these Rationalist understandings of the person entails a form of metaphysical realism. The governing idea is that human beings have a real essential nature which is defined by the human capacity for reason and that law should directly reflect this human reality in its conception of its person and its corresponding recognition of rights and duties. Legal personification should be calibrated to the past, present or future degree of reason, depending on the condition and circumstances of the particular human being. Concomitantly, law should not waste its time with those who have no reason at all and who will never have it. Not surprisingly, this last view has attracted a good deal of scholarly critical attention, especially from those of a religious disposition who say that all human life is sacred. (These believers in the sanctity of human life will form the subject of the next chapter.)

Law does not entirely accede to the demands of strict Rationalism, insisting that brain death is necessary for the death of the person in law and for the extinguishment of most rights. (Not all rights are extinguished at death: the will of the testator endures long enough to ensure that property

[4] Ronald Dworkin, *Life's Dominion: an Argument about Abortion and Euthanasia* (London, Harper Collins, 1993).

is distributed to the designated beneficiaries.) Law does, however, condition its response to persons according to their cognitive abilities and will demand less of those of impaired or limited intellect.

Law places a variety of demands on reason and recognises a variety of levels of reason in its subjects. Sophisticated reason is not required for every type of legal decision, as some decisions are complex, others simple. Also, some legal decisions seem to have a greater bearing on human dignity than others, and so they call for more sustained legal effort to comprehend and respect the wishes of the decision-maker. For example, Australia's legal and ethical guidelines on the use of artificial reproductive technology (such as IVF) require providers of such services to communicate with prospective mothers and fathers 'in plain language' and 'in a way that is accessible to those with low literacy or disability'.[5] High-level reason is not needed for effective legal decision-making in this context and indeed it is incumbent on those delivering such highly personal services to tailor their legal communications to the capacities of the recipient.

When it comes to decisions about what is to be done with one's own body, when human dignity is most at stake, courts have been willing to recognise the legal capacity for rational self-government in even quite young children and in the intellectually impaired and the diseased. Similarly, legal theorists have been willing to adjust their demands for reason, if legal context and legal relation permit. Those with an interest in the mentally and physically infirm (such as medical patients or children) have insisted that the diminution of reason does not necessarily diminish legal personhood and the ability to make legally-effective decisions. Here, the desire is to preserve what Mill called the 'sovereignty' of each of us over our body and our mind.[6] When it comes to matters which merely concern ourselves, the idea is that law should make a considerable effort to recognise the exercise of even simple reason.[7]

[5] National Health and Medical Research Council, *Ethical Guidelines on the Use of Assisted Reproductive Technology in Clinical Practice and Research* (Australian Government, September 2004) s 9.1.3.

[6] JS Mill, *On Liberty* (London, Longman, Roberts & Green, 1869).

[7] When we are sick and vulnerable, the endorsed legal principle (and the view advanced by legal scholars) is still one of patient choice and patient autonomy. This remains true as long as there is a basic capacity to understand what is proposed and its implications. The Rationalist idea is that it is up to us to decide what is to be done to ourselves. The patient is thus to be treated as a moral agent and her choices respected, even when exercised by an individual of very limited mental ability, which we are all at some time in our lives. Only thus do we respect the patient as a person. The courts have even upheld the right of patients to make what they call 'irrational decisions' about how they are to be treated, if it is clear that the person has sufficient reason to be considered legally competent. One is supposed to have the right to make an irrational decision about one's own person. There is, of course, a Catch 22. The more irrational the decision, the less likely will it be that a court will find sufficient competence to make such a decision.

This chapter is about Legal Rationalists and their variable responses to the vicissitudes of reason. It considers, in the first instance, the problem of the disappearing rational self and the prospective death of the person, conceived in a strict Rationalist sense. It then reflects on a Rationalist approach to babies and young children in which they are treated as future persons—as persons in waiting. It goes on to examine the nature of the personhood of maturing children who are acquiring the skills of the sophisticated reasoner, but still only possess a modest level of reason: the trainee persons. And finally it canvasses the predicament of the fully and enduringly irrational, those whom law cannot engage with at all and whom certain Rationalists would therefore characterise as non-persons.

Ronald Dworkin on the Patient as Author of a Life

There is always a problem of delimiting reason, of deciding the moment at which someone is no longer enough of a rational person to guide their own life, when their personhood is effectively lost. The medical legal literature has formed the setting for a particularly poignant discussion about what is to be done when someone loses their senses and it speaks directly to the problem of what constitutes a person in law. Specifically, if someone has given instructions, while rational, about how they wish to be treated should their reason be impaired some time in the future, should those instructions made while rational be honoured after reason is diminished or lost, especially if those instructions no longer seem to reflect the interests and desires of the new irrational individual?

While rational, for example, the person may say that no heroic measures should be taken to keep them alive after they have lost the capacity to make decisions; or they may say that life support should be withdrawn should they become thus dependent and in a state of much diminished mental capacity. Whose medical wishes should prevail: those of the rational person or those of the irrational patient who may at the later, impaired, stage want the treatment? Which individual should prevail? Who should law address? Indeed, are there two persons here, or only the one: the rational person prior to loss of competence? Anglo-American legal philosopher Ronald Dworkin has sought to answer these questions.

Dworkin has entered into some of the most controversial debates about beginning and end-of-life decisions. Most importantly, for present purposes, Dworkin has endeavoured to ground his arguments about these life-defining decisions on a sustained, reasoned and persuasive account of the nature of the person in law. As a liberal, who believes in the primacy of choice, Dworkin has accentuated the right of the person, while rational, to engineer her own life and the vital role of law in securing this opportunity for self-engineering, this autonomy. To Dworkin, what most defines the person is her capacity for reason and her consequent capacity for self-governance. In this respect, he fits squarely within the Rationalist tradition.

As a political and legal thinker steeped in the Judeo-Christian tradition, however, Dworkin has also defended what many would regard as a religious understanding of the person and, more particularly, he has endorsed the idea of human sanctity. I will return to his influential ideas about sanctity and human value in the next chapter, where I consider the idea of the sacred legal person. Dworkin has also embraced a naturalistic account of the person, ostensibly informed by Darwinian thought. I will therefore visit Dworkin, once again, when I examine the influence of evolutionary thinking on legal ideas of the person. Indeed, Dworkin is distinctive in his endeavour to effect a *rapprochement* of all three metaphysical approaches to the person which form the subject of this book (the Rationalist, the Religionist and the Naturalist) which have characteristically stood in stark opposition; to show how they can be interlinked and support one another. Whether he manages this Herculean task is another matter, which I will also consider.

For the moment, I will look at Dworkin's understanding of the person as a rational self-governing patient, as author of a life, and his particular interest in what the responsible agent should do when facing fundamental life decisions, and especially when anticipating the loss of reason and the loss of life. But Dworkin's Rationalism is not easily disentangled from his more mystical thinking about the nature and innate value of human life. Our human reason, he believes, must be directed to living life well: each life is of such incalculable value that it must not be squandered.

The mysticism, even religiosity, of Dworkin (again more on this in the next chapter) comes from this foundational assertion that human life has intrinsic value—it is simply there, this innate *human* value—and that it imposes a great responsibility on us as thinking agents. We have been given a life of innate, even 'cosmic', value (he says) and this is why it is deeply wrong to waste it. As thinking agents, we are obliged to use our lives fruitfully.

Dworkin advances an essentially liberal Rationalist argument about what flows from the innate value of the lives we have been given. One might expect him to say that if human life is of intrinsic value, then life must always be preserved; certainly this is the view we tend to associate with those who defend the sanctity of life (such as natural lawyer John Finnis, whose views on human sanctity I will also consider in the next chapter). But Dworkin does not say this. Instead, he concludes that the life we are given imposes on us an obligation to use it well, *not* to preserve it at all costs or have it preserved for us at all costs. It is intrinsically wrong to waste it, but it is not intrinsically wrong to decide to end it if it has ceased to have value or no longer corresponds with our conception of a life well lived, as understood by our rational selves.

As a liberal, Dworkin believes that the means by which we respect the value of our life is something for each of us to decide. We each must determine how our own life is best lived. Life's sanctity means that we must use this life well; we must not waste it. But as agents, as sophisticated reasoners and therefore as the authors of our own individual lives (and he is deeply committed to ethical individualism), we are obliged to decide how to respect and give meaning to our lives. Dworkin thus places great store by the ability of an individual to construct a complex autobiography and it is this autobiographical self which makes each of us a person who commands respect and who must be addressed as such by others, including by legal institutions. According to Dworkin:

> In our society, a society that is marked by the point of view [of] . . . ethical individualism, one master idea is accepted: that it is not only the case that human beings each have a life to live, but that each human being has a life to make something of—responsibility to create a life such that he or she can look back on that life with pride rather than misery and take pride in it rather than account it a waste. This is a fundamental human responsibility.[8]

The responsibility to make something of one's life, not to waste it, therefore brings with it the responsibility that 'in our moral tradition . . . is often referred to as autonomy or self respect'.[9] What Dworkin calls 'the nerve of that responsibility' is the right to determine what is best for ourselves, what is good for us. He insists that:

> so far as decisions are made primarily affecting a person's life, and so far as those decisions are made with the aim that that person's life go better, be more successful, run less risk of waste, then those decisions must be made by the person whose life it is or, when that's not possible, in accordance, so far as this is possible, with the standards that that person chose.[10]

This responsibility is then linked to a fundamental right: 'the right to make personality-defining or life-defining decisions for oneself'.[11] To Dworkin, this is 'a deep humanist idea of individual liberty'.[12] We must determine our own fate but we must do so responsibly; or as Dworkin eloquently expresses it:

> [w]e have ultimate responsibility one by one, person by person, for deciding what an appropriate life for us is, and for doing our best to live that life.[13]

[8] Ronald Dworkin, 'Euthanasia, Morality and Law Transcript' (1998) 31 *Loyola LA Law Review* 1147.

[9] *Ibid.*

[10] *Ibid.*

[11] *Ibid.*

[12] *Ibid.*

[13] Ronald Dworkin, 'Politics, Death and Nature' (1996) 6(2) *Health Matrix* (Summer)201, 206–7.

This great obligation we bear as rational beings, to respect our innately valuable life, but also to decide what meaning it should have if we are to respect it—in effect to decide, as thinking agents, how best to respect this sacred life, to decide *our* meaning of life—is for Dworkin our great responsibility as persons.[14] It cannot and should not be decided for us. Our rational autonomy, our personhood, is realised in the decisions that *we* make about how to give *our* life value, how to respect it, how to give it meaning. In Dworkin's view, the processes of rational deliberation, over a lifetime, make us what we are. Through our 'human creative intelligence', we make ourselves; our 'own creative choices progressively determine [our] thoughts, personality, ambitions, connections and achievements'.[15]

This has at least two practical legal consequences. One is in relation to abortion, a subject I will return to in the next chapter, because it bears directly on the question of foetal sanctity.[16] The second is in relation to end-of-life decisions. In his major work on moral and legal rights at the two ends of life, *Life's Dominion*, Dworkin specifically considers the nature of the rights and interests 'not of someone who has always been demented, but of someone who was competent in the past'.[17] He asks, pointedly:

> Does a competent person's right to autonomy include, for example, the power to dictate that life-prolonging treatment be denied him later, or that funds not be spent on maintaining him in great comfort, even if he, when demented, pleads for it?[18]

To Dworkin, the real person, the one who carries moral and legal authority, is the thinking agent. It follows that the present rational person can dictate to the later (non)person who has lost their capacity for reason. It is a personal decision, to be made by the agent, as to whether, and at what point, life can still be lived in a manner which is consistent with the agent's conception of their own life well lived. A life reduced to endless pain or sedated to the point that agency is no longer possible may be intolerable, even in anticipation. It is not a life that should be lived and it is not an end that an agent would choose.

[14] The fact that our life has intrinsic value is not a matter of personal choice or interests. It is objectively true. It is not up to us. But how that intrinsic value is then given meaning, and respected, is a matter of personal choice.

[15] Dworkin, above n 4, at 82–3.

[16] According to Dworkin, because human life has intrinsic value, a foetus has value but not such that its life must also always be preserved. The mother's life also has intrinsic value and as an agent she has an obligation to decide how that value is to be realised and the continuation of a pregnancy may be inconsistent with that meaning. It may be a blight on her life as she understands and gives meaning to her life. So although it is a shame that the abortion goes ahead it might be necessary for the woman's life to have meaning, and this is a decision for her to make.

[17] Dworkin, above n 4, at 221.

[18] *Ibid.*

Dworkin is clear that the person as thinking agent exercises authority over the later person whose reason is reduced or effaced. For Dworkin, the demented person does not satisfy the 'conditions of autonomy'[19] because they are incapable of reflecting on the 'the overall shape' of their life. In effect, there is no person left whose views must be listened to. Alzheimer victims, he says, have lost their 'critical interests'. They no longer have:

> the capacity to think about how to make their lives more successful as a whole. They are ignorant of self . . . they have no sense of a whole life, a past joined to a future, that could be the object of any evaluation or concern as a whole . . . They therefore have no contemporary opinion about their own critical interests.[20]

Dworkin explicitly links his analysis to the Rationalist philosophy of Kant; he believes that his is 'a useful reading of the Kantian principle that people should be treated as ends and never merely as means'.[21]

Dworkin writes of 'our moral tradition',[22] of our ethic of individualism, which might suggest that he is deferring to local conventions in his conception of human agency. And yet in other places he declares that our most basic moral rights transcend the merely conventional; they are not merely the product of a liberal and enlightened society but rather they are '"out there" in the fabric of the universe'.[23] Dworkin's moral absolutism is particularly in evidence when he is trying to give meaning to the idea of human sanctity, or innate value: that which imposes on us the obligation as thinking agents to use our lives well. In the next chapter, I will consider more closely what human sanctity means to Dworkin and how he would seek to distinguish himself from others who pursue the sanctity of (human) life argument.

Safeguarding the Future Person: Dena Davis and the Child's Right to an Open Future

Rationalists have a natural interest not only in the extinguishing person slipping into dementia (and the threat she may pose to her former rational self) but also an interest in the future person (and the perceived need to safeguard the prospects of a full intellectual flourishing). More specifically, there is a logical desire to preserve the full cognitive potential and freedom of choice of the sophisticated reasoner who will not come on to the scene until adulthood and so must live through a long period of vulnerability to the decisions of others. American Rationalist lawyer Dena Davis has

[19] Dworkin, above n 4, at 227.
[20] *Ibid* 230.
[21] *Ibid* 236.
[22] Dworkin, above n 8.
[23] Ronald Dworkin, 'In Praise of Theory' (1997) 29 *Arizona State Law Review* 353, 361.

described and defended this future person in a spirited critique of the 1972 American Supreme Court decision of *Wisconsin v Yoder*.[24]

Wisconsin v Yoder[25] concerned the efforts of a group of Older Order Amish to obtain an exemption from the Wisconsin State requirement that children attend school until they were 16 or until they graduated from high school. The Amish wanted to secure their right to insulate their children from the broader culture and to inculcate them in traditional Amish ways and beliefs which entailed self-reliance and the acquisition of farming and housewifery skills (depending on the sex of the child). As Davis explains, the Amish in question:

> framed the issue in the starkest manner: to send their children to any school, past eighth grade, would be antithetical to their religion and their way of life, and might even result in the death of their culture.[26]

Higher learning, it was thought, encouraged the acquisition of values which could 'alienate man from God'.[27] The court accepted this framing of the legal question, as essentially one of freedom of religion, which was to be weighed against the state's rights to have its citizens educated. And accepting that this was essentially a matter of religious freedom, the court found in favour of the Amish.

Davis objects strongly to the decision of the US Supreme Court because, in her view, it did not take proper account of the right of the child 'to an open future'.[28] Davis describes what she sees as a judicial failure to recognise the needs and rights of the future person, the future adult reasoner and choice-maker. In essence, she provides a strong Rationalist defence of the sophisticated reasoner as a paradigm person. She defends the right of this person to come into existence, and to ensure that choices are not made for her which will hamper her eventual full flourishing. Of the US Supreme Court, she says that:

> No justice squarely faced the question of whether the liberal democratic state owes all its citizens, especially children, a right to a basic education that can serve as a building block if the child decides later in life that she wishes to become an astronaut, a playwright, or perhaps to join the army . . . without a high school diploma one's future is virtually closed. By denying them a high school education . . . parents are virtually ensuring that their children will remain housewives and agricultural laborers. Even if the children agree, is that a choice parents ought to be allowed to make for them?[29]

[24] Dena Davis, 'Genetic Dilemmas and the Child's Right to an Open Future' in *Hastings Center Report* (March–April 1997) 7, 9.

[25] 406 US 205 (1972).

[26] Davis, above n 24.

[27] *Wisconsin v Yoder*, 406 US 205, 211 (1972).

[28] Davis, above n 24.

[29] *Ibid* 9–10.

To Davis, there is a positive obligation on the state to secure a rich adult future for the child, particularly through the provision of education. 'It should send him out into the adult world with as many open opportunities as possible, thus maximizing his chances for self-fulfillment'.[30]

In 1995, in *B(R) v Children's Aid Society of Metropolitan Toronto*,[31] the Supreme Court of Canada employed similar reasoning and declared that the future person must be protected from those who would cut off her future life choices as a sophisticated reasoner (as well as her very life). Richard and Beena B were the parents of a baby girl who was born prematurely with a number of serious physical ailments. Richard and Beena were Jehova's Witnesses who, on religious grounds, objected to the transfusion of blood for their baby, despite its obvious medical need. Against their wishes, their baby was transfused. The question asked of the Canadian Court was whether an Ontario Statute which permitted such medical interventions against the parents declared wishes was in breach of the Canadian Charter of Rights and Freedom and its guarantee of freedom of religion and if it was in breach, was that breach justifiable.

The Court agreed that:

> [t]he right of parents to rear their children according to their religious beliefs, including that of choosing medical and other treatments, is a fundamental aspect of freedom of religion, guaranteed by . . . the Charter.[32]

But this freedom was constrained by the rights and freedom of others. Critically, the Court declared that:

> [s]ince SB [the baby girl] has never expressed any agreement with the Jehovah's Witness faith or any religion, there is an impingement on her freedom of conscience, which arguably includes the right to live long enough to make one's own reasoned choice about the religion one wishes to follow as well as the right not to hold a religious belief. 'Freedom of religion' should not encompass activity that so categorically negates 'the freedom of conscience' of another.[33]

The future person, the future reasoning chooser, was to be shielded from the parents and present life and intellectual potential preserved. It was not simply the life of the present baby at stake. There was another figure to be considered, one who would inhabit the future as a mature thinker and who must be permitted then to make her own life-governing decisions.[34]

[30] Davis, 11.

[31] [1995] 1 SCR 315.

[32] *B(R) v Children's Aid Society of Metropolitan Toronto* [1995] 1 SCR 315, electronic copy at 10.

[33] *Ibid*, electronic copy at 11.

[34] For a fine analysis of this decision and its implications for the child's right to autonomy, see Benjamin L Berger, 'Law's Religion: Rendering Culture' (2007) 45 *Osgoode Hall Law Journal* 277.

Persons in Training: Mrs Gillick and the Contraceptive Advice

There comes a time when children can reason perfectly well on their own about some matters, if they are permitted to do so. Moreover, practice at reasoning is needed if the capacity for mature reason is to be acquired. The sophisticated reasoner requires a period of training.

In 1986, the House of Lords directly confronted this problem of the person in preparation and when and how to acknowledge the decisions of the intellectually maturing child. The appellant in the case was Mrs Victoria Gillick, mother of 10 children, five of whom were girls under the age of 16. She objected strongly to advice given by the Department of Health to local health authorities to the effect that doctors could lawfully prescribe contraception to girls under 16, without the consent of their parents.[35] Mrs Gillick sought assurance that her own daughters would not be given such services (not that they were seeking them nor were likely to challenge their mother's authority), and a declaration of their unlawfulness. She regarded them as an infringement of her rights and duties as a parent.

The House of Lords disagreed with Mrs Gillick and endorsed the idea of the emerging and maturing person as reasoner and choice-maker. In the words of Lord Scarman:

> parental right yields to the child's right to make his own decisions when he reaches a sufficient understanding and intelligence to be capable of making up his own mind on the matter requiring decision.[36]

The mature reasoner must be given sufficient opportunity to emerge. Parental rights over the child were not sovereign. The law had never treated the child 'as other than a person with capacities and rights recognised by law'[37] and when the child could think for herself, parental rights must diminish and dwindle. 'The law relating to parent and child is concerned with the problems of the growth and maturity of the human personality', affirmed Lord Scarman:

> If the law should impose upon the process of 'growing up' fixed limits where nature knows only a continuous process, the price would be artificiality and a lack of realism in an area where the law must be sensitive to human development and social change.[38]

[35] *Gillick v West Norfolk and Wisbech Area Health Authority* [1986] 1 AC 112.
[36] *Ibid* 186.
[37] *Ibid* 184.
[38] *Ibid* 186.

Rationalists on Non-persons

But what of the human being who cannot reason at all? How are we to think of the individual who will never acquire the capacity to reason, because of brain damage or mental disease? And what of the human being who once reasoned but has now lost this capacity forever (Dworkin's particular concern)? What of their personhood?

There is a palpable reluctance among nearly all styles of Rationalist to take Rationalism to its logical conclusion and say that legal personhood disappears altogether in the complete absence of reason. Among lawyers it is hard to find anyone who will say that the fully irrational should not attract basic human rights and, of course, the law, as a matter of doctrine and practice, protects all human beings. The almost universal view is that the irrational cannot participate as legal persons in law's community of legal actors, but they must still be protected. They remain law's beneficiaries but they cannot be its addressees. (Why law should worry about such irrational human beings is the subject of the next chapter on human sanctity.)

Once the person slips below the threshold of mental capacity considered necessary to make minimally-rational medical decisions, then another person must assume the patient's persona. They may do this by trying to work out what the rational patient would have wanted or they may decide what is now best for the patient, in their reduced form, and the persona of the patient effectively disappears. There is no real legal person left in the sense of an agent governing their own life. And to those who demand agency from their legal person, there is no person left either. This was essentially Dworkin's message.

The courts, however, have continued to insist that a live human being who is entirely devoid of reason remains a legal person and so a beneficiary of law's protection. In the case of *A (Children)*,[39] the English Court of Appeal was asked to decide whether surgery to separate conjoined twins, which would certainly kill one of them, would constitute the crime of murder. At the outset, the court considered whether the twins, Jodie and Mary, were both legal persons: law's beneficiaries. It would vastly have simplified their job if they had agreed either that there was only the one person present (who would be Jodie, the stronger twin, upon whom Mary depended) or that there were no persons at all (in accordance with the will theory). A surgeon commenting on the case declared that there was indeed only one person, that physiologically Mary 'was not a human being but a tumour'.[40] However, the court declined to take this view, declaring that Jodie and Mary were both persons.

[39] *Re A (Children) Conjoined Twins: Surgical Separation* [2000] 4 All ER 961.

[40] H Watt, 'Conjoined Twins: Separation as Mutilation' (2001) 9 *Medical Law Review* 237.

Other legal analysts have objected to the decision saying that, in truth, neither twin was a person. John Harris, for example, has plumped for a definition of a person based on the 'cognitive capacity . . . to sustain a biographical life' (a rather less stringent definition than Moore's), with the effect that 'neither Mary nor Jodie were persons at the time of the operation'.[41] The final decision to approve the separation of the twins (thus saving Jodie but killing Mary) was therefore, in his reasoning, ethically justified. In effect, Harris is saying that Mary was neither an addressee nor an appropriate beneficiary of law. She was not a person at all.

Few lawyers subscribe to this view that the person devoid of reason, or with only the capacity for the most primitive thinking, is not a person in the sense of an appropriate beneficiary of basic legal rights. A handful of philosophers has done so. Australian philosopher Michael Tooley, for example, has pursued the logic of Rationalism to its natural end.[42] He has argued that in the absence of any capacity for reason, of any sense of self (the sort that Locke demanded), there is no person at all and so there cannot be said to be even the most basic legal right of a person: the right to life.

In his now famous philosophical treatise on what it is to be a person, *Abortion and Infanticide*,[43] Tooley asked, provocatively, whether 'new-born humans' are persons and concluded that they are not because there is 'no ground for attributing higher mental capacities to them'.[44] According to Tooley, we have no reason to believe 'that new-born humans possess a capacity for thought, or for self consciousness, or for rational deliberation'.[45] For this reason, infanticide of a very young baby, in the first few weeks of life, is not morally wrong. For a very young human to possess the right to life, it must have a sense of itself and must have more than momentary interests; it must have a 'unification of consciousness over time'.[46] From this it follows that neither foetuses nor neonates are moral persons and neither possesses a right to life. This is not the position law takes. But arguably it is one which takes Rationalism to its logical conclusion and so it has the merit of intellectual and moral consistency.

Against this strong Rationalism, Michael Ignatieff has invoked its unfortunate implications for the entire structure of civil society:

> [T]he humanism of our day believes . . . [that] We are creatures of reason and speech, and it is as creatures who, alone of all the species, can create and exchange meaning that we all have intrinsic needs for respect, understanding, love

[41] John Harris, 'Human Beings, Persons and Conjoined Twins: an Ethical Analysis of the Judgment in Re A' (2001) 9 *Medical Law Review* 221.

[42] This position is also associated with the work of Peter Singer, who will be considered in the chapter on the legal status of animals.

[43] M Tooley, *Abortion and Infanticide* (Oxford, Clarendon Press, 1983).

[44] *Ibid* 407.

[45] *Ibid.*

[46] *Ibid* 410.

> and trust . . . [but] As soon as one enlarges the definition of the human, real human beings begin to be excluded: the Tom O'Bedlams of our time, the mad kings, the insane, the retarded, the deaf and the dumb, the crippled and the deranged. Those doctors and magistrates who have taken upon themselves the awesome business of deciding who is human—ie who is rational—have created a vast array of institutions designed to make Tom O'Bedlam and the mad king human again. The converse of the rational man has turned out to be man the disciplinarian, the man who takes upon himself the godly power of deciding who is in the sacred circle of reason and who is without.[47]

Recognising Reason

The view that persons must be engaged with as rational beings and not simply instructed is important and dignifying. Dworkin is persuasive on this. It puts an onus on the law and its institutions to make a substantial effort on behalf of us all.[48] Even as an aspiration, it seems important to set conditions of proper engagement between the law and the people. The justice system can then be judged, as fair and just or otherwise, by its willingness and its capacity to provide opportunities for rational agents to engage in reasoned discourse and to explain their actions and decide their own life course: to be treated as persons.

This may be regarded as the best case for intelligent agency as the hallmark of personality. It confers respect on the individual; it places obligations on the state to provide the means of engaging in intelligent discourse with the individual before the law; it sets dignifying standards of thought and conduct both for the law and for us; and it is supported by a revered and broadly-endorsed philosophical tradition.

But to be fair and just, Rationalism must be fairly and evenly applied. Those who subscribe to this philosophy should treat as rational those who are actually rational and they should temper their demands when reason is found to be diminished. A serious problem with Rationalism, however, lies in the unevenness of its application. The animal rights lawyers, who will be considered later in the book, are particularly exercised by the failures of Rationalists to apply their principles, at all, to other species. Dworkin is an obvious offender here. He is concerned about animals *en masse*, as species, but not as individuals. It appears that they are utterly disqualified from the benefits of Rationalism because they are not human. The growing body of evidence of animal intelligence, of the presence of child-like reason in apes and even in parrots, does not seem to alter his thinking on the species of rights holders. The problem is one of consistency; recognising reason and permitting it to do its work in relation to all beings that can reason. If

[47] Michael Ignatieff, *The Needs of Strangers* (New York, Viking, 1984) 43–4.

[48] Martin Krygier has written extensively on the obligation of the state to reason with its citizens, not merely instruct them. So too has HLA Hart.

modest reason is recognised in humans as a basis of legal decision-making and legal personification, then why not in animals?

Feminists have also been exercised by the failures of Rationalists to apply their principles consistently to women. This was once quite blatant. When women were not considered to be persons for many public offices, it was their reason which was found wanting. In 1875, a Wisconsin court thus explained the problem with women:

> The law of nature destines and qualifies the female sex for the bearing and nurture of the children of our race and for the custody of the homes of the world . . . The peculiar qualities of womanhood, its gentle graces, its quick sensitivities, its tender susceptibility, its purity, its delicacy, its emotional impulses, its subordination of hard reason to sympathetic feeling, are surely not qualifications for forensic strife.[49]

Well into the twentieth century, women were permitted to demonstrate their powers of reason at medical and law schools but they were not permitted to take the relevant degrees, as they were not persons for these legal purposes. They were effectively denied public citizenship.

But the most egregious refusals to recognise reason in women (and its most important corollary, rational self-government), are far more recent and some persist to the present day. The husband's immunity from prosecution for the rape of his wife was honoured in England until 1991.[50] The right to refuse sexual intercourse, arguably the most basic human right to bodily sovereignty which is recognised in those of very modest reason, was not permitted to a wife, whatever her intelligence.[51]

Feminists remain concerned that women in the labour ward are still vulnerable to exclusion from the population of rights-bearing reasoners, those who have a basic right to determine what is done to their bodies. The current formal legal position is that women when pregnant retain an absolute right to refuse medical intervention, even if their foetus is at risk. However, there is a much-discussed line of cases which demonstrates the fragility of this right.

The right of pregnant women to refuse medical treatment considered beneficial or necessary for the welfare of the foetus has always been precarious. In some early American decisions, it was explicitly denied and thus were women denied rational self-government in a manner which has no parallel for men. The more recent medical jurisprudence has formally affirmed

[49] *In re Goddell*, 39 Wisc 232, 245 (1875).

[50] The presumptive immunity was lifted by the House of Lords in 1991: *R v R* [1991] 3WLR 767.

[51] South Australia was one of the first jurisdictions to permit the prosecution of a husband for the rape of his wife but there was such concern about the threat this represented to marriage that only aggravated marital rape was criminalised. Basic marital rape was not a crime. It was the intrusion of rape law into marriage that was unthinkable.

the rights of pregnant women to make their own medical decisions, whether or not the life of the foetus is at stake, and yet the courts remain practically uncertain about whether such women possess unqualified autonomy. Women in late pregnancy and in labour still seem to constitute a class of persons of suspect reason when they make decisions which may jeopardise the foetus.

In *Re MB (Medical Treatment)*,[52] for example, the English Court of Appeal had to decide whether to respect the wishes of a pregnant woman who refused a medically-indicated Caesarean section because of her fear of needles. The court affirmed the general principle that a:

> mentally competent patient had an absolute right to refuse to consent to medical treatment for any reason, rational or irrational, or for no reason at all.[53]

However, MB was found to be *temporarily* incompetent and thus the right was forfeited. The court approved a judicial declaration to proceed with a Caesarean against her wishes, with the use of force if necessary. In *St George's Healthcare NHS Trust v S*,[54] the English Court of Appeal disapproved a judicial declaration dispensing with the woman's consent to a Caesarean section (the judge who issued the declaration deemed her incompetent despite a highly articulate written and verbal refusal of consent), but only after the Caesarean had been performed. Here, the court recognised the unqualified autonomy of the woman as competent rational legal agent. But then the court said that '[i]t does not follow . . . that this entitles her to put at risk the healthy viable foetus which she is carrying'.[55] Rational self-determination was not an unqualified right of the pregnant woman.

These represent deep and yet changing ways of thinking about half the population of rational adults who are supposed to be paradigm rational subjects. At different times, common adult female conditions (marriage and pregnancy in particular, though at the start of the century, just being a woman) have significantly compromised the assignment of reason and the rights which are supposed to flow from its presence. We remain in a way of thinking which finds Rationalism not always fully applicable to female human beings.

And of course there is also a deep speciesism evident among Rationalists generally. As we will see in the chapter on animal rights, most Rationalists would not dream of applying their principles to non-human animals of modest but demonstrated reason. It is simply beyond contemplation.

[52] *Re MB (Medical Treatment)* [1997] 2 FLR 426.
[53] *Ibid.*
[54] *St George's Healthcare NHS Trust v S* [1998] 3 WLR 913.
[55] *Ibid* 951.

Emotional Intelligence

My final concern about Rationalism is its central dogma that dispassionate reason best defines the character of human beings and endows us with value. An alternative way of conceiving of human beings has been hinted at throughout this chapter and this is as affectionate, caring, social and interdependent beings who are most defined by their feelings for others, not their mature capacity for formal reason. Human life could not get going and could not be sustained were it not for the efforts of carers—those who tend to the needs of those who have yet to achieve an autonomous rational state. And care without affection is not truly care.

I do not wish to suggest that it is as loving altruistic beings that we are necessarily best understood, although others have made this interesting claim.[56] I do not wish to suggest that this is necessarily a better, truer way of thinking of human beings. Nor do I want necessarily to retain the idea that there is an essential ingredient of human nature which law should reflect, if it is to be true to human beings. However, the clear presence of an alternative way of thinking about what most defines us must bring Rationalism into doubt. For it is not the case that the capacity for sophisticated reason is indisputably the one and only way of conceiving of us. Nor is it necessarily that which most ennobles us, as Kant believed.

Those who have friends or family members with Downs Syndrome will know that these intellectually-disadvantaged individuals can still display a particularly well-developed sense of loving empathy which can be lacking in other persons of high formal intellect. Those with Downs Syndrome can be very good at reading people and responding sensitively to their emotional states. Chief Sportswriter for *The Times*, Simon Barnes, has recently written affectingly about his son Eddie, who has Downs Syndrome, and why he is a delightful and valued member of his family.[57] He describes Eddie's warm, responsive nature and why Eddie greatly enriches the life of those around him. Barnes' larger point is that such persons are not best regarded as defective and afflicted beings, purely a cost to society, a view that strict Rationalism might encourage. Rather, they are persons with particular strengths and abilities but those strengths are not sufficiently appreciated by Rationalists.

Persons with Downs Syndrome are therefore particularly interesting in the current context because they lack precisely the ability which Rationalists

[56] There is an extensive literature on what has come to be known as an 'ethic of care'. It is built upon the foundational work of Carol Gilligan, *In a Different Voice* (Cambridge, Mass, Harvard University Press, 1981) and has been developed by such social analysts as Nel Noddings.

[57] Simon Barnes, 'Living with Eddie', *The Weekend Australian Magazine*, 14–15 April 2007, 31.

find most important in us—that is sophisticated reason—but may possess another ability: emotional intelligence. These people show us that we are making a choice when we say that high-level reason is most valuable and most human-defining and the human characteristic which should most find expression in law's conception of its person. These people show us that we could make another choice. Their presence does not demonstrate that Rationalism is wrong. It does show us that Rationalism entails a decision about what to value in us, in society and in law, and that we could well choose another.

A related objection to Rationalism, with its current emphasis on cool-headed sophisticated reason as the hallmark of personhood, is that it takes too little account of the role of empathy and compassion and even raw intuition in the effective exercise of mature reason.[58] The Rationalists I considered in this chapter and the last said little about the need for a developed sense of fellow feeling or empathy in making rational determinations. They also said little about the gut reactions or intuitions which often accompany or inform our best decisions. And yet legal determinations which are devoid of any sense of compassion for defendants or plaintiffs may well be wanting. So too may be legal determinations which demonstrate little sense of repugnance towards certain types of behaviour; that is, good decisions may call for appropriate feelings, for appropriate intuition and affect. As Jennifer Nedelsky has suggested, 'good judgment' may well require 'learning appropriate affective responses' so that the good judge also has the right 'gut feelings'; so that she can judge with the heart, the body and the mind.[59]

[58] The operation of these human properties has been a sustained concern of Martha Nussbaum. See, eg *Love's Knowledge: Essays on Philosophy and Literature* (New York, Oxford University Press, 1990).

[59] Jennifer Nedelsky, 'Embodied Diversity and the Challenges of Law' (1996–1997) 42 *McGill Law Journal* 91, 105.

7

The Divine Spark: the Principle of Human Sanctity

> [W]e are born free and equal in dignity and rights because there is a divine Creator, and there is a divine spark in men.
>
> Eleanor Roosevelt[1]

> The divine image is present in every man.
>
> Catechism of the Catholic Church[2]

Legal doctrine and legal philosophy are replete with assertions about the intrinsic value of human life and the need to respect it. It is often said that the human being is 'inviolable' and that human life is of infinite worth. There are frequent references to such things as innate human value, dignity and integrity. It is also commonly said that law must respect 'the sanctity of human life'. It is difficult to find a quarrel with any of these propositions. And yet it is far from clear what such statements really mean and why it is thought that human life is so very valuable. Most perplexing is this property of sanctity that is often said to constitute human value. Typically, these evaluative claims about human beings are simply taken as a given.

Respect, even reverence, for human beings can derive from a number of sources. In the last two chapters, I considered one highly respected source of legal reverence for human life. I examined the role of reason in defining the human, endowing her with value and so engendering respect for her as a legal person. I reviewed the character of rational articulate legal actors, often imagined in a criminal courtroom, asserting their rights and being called to account. This was thought to be the full flourishing of the human and legal person because the capacity for sophisticated reason was regarded as the source of human value: the seat of our personhood. I reflected also on the moral and legal nature of more modest reasoners who were thought to derive their value from their future capacity for reason. Individuals who were permanently incapable of reason clearly posed a problem for the

[1] Eleanor Roosevelt, 'Making Human Rights Come Alive', in *What I hope to Leave Behind: the Essential Essays of Eleanor Roosevelt* (Allida Black (ed), Brooklyn, Carlson Publishing Inc, 1995) 559, quoted in Mary Ann Glendon, *A World Made New: Eleanor Roosevelt and the Universal Declaration of Human Rights* (New York, Random House, 2001) 147.

[2] *Catechism of the Catholic Church* (Homebush NSW, Society of St Paul, 1994) 425.

Rationalists. It was difficult to find value in them according to the strict requirements of Rationalism.

It is when reason runs out, when there is absolutely no prospect of a human being ever becoming a rational subject or being one again, that law and legal thinkers need another source of human value if they are to remain committed to the idea of a deep and enduring respect for all human life.[3] (Some Rationalists would also argue that when there is no present capacity for reason, as with the foetus, there is no person present and therefore no fundamental obligation to respect that entity or being.) When reason expires, when it cannot do its work of creating human value because there is no present or future capacity for reason, 'human sanctity' is typically invoked. Often the term is employed to conjure up a mysterious essence of human beings which is indwelling and calls for reverence, notwithstanding the absence of reason. The invocation of 'human sanctity' is intended to tell us that human beings are innately special and that we are somehow always elevated above the animal world, regardless of our individual abilities and capacities. The sacred human person is said to possess inherent value with or without law expressing that value and with or without the human in question possessing any particular characteristics, beyond their raw humanity.

The term 'sanctity' is borrowed from religious language and seems to have strong religious connotations. Indeed, the very notion that human beings are of infinite value, irrespective of their quality as individuals, seems to be implicitly religious. According to Ronald Dworkin:

> the belief that the value of human life transcends its value for the creature whose life it is—that human life is objectively valuable from the point of view, as it were, of the universe—is plainly a religious belief, even when it is held by people who do not believe in a personal deity. It is, in fact, the most fundamental purpose of traditional religions to make exactly that claim to its faithful, and to embody it in some vision or narrative that makes the belief seem intelligible and persuasive.[4]

And yet in much legal writing that applies the term 'sanctity' to humanity, its religious nature remains unexamined. It is difficult to find extended disquisitions on the nature of 'the sacred' or 'the soul', for example, and their significance for law's person. Often the term 'human sanctity' is used loosely by jurists as just another way of expressing respect or reverence for all human beings, including those who are presently incapable of reason. Rationalists might well use the term without anyone looking askance and accusing them of inconsistency or asking them to explain themselves, so commonplace is the legal usage. In the legal invocation of the term 'human sanctity', there can therefore be a blurring of the distinction between the religious and the secular, and a vagueness about the precise source of

[3] I thank Ben Berger for pointing this out to me.

[4] Ronald Dworkin, 'Unenumerated Rights: Whether and How *Roe v Wade* Should be Overruled' (1992) 59 *University of Chicago Law Review* 381, 414.

respect for human beings. Human value is something which is simply agreed upon and the secular Rationalist need not come to blows with the religious believer when the term 'sanctity' is employed to designate that value.

For most of the time this fuzzy articulation of the source or seat of human value, especially its notional sanctity, and its expression in law, does not seem to matter. Notwithstanding their commitment to the primacy of reason, most Rationalists still want to protect human beings who are incapable of rational thought and seem content to let the term 'human sanctity' do its work of expressing the value of all human beings regardless of their individual abilities. However, there do arise moments of sharp disagreement between Rationalists and religious believers, especially at the beginning and end of life when the interests of the rational person may compete directly with those of a being lacking all rational capacity (typically the foetus). It is at these times that we can see more clearly the role of the religious in conceptualising the person in law. This is when a religious understanding of what we are is brought into sharp relief.

This chapter is about the role of religion in helping to define law's person. In the first part, I will consider how the idea of reverence for human life, the supposed innate preciousness of humanity, has found strong expression in law and legal theory, but in a manner which tends to blur Rationalist and religious understandings of human value, because there is no obvious bone of contention. The same practical legal results are sought: the legal protection of all human beings. In the second part, I will concentrate more on the areas of strong disagreement between Rationalists and believers, when the religiously-inclined assert separate and distinctive moral and legal principles about the nature of personhood. It is here that some religious believers raise their heads above the parapet, declare that all 'ensouled' beings must be protected and that law must change dramatically as a consequence.[5]

The Human Rights Movement and the Revival of Belief in Human Preciousness

The view that legal rights necessarily map onto a natural human subject, one that possesses innate and absolute value regardless of actual ability, is implicit in the basic human rights instruments. The central idea is that law does not create human value; it simply acknowledges it. It is probably not drawing too long a bow to say that the idea of the sacred implicitly forms

[5] As we will discover, the possession of a soul is seen by some jurists, perhaps most notably John Finnis, to be determinative of personality. For an account of the fascinating theological debates on the timing and significance of 'ensoulment', see Norman M Ford, *When Did I Begin? Conceptions of the Human Individual in History, Philosophy and Science* (Cambridge, Cambridge University Press, 1988).

the basis of all human rights law, generally, for the underlying idea is that human life is innately precious. It is enough that we are human. This idea is sometimes expressed as innate or inherent human dignity or human inviolability, but the message is largely the same.[6] As leading American bioethicist Leon R Kass says of the relation between the terms 'sanctity of life' and 'human dignity' (from a Christian perspective): 'Each rests on the converse of the other. Or, rather, they are mutually implicated, as inseparable as the concave and the convex'.[7]

If anything, with the flourishing of the human rights movement in the second half of the twentieth century, and the articulation of human rights in a variety of international documents, there has been a fortification of the tendency among lawyers to ascribe inherent (and necessarily pre-legal) spiritual value to human beings. Thus, it is not unusual to find it said that rights 'inhere in the natural condition of being human'.[8] There is no felt need to say why because the value is thought to be immanent.

For many human rights lawyers this is almost axiomatic, this mapping of legal rights onto an antecedent human subject.[9] No further justification is needed. This deep conviction in the innate preciousness of *human* life is most clearly expressed in the Preamble to the Universal Declaration of Human Rights[10] which simply declares, without further supporting explanation or argument, that the 'recognition of the inherent dignity and of the equal and inalienable rights of all members of the human family is the foundation of freedom, justice and peace',[11] while Article 1 of the Declaration declares that: 'All human beings are born free and equal and in dignity'.[12] The Declaration thus 'traces its legitimacy to fundamental characteristics of human nature'[13] with human dignity being described as 'inherent'. In this view, dignity resides in the condition of being human.[14] It is intrinsic to humanity.

[6] Indeed, *Roget's Thesaurus* provides as synonyms for 'inviolable': adored, beatified, consecrated, divine, enthroned, exalted, glorified, hallowed, holy, inviolable, redeemed, religious, resurrected, revered, rewarded, sacred, sacrosanct, saved, spiritual, unprofane.

[7] Leon R Kass, *Life, Liberty and the Defense of Dignity: the Challenge for Bioethics* (San Francisco, Encounter Books, 2002) 243.

[8] D Kinley (ed), *Human Rights in Australian Law: Principles, Practice and Potential* (Sydney, Federation Press, 1998) 5.

[9] *Ibid* 4.

[10] Universal Declaration of Human Rights, GA Res 217(III), UN GAOR, 3rd sess, Supp No 13, UN Doc A/810 (1948) 71.

[11] The Preamble to the International Covenant on Civil and Political Rights (1966) employs precisely the same language.

[12] Universal Declaration of Human Rights, above n 10, art 1.

[13] Mary Ann Glendon, *A World Made New: Eleanor Roosevelt and the Universal Declaration of Human Rights* (New York, Random House, 2001) 175.

[14] For a recent discussion of the philosophical foundations of human rights, see Jerome J Shestack, 'The Philosophical Foundations of Human Rights' (1998) 20 *Human Rights Quarterly* 201.

Eleanor Roosevelt and her commission, formed in 1947 under the auspices of the new United Nations, formulated the Universal Declaration of Human Rights. Chairman Roosevelt was mindful of the fact that this document was to set the standard for all other human rights documents.[15] She called it:

> a declaration of basic principles of human rights and freedoms, to be stamped with the approval of the General Assembly . . . to serve as a common standard of achievement for all peoples of all nations.[16]

The thinking behind this document, and in particular its underlying views of human nature, are examined in some detail by Mary Ann Glendon in *A World Made New*.[17]

Glendon chose as the title of her book a phrase from the nightly prayer of Roosevelt in which she asked 'Our Father' to '[s]ave us from ourselves and show us a vision of a world made new'.[18] Roosevelt was an avowed Christian. We are told that when she summed up the attitude of the framers of the Declaration, in her General Assembly speech of December 1948, she said that it 'is based on the *spiritual* fact that man must have freedom in which to develop his full stature and through common effort to raise the level of human dignity'[19] (emphasis added).

In a later address to an American audience, Roosevelt explained 'why the Declaration contained no reference to the Creator'.[20] Roosevelt was happy in this setting to declare her own belief 'that we are born free and equal in dignity and rights because there is a divine Creator, and there is a divine spark in men'.[21] And clearly she saw the Declaration as fully consistent with this belief. The reason that the Creator was not explicitly mentioned is that it allowed the Declaration to speak for and to a broader community of belief.[22] The particular wording of the Declaration, she said, 'left it to each of us to put in our own reason, as we say, for that [human] end'.[23]

The Universal Declaration, as with other human rights instruments, reflects the natural law view that rights inhere naturally in human beings:

[15] And as Glendon observes, it was to become 'the parent document, the primary inspiration, for most rights instruments in the world today' (above n 13, at xvi).

[16] 'Statement by Mrs Franklin D Roosevelt', *Department of State Bulletin* (December 1948) 751, quoted by Glendon, above n 13, at 177.

[17] Glendon, above n 13.

[18] This prayer begins the book and sets its tone.

[19] 'Statement by Mrs Franklin D Roosevelt', above n 16.

[20] Glendon, above n 13, at 147.

[21] Roosevelt, above n 1.

[22] This indeed was essential in view of the constitution of the Declaration's Drafting Committee. It included the influential Chinese delegate, Peng-chun Chang, who referred often to the teachings of Confucius. It also included Lebanon's Charles Malik, as rapporteur and secretary. Compromise about the sources of human value was essential for agreement to be reached.

[23] Roosevelt, above n 1.

rights are not legal constructs as the strict Legalists of Chapter 3 insist. They are not the product of law, they are not posited into being by law, but rather precede law and indwell in human beings as a natural property. As John Finnis advances this view of natural rights:

> one cannot reasonably affirm the equality of human beings, or the universality and binding force of human rights, unless one acknowledges that there is something about persons which distinguishes them radically from sub-rational creatures, and which, prior to any acknowledgement of 'status', is intrinsic to the factual reality of every human being, adult or immature, healthy or disabled.[24]

As Glendon observes of the Universal Declaration, the founding rights document, it 'implicitly rejected the positivist position by stating that fundamental rights are recognized, not conferred'.[25] This commitment to the natural (rather than legal) basis of human rights Glendon attributes to the:

> legally sanctioned atrocities committed in Nazi Germany [which] had caused many people to reevaluate the proposition that there is no higher law by which the laws of nation-states can be judged.[26]

As the Preamble to the Declaration itself proclaims, 'disregard and contempt for human rights have resulted in barbarous acts which have outraged the conscience of mankind'.[27]

In a similar vein, the American Convention on Human Rights (1969) asserts in its Preamble that 'the essential rights of man are not derived from one's being a national of a certain state',[28] that is, they are not derived from the posited law of a given state. Rather they 'are based upon attributes of the human personality'. The African Charter on Human and Peoples' Rights (1981) similarly avows 'that fundamental human rights stem from the attributes of human beings'.[29] The European Convention for the Protection of Human Rights and Fundamental Freedoms (1950) expresses a 'profound belief in those fundamental freedoms which are the foundation of justice'.[30] The significance of 'the inherent dignity and of the equal and inalienable rights' is cited by the International Covenant on Civil and Political Rights (1966).[31] Such rights 'derive from the inherent dignity of the human person' not, by implication, from law.[32]

[24] John Finnis, 'Natural Law: the Classical Tradition' in Jules Coleman and Scott Shapiro (eds), *The Oxford Handbook of Jurisprudence and Philosophy of Law* (Oxford, Oxford University Press, 2002) 4.

[25] Glendon, above n 13, at 176.

[26] *Ibid.*

[27] Universal Declaration of Human Rights, above n 10.

[28] American Convention on Human Rights (1969) 1144 UNTS 123.

[29] African Charter on Human and Peoples' Rights (1981) 1520 UNTS 217.

[30] European Convention for the Protection of Human Rights and Fundamental Freedoms (1950) 213 UNTS 222.

[31] International Covenant on Civil and Political Rights (1966) 999 UNTS 171.

[32] *Ibid.*

Although there is talk of human 'attributes', these are not intended to denote actual abilities or distinctive observable qualities of real human beings. It is simply being human that matters and somehow that humanity entails intrinsic dignity. The term 'human' refers to a species, but here it is neither animal nature that is being invoked nor specific natural attributes, which are obviously highly variable and sometimes anything but dignified. The value asserted is more mystical, more metaphysical; it is indwelling, innate, inherent, just there, because we are the right kind of species. It is not susceptible to proof. It is not open to question. It is intended to be non-negotiable. It is to be taken on faith and indeed it is a matter of faith.

Human rights instruments consistently declare this underived, intrinsic and universal value of human beings and use the term 'human being' and the dignifying honorific 'person' interchangeably. The one is equated with the other. Article 6 of the Universal Declaration asserts that everyone is 'a person before the law'—morally and legally.[33] The American Declaration of the Rights and Duties of Man (1948) begins with the proposition that: 'Every human being has the right to life, liberty and the security of his person'.[34] Article 2 then asserts that 'All persons are equal before the law'.[35] The American Convention on Human Rights conflates the two terms quite explicitly. Article 1 maintains that: 'For the purposes of this Convention, "person" means every human being'.[36] Article 3 then states that: 'Every person has the right to recognition as a person before the law'.[37] The rest of the Convention then employs either the term person or 'one' (as in everyone) to designate its subject.

The Canadian Charter of Rights and Freedoms, enshrined in the Canadian Constitution in 1982, uses a variety of terms as if they were synonyms. It begins with an assertion of the fundamental freedoms of 'everyone' but goes on to declare the rights of 'any persons' in criminal and penal matters. Later there is mention of the equality rights of 'every individual' before and under the law.[38] The message clearly conveyed by these basic rights documents is that law's persons and human beings are one and the same and that it is the innate preciousness of human beings which demands law's protection through the endowment of personality.

For Eleanor Roosevelt, who began the process of recognising human rights in this fundamental and unqualified manner, there was no doubt that human preciousness came from the Creator. However, Roosevelt also recognised the dangers of pressing a strong clearly-articulated Christian view of the person on the founding human rights instrument, preferring to

[33] Universal Declaration of Human Rights, above n 10, art 6.

[34] American Declaration of the Rights and Duties of Man (1948) OAS Res XXX.

[35] *Ibid* art 2.

[36] American Convention of Human Rights, above n 28, art 1.

[37] *Ibid* art 3.

[38] Canadian Constitution Act, Sch B, Part I.

let each arrive at their own view of the basis of human preciousness. She believed that the document would attract broad support only in this way. The modern legal thinker who has sought a similar compromise between the religious and the secular in his analysis of human sanctity, and its import for law and the legal person, is Ronald Dworkin.

Ronald Dworkin on Human Sanctity

Ronald Dworkin takes human sanctity to be a fundamental universal verity, one that he intuits directly. 'The fact is', he says, 'I look at the sanctity of life as true. I feel this. It is my conviction that we do wrong to insult the inherent, objective value of life'.[39] Dworkin believes that we nearly all think this way about our species, whether or not we are religious believers: 'that individual human life is sacred', he declares, is 'a fundamental idea we almost all share in some form'.[40] This is a view he reaffirms throughout his writing, this belief that we are essentially of a common mind in our belief in human sanctity:

> I think we all possess a conviction that the life of each member of our species has intrinsic, or, as some prefer, sacred value. This means that we consider an individual life valuable not only to itself, but *objectively*. That idea is quite central to our culture.[41]

However, as a committed Rationalist, Dworkin is keen to insert two other ideas into his theory of the person. One is the critical importance of human reason and choice in giving meaning to a life, in creating the person, a view I examined in the last chapter. To Dworkin, a life which is not governed by reason, by personal deliberation, is not a life worth having; without reason there is no person and he means this in a moral and legal sense. Dworkin is also keen to acknowledge the viewpoint of the religious sceptic, who may not see life as a gift from God, and yet to retain the idea of the intrinsic worth of human life. He does this partly by recognising the role of reason and individual human investment in imparting meaning and value to a life and partly by recognising the role of evolutionary forces in endowing us with value, and so appearing to embrace the biological sciences. To Dworkin, the processes of random mutation and natural selection have resulted in something wonderful, something of absolute value. We do not have to believe in God to recognise that the human species is a remarkable achievement of biology and that we are now set above the animal kingdom,

[39] Ronald Dworkin, 'Tyranny at the Two Edges of Life: a Liberal View' (2004) *New Perspectives Quarterly* (Winter) 16, 19.

[40] Ronald Dworkin, *Life's Dominion: an Argument about Abortion, Euthanasia and Individual Freedom* (London, Harper Collins, 1993) 13.

[41] Dworkin, above n 39, 16.

each one of us now possessed of intrinsic worth. We are nature's 'masterpiece'.[42]

Some interesting conclusions are drawn from this package of ideas about the nature and value of being human. To Dworkin, 'the intrinsic value of human life'[43] extends to the human foetus, which is 'a living, growing human creature' and so 'it is intrinsically a bad thing, a kind of cosmic shame, when human life at any stage is deliberately extinguished'.[44] However, the early foetus can have no rights and interests which necessarily derive from the ability to think and feel, because it cannot think and feel. And to Dworkin:

> It makes no sense to suppose that something has interests of its own—as distinct from its being important what happens to it—unless it has, or has had, some form of consciousness: some mental as well as physical life.[45]

It is therefore wrong to think of the foetus as a person and it is wrong to cast the debate about foetal status as a debate about its personhood. And indeed according to Dworkin, 'very few people . . . actually believe that [the foetus is a full moral person from conception] whatever they say'.[46]

But the foetus does possess what Dworkin calls 'detached' value; this is its 'cosmic' significance, its intrinsic worth, which is detached from any direct interests it might have (but doesn't, if it can't think and feel) and which is simply there, existing independently in the universe. Here, it is worth noting, we are purely in the realm of assertion.

All this means that American law is right not to regard the foetus as a constitutional person, but it is also right to offer protections to the late-term foetus which has begun to develop interests. Dworkin, therefore, agrees with the finding of the leading US Supreme Court decision on abortion, *Roe v Wade*,[47] that foetuses are not constitutional persons: that is, they are not persons for the purposes of the US Constitution. When this document refers to persons, it does not mean foetuses. Dworkin also agrees with the court's determination that although foetuses are not persons, the state nevertheless acquires an interest in their protection as they mature, and develop interests, so that in the third trimester of pregnancy it may interfere in a fundamental way with the acknowledged privacy of pregnant women and prohibit abortion.

To Dworkin, American law is also right to permit the withdrawal of treatment from the permanently comatose, for 'we might well doubt that an

42 *Ibid* 92.
43 Dworkin, above n 40, at 12.
44 *Ibid* 13.
45 *Ibid* 16.
46 *Ibid* 13.
47 *Roe v Wade*, 410 US 113 (1973).

insensate, vegetative life has any value at all'.[48] But law is wrong not to grant a positive right to die because there can come a time when a life is not worth having; instead it is a positive burden.

Dworkin endeavours to speak to both the religious believer and to the secular evolutionist. He tells us that it is axiomatic:

> that we treat the preservation and prosperity of our own species as of capital importance because we believe that we are the highest achievement of God's creation, if we are conventionally religious, or of evolution, if we are not, and also because we know that all knowledge and art and culture would disappear if humanity did.[49]

However, Dworkin's understanding of evolutionary theory is not without its own problems. In particular, his view that we represent the high point of evolution carries with it a host of assumptions about the meaning of humanity which, to some, remain irredeemably religious. I will return to Dworkin and his tendentious reading of evolution in the next chapter.

Dworkin uses the term 'sanctity' to invoke 'the inherent, objective value of life'.[50] He maintains also that '[s]omething is sacred or inviolable when its deliberate destruction would dishonor what ought to be honored'.[51] And further that:

> [t]he hallmark of the sacred as distinct from the incrementally valuable is that the sacred is intrinsically valuable because—and therefore only once—it exists. It is inviolable because of what it represents or embodies.[52]

But, for Dworkin, it does not follow that all life must be preserved and that it is always better to choose life over death. What sanctity does mean, to Dworkin, is that 'once each life begins it is important that it not be wasted';[53] that 'once a human life has begun, it is very important that it flourish'.[54]

The challenge, for Dworkin, is how best to acknowledge the inviolable or sacred nature of a human life. This, he concedes, is subject to great personal disagreement. We are bound together in our shared view of human life's intrinsic value but also 'deeply and consistently divide[d]' about 'what that idea means'.[55] We each have our own understanding of how best to respect life. Dworkin insists that *Roe v Wade* got it right: that a woman, as

[48] Ronald Dworkin, *Freedom's Law: the Moral Reading of the American Constitution* (New York, Oxford University Press, 1996) 141.
[49] Dworkin, above n 40, at 82.
[50] Dworkin, above n 39.
[51] Dworkin, above n 40, at 74.
[52] *Ibid* 73–4.
[53] Richard Stith, 'The Right to Death', Reply by Ronald Dworkin, 38(6) *New York Review of Books*, 28 March 1991.
[54] Dworkin, above n 40, at 73–4.
[55] *Ibid* 28.

a thinking agent, an author of a life, should remain free to decide whether to terminate a pregnancy in its early stages because a termination may well be the best way of respecting life as she sees it. If, for example, a pregnancy is regarded as a major impediment to her realisation of her goals, if she feels it will blight her life, then an abortion may best respect the human investment that has gone into her life and her right to shape that life through her life choices.

Though Dworkin gives us an apparently qualified, muted and, to his mind, balanced view of human sanctity (offering us the term 'inviolable' if we are unhappy with the overtly religious term 'sanctity')[56] there remains nevertheless a mystical and intuitive element to his thinking. Thus, it is 'a kind of cosmic shame, when human life at any stage is extinguished'.[57] Dworkin is thinking at the level of the cosmos, the universe, not England and the United States late in the twentieth century, the time when he is writing. And he is paying little attention to the views of those who are closer to home (whom we will meet in the next chapter), those for whom humans are not exceptional and who question the logic and morality of this way of exalting and preferring our species over others.

And despite his concerted endeavours to marry the religious and the secular in his conception of the person, Dworkin is in fact jarringly at odds with orthodox Catholic thinking, as we will shortly see. Dworkin endorses the principle of human sanctity but believes that it can be interpreted both religiously and non-religiously, as that which emerges with human effort and planning. Because human investment can give value, or add value, to a human life, the desires and interests of the pregnant woman carry greater weight than the interests of her foetus. As a Rationalist, Dworkin believes that human sanctity is qualified, developmental and related to the intellectual capacities of the individual. But this is not in fact how orthodox Catholics view the person. I now turn to consider this less compromising religious view of the person both within the traditional teachings of the Church and in the writings of Catholicism's chief legal defender, John Finnis.

The Human Person and the Catholic Church

The *Compendium of the Social Doctrine of the Church* is prepared by the Pontifical Council for Justice and Peace 'in order to give a concise but complete overview of the Church's social teaching'.[58] It is a rich and authoritative source of information on the Roman Catholic understanding of the

[56] *Ibid* 25.

[57] *Ibid* 13.

[58] Pontifical Council for Justice and Peace, *The Compendium of the Social Doctrine of the Church* (Strathfield NSW, St Paul's Publications, 2004).

person. It purports to contribute to 'the full truth about man',[59] not just offer one view of human beings. The *Compendium*'s great merit, for current purposes, is that it explains precisely why it is that human beings have intrinsic value and are therefore persons. The reason is this:

> The Church sees in men and women, in every person, the living image of God himself. This image finds, and must always find anew, an ever deeper and fuller unfolding of itself in the mystery of Christ, the Perfect Image of God, the One who reveals God to man and man to himself. It is to these men and women, who have received an incomparable and inalienable dignity from God himself, that the Church speaks . . . Christ, the Son of God, 'by his incarnation has united himself in some fashion with every person'.[60]

We are instructed that the entire social doctrine of the Church 'develops from the principle that affirms the inviolable dignity of the human person'.[61] This human person 'is a creature of God' and is made 'in the image of God'.[62] *Genesis* declares this foundational truth about human life:

> God created man in his own image, in the image of God he created him; male and female he created them.[63]

Moreover, 'God places the human creature at the centre and summit of the created order'.[64] Of all God's creatures, 'only man has a "capacity for God"'.[65] Being made in God's image, man is a person, 'a someone', not just a 'something'.[66] This human person 'is superior to the material world'. He is not just 'a speck of nature' for he possesses 'a spiritual and immortal soul'.[67] Though he is 'a material being', he is also 'a spiritual being' which means that he is 'open to transcendence'[68] and 'shares in the light of the divine mind'.[69] The *Compendium* is clear that, *contra* the Rationalists, 'it is not intellect, consciousness and freedom that define the person' and that the faculties of reason 'can even be absent, for even without them man does not cease to be a person'.[70]

The natural dignity with which each human person is endowed, as God's creature, provides the foundation of human rights and such rights are said to apply 'to every stage of life'.[71] The most basic human right, the right to

[59] Pontifical Council for Justice and Peace, *The Compendium of the Social Doctrine of the Church* (Strathfield NSW, St Paul's Publications, 2004) 7.
[60] *Ibid* 55.
[61] *Ibid* 55.
[62] *Ibid* 56.
[63] *Genesis* (1:27).
[64] Pontifical Council for Justice and Peace, above n 59, at 56.
[65] *Ibid* 56.
[66] *Ibid* 56.
[67] *Ibid* 64.
[68] *Ibid.*
[69] *Ibid* 65.
[70] *Ibid* 66.
[71] *Ibid* 77.

life, endures 'from conception to its natural end' and so 'implies the illicitness of every form of procured abortion and euthanasia'.[72] In the order of things described by the *Compendium*, 'God alone is Lord of life and death'.[73]

From this brief account of the authoritative orthodox Catholic view of the person,[74] it should be readily apparent that there are substantial differences between the social teachings of the Church and actual positive law and certainly differences with the thinking of Dworkin. Abortion in the early stages of pregnancy is not generally outlawed as the Church demands. Human legal rights do not commence at conception (most legal rights of the person instead commence at birth). Withdrawal of medical treatment is lawful if it is thought no longer to be in the interests of the person (an idea which seems to make no sense according to Catholic teachings). However, euthanasia in most places remains subject to the law of murder. The legal thinker who has most conspicuously and vigorously taken up the Catholic cause against the current body of law and in thc name of the sacred person is Anglo-Australian jurist, John Finnis.

John Finnis on Law's Person

John Finnis is a devout Catholic and a natural lawyer, best known for his influential book *Natural Law and Natural Rights* published in 1980.[75] This has been described as 'a major restatement of classical natural law theory'.[76] Finnis has sustained a natural law position over many years and in many places. Consistently, he has maintained a view of our natures which is greatly at variance with both Rationalist philosophical and strictly legal views of the person. As we saw in the last chapter, the well-accepted philosophical view of the person is that of a conscious, thinking, rational agent. The strictly legal view of the person is that of a rights-and-duty bearer, essentially an abstract and technical device, which comes into formal existence at birth and ceases, in most ways, at death.

For Finnis, law must capture and reflect the truth of what we are, what he calls 'the realities of personal existence'.[77] But what are these natural realities? In his early and seminal text, he tells us that we are the sort of beings that require knowledge, life, play, aesthetic experience, practical

[72] *Ibid* 78.

[73] *Ibid* 58.

[74] And for a bracingly sceptical account of Christian theology, see Richard Dawkins, *The God Delusion* (Boston, Houghton Mifflin, 2006).

[75] John Finnis, *Natural Law and Natural Rights* (Oxford, Clarendon Press, 1980).

[76] Raymond Wacks, *Understanding Jurisprudence: an Introduction to Legal Theory* (New York, Oxford University Press, 2005) 28.

[77] John Finnis, 'The Priority of Persons' in Jeremy Horder (ed), *Oxford Essays on Jurisprudence* (4th series, Oxford, Oxford University Press, 2000) 1, 9.

reasonableness, friendship and religion and that law must be put in service to these values.[78] Here, Finnis does not dwell on human sanctity or on the nature and significance of the soul. His religious sentiments and commitments remain muted.

In his more recent writing, however, Finnis squarely asserts that it is as ensouled beings that we are the sort of creatures that law must naturally serve and personify. He arrives at his existential conclusion in much the same way as Descartes did in his *Meditations*[79] and Hume did in his *Enquiry Concerning Human Understanding*.[80] Thinking aloud, perhaps sitting at his desk or in an armchair, Finnis struggles with the mystery of being human. Descartes concluded after his solitary but recorded struggle that he was a thinking thing. Hume concluded that he was nothing more than a series of sensations. Finnis arrives at yet another conclusion and draws on the authority of Thomas Aquinas (Finnis is a Thomistic scholar). But first Finnis enjoys a stream of consciousness. He imagines himself in a variety of conversations, speaking to his partner, to a court of law, or to a client. He reflects on his choices of what to say, the reaction of his audience, and his ongoing desire to get his meaning across despite possible misunderstandings. He reflects on the subjective nature of what is going on:

> This experience of the unity . . . of my being—as a feeling, willing, remembering, understanding, physically active and effective mover or cause of physical effects and equally an undergoer and recipient of such effects.[81]

To Finnis this 'intelligible presence of [his] many-faceted acting self to [him]self', this 'unified self', is his 'human being'.[82] Without much further ado, he concludes that what he is really describing is a soul and that it exists from 'the very outset' of his existence. Thus, 'the essence and powers of the soul seem to be given to each individual complete (as wholly undeveloped, radical capacities) at the outset of his or her existence as such'.[83] Finnis makes quite clear that the outset of the soul and of the human being and of the moral and legal person[84] is at the moment of conception.

These views are not held lightly, and although Finnis describes an intellectual process of sober reflection, of arriving at a considered conclusion, his views come from a deep faith and appear to be non-negotiable. His convictions about our nature are said to be the result of:

[78] Finnis, above n 75, at 88.

[79] René Descartes, *Meditations on First Philosophy* (John Cottingham (ed), Cambridge, Cambridge University Press, 1992).

[80] David Hume, *An Enquiry Concerning Human Understanding* (Montana, Kessinger Publishing, 2004).

[81] Finnis, above n 77, at 14.

[82] *Ibid.*

[83] *Ibid.*

[84] We may see Finnis using the term 'human being' and 'person' as synonyms and interchangeably.

> a close attention to the solidity and depth of the universe . . . the kind of close attention which is the cause of religious belief—and also of good science—rather than a mere resultant of them.[85]

And yet they do not appear to be susceptible to either proof or falsification or even open to secular modes of argument. They are the truth as witnessed by a believer; they are taken on, and a matter of, faith. Thus, Finnis asserts, by fiat, that the soul and its powers are 'the root of the dignity we all have as human beings'.[86] This is, to him, an unalterable universal timeless metaphysical truth; it is the natural but underived fact 'which should inform juristic thought about the persons whom law exists to serve'.[87]

It is not easy to grasp the nature of the soul as Finnis expounds it, and yet it is arguably to his credit that he is one of the few legal philosophers who not only writes about human sanctity but who also endeavours to say what the soul is and to give it clear work to do, at least in his later writing. We are told in a recent discourse on the subject that:

> [t]he principle—principium, fundamental element and source—of this life, giving unity and continuity to the shifting material components of the organism, is the factor that Aquinas, like Aristotle, calls soul.[88]

What follows, by way of clarification, is still not easy to follow, and perhaps requires mastery of Catholic theological principles to comprehend its meaning. For the soul is then described as:

> the very form and lifelong act(uality) by which the matter of one's bodily makeup is constituted the unified and active subject/object, this organism, this human being, this person, from one's outset until one's death.[89]

In an explanatory footnote to this definition, we are told that:

> from the moment of the insemination of the ovum . . . the specifically human, rational (and sensitive and vegetative) animating form and act (soul)—and therefore personhood . . . can be and doubtless is present.[90]

Finnis then refers to 'the unity of soul and body . . . as the principle of one's soul's individuality'[91] and adds that 'one's bodiliness is the foundation of one's personal identity, a subsisting identity that precedes consciousness and lasts through even protracted terminal consciousness until death'.[92]

[85] John Finnis, 'Public Reason, Abortion and Cloning' (1998) *Valparaiso University Law Review* 361, 378.

[86] *Ibid.*

[87] Finnis, above n 77, at 13.

[88] John Finnis '"The Thing I Am": Personal Identity in Aquinas and Shakespeare' in Ellen Frankel Paul, Fred D Miller Jr and Jeffrey Paul (eds), *Personal Identity* (Cambridge, Cambridge University Press, 2005) 250, 253.

[89] *Ibid.*

[90] *Ibid* 253.

[91] *Ibid* 254.

[92] *Ibid* 255.

It seems that, to Finnis, the soul is a life force which is somehow present from conception until death; it requires a human body and yet is fully present in a fertilised human egg; it entails the 'radical capacity' to reason but is nevertheless to be found in the embryo and the terminally unconscious.[93] The soul appears to be full of paradoxes. Finnis himself admits that the soul is inherently mysterious. For it is 'that which—we know not how—unifies all the irreducibly distinct but interpenetrated aspects of the person'.[94] That this is a Christian and a Catholic idea of a soul, the view of a certain kind of Christian believer, is confirmed by the authoritative invocation of the Second Vatican Council.[95]

The practical import of Finnis's convictions is dramatic. It means that law in permitting the termination of pregnancies is party to the deliberate destruction of those with 'the essence and powers of the soul' which are given 'to each individual complete . . . at the outset of his or her existence as such'.[96] It is (to Finnis) obscenely disrespectful of these basic spiritual facts about human nature and so should, as a matter of urgency, be made to conform to what we are. Finnis is convinced that our law sanctions the murder of innocent human persons, repeatedly and routinely, and no doubt this causes him immense grief as a lawyer and as a person of faith. He has written at length on the perceived evils of abortion,[97] especially on the supposed evils of the US Supreme Court decision of *Roe v Wade* which protected a woman's right to abortion in the early stages of pregnancy.[98] Finnis has also expounded on the supposed evils of the withdrawal of life support equipment from those in a persistent vegetative state. This, too, is said to represent the deliberate destruction of human beings who, in his view, are sacred persons.

A case that has especially provoked the ire of Finnis is one of the most publicised English decisions on the legality of the termination of life support: the case of Tony Bland.[99] At the time of the Hillsborough football ground disaster in 1989, Bland was 17.[100] Then, as a consequence of a crowd stampede, he was pressed against the front fence and suffered catastrophic and

[93] Finnis states that 'each living human being possesses actually and not merely potentially, the radical capacity to reason, love, laugh and repent'. Further that 'personhood . . . subsists . . . even while its operations come and go'. Above n 85, at 377.

[94] Finnis, above n 88, at 280.

[95] *Ibid* 256.

[96] Finnis, above n 77, at 15.

[97] See, eg John Finnis 'The Rights and Wrongs of Abortion: a Reply to Judith Jarvis Thomson' (1973) 2 *Philosophy and Public Affairs* 117; John Finnis, 'The Legal Status of the Unborn Baby' (1992) 43 *Catholic Medical Quarterly* 5; John Finnis 'Abortion, Natural Law and Public Reason' in Robert P George and Christopher Wolfe (eds), *Natural Law and Public Reason* (Washington, DC, Georgetown University Press, 2000) 71–105.

[98] See his discussion of this case in Finnis, above n 77, at 15.

[99] John Finnis, '*Bland: Crossing the Rubicon?*' (1993) 109 *Law Quarterly Review* 329.

[100] See *Airedale NHS Trust v Bland* [1993] AC 789.

irreversible damage to his higher brain centres. Although he could breathe and had basic reflexes, he had no awareness at all. He was diagnosed with persistent vegetative syndrome. The treating doctors and Bland's family wanted artificial feeding stopped which would cause him to die in about a fortnight and the hospital sought a declaration that this was lawful. The Official Solicitor as guardian *ad litem* for Bland opposed it, saying that it would amount to at least the crime of manslaughter and was possibly murder.

What is interesting for present purposes is the manner in which the House of Lords approached the principle of human sanctity. Lord Goff asserted that the applicable legal principle was indeed that of the sanctity of life, which was fundamental, but not absolute.[101] The principle of the sanctity of life yielded to the principle of self-determination when the patient was conscious and competent. Doctors could not force patients to accept treatment in order to stay alive. The person of sound mind could therefore instruct that life support be removed. In circumstances such as those of Bland, however, when no prior instructions had been given, it was lawful to withdraw treatment if he had no interests in being kept alive.[102] And here the Lords described his condition as a sort of living death. Thus, a competent patient had every right to refuse life-saving treatment. But in the case of Bland, there was no capacity for reason and so no autonomy to be exercised on his part. There was not even a life worth living which could form the basis of a duty on the treating doctors to sustain life support. To Finnis, this case represents a travesty of justice because all human life is sacred and demands protection and preservation until God, not man, determines the moment of death.[103] Thus do the law and Finnis part company.[104]

Implications

At its noblest, a commitment to human uniqueness, to human sanctity, lies behind the estimable demand that all who are human be treated with

[101] The House of Lords in *Pretty v DPP* [2001] UKHL 61, especially Lord Steyn, similarly endorsed 'the deeply-rooted sanctity of life principle' in English law (at para 65). Mrs Diane Pretty, who suffered from motor neurone disease, sought a declaration from the DPP that if her husband assisted her suicide, he would not be prosecuted under the Suicide Act 1961. She was denied her request.

[102] In the case of *Bland*, 'his best interests no longer require[d] that' his life should be prolonged artificially because 'the treatment [was] of no benefit to him because he [was] totally unconscious and there [was] no prospect of any improvement in his condition' (at 868). Treatment was 'futile', of 'no therapeutic purpose'.

[103] See John Finnis 'A Philosophical Case Against Euthanasia' in J Keown (ed), *Euthanasia Examined: Ethical, Legal and Clinical Perspectives* (Cambridge, Cambridge University Press, 1997) 32.

[104] In 'Euthanasia, Morality, and Law' (1996) 31 *Loyola LA L Rev* 1123, 1143, Finnis says 'I think we should judge, and act on the basis, that: Persons keep their radical dignity until death—all the way through'.

dignity and kindness. This was the moral and spiritual impetus for the Universal Declaration of Human Rights which spoke of a deep revulsion towards the 'barbarism' of the Holocaust and declared a commitment to the moral treatment of all humans because of (what was said to be) their innate dignity. All (humans) should be included, no one excluded; all possessed absolute, universal value. Human rights were not to depend on the particular attributes of the particular human being: health, intelligence, age, race, sex were to make no difference to this value. Simply to be human was to have unqualified value. Thus, the Declaration was intended as a statement of complete inclusion: a reply to any society (Nazi Germany in particular) in which human beings were divided into those who mattered and those who did not. No one was to be 'unpersoned'.[105] In the words of Article 6 of the Declaration: 'Everyone has the right to recognition everywhere as a person before the law'.[106]

And yet a dogmatic belief in human sanctity can have less beneficent, more illiberal effects. It lies behind attempts to impose severe constraints on human choice about some of the most personal aspects of existence, at some of the more vulnerable human moments: in pregnancy and at times of great suffering and in dying. Necessarily this places great strain on what is often said to be the first principle of our Rationalist liberal law, which is respect for individual autonomy and personal choice, which in turn provides the basis of individual responsibility (the set of ideas documented in the last two chapters).

Christian moral conservatives, such as Finnis, have campaigned vigorously against any sort of right to terminate a pregnancy, at any stage, regardless of the costs to women.[107] They have campaigned against a right to withdrawal of life support when it is no longer wanted or needed; and against a right to die (voluntary euthanasia), no matter the suffering entailed in living, maintaining that human freedoms and choices do not extend to personal governance over life itself because life is of supreme value—a gift from God. It is not ours to meddle with. It must be endured, if God is so minded.

A Christian conviction that it is only human beings that truly matter, because animal beings are not touched by the Holy Spirit, can also countenance cruelty to animals (as we will see in the next chapter). In the traditional and orthodox Christian view, animals are put on earth for our use; they do not have ends of their own that count. Thus, to say that humans,

[105] The most memorable fictitious evocation of unpersoning has been provided by George Orwell in his novel *Nineteen Eighty-Four*. An 'unperson' was a person who had been 'vaporised' by the government and said never to have existed (London, Secker and Warburg, 1949) 40.

[106] Universal Declaration of Human Rights, above n 10, art 6.

[107] And perhaps the principal cost is the butchery of the backyard abortion to which women may be driven if denied a lawful termination.

and only humans, possess special value and fundamental rights *simply* because we are human is in itself to say that our species matters and that other species do not. The term 'human' is intended as a gesture of inclusiveness but the very term 'human rights' refers to our species. Thus, to those concerned about the treatment of other species, the term 'human rights' appears as a term of exclusion. To the advocates for animals, it does not embrace the full moral community. I will return shortly to this moral problem of other species.[108]

The association of certain strands of Christianity with moral dogma, rather than moral engagement and open bracing dialogue, has prompted some believers to avoid the explicit language of religion and to find other ways of expressing the value of humanity and why it demands legal protection. They avoid overt references to the soul or the human spirit. They may or may not invoke the term 'human sanctity' (as for some, like Dworkin, it has acquired a secular meaning). Roosevelt herself trod carefully when it came to the overt expression of her religious beliefs. Dworkin sought to reconcile the believer with the religious sceptic in his conception of the person. But orthodox believers, such as Finnis, question whether this is possible, this avoidance of the religious dimensions of the assertion of absolute human value. They insist that true expression of what makes humans innately precious depends on the use of religious terms such as sanctity, or the sacred, or the soul, and strict legal adherence to the teachings of the Church.[109] After all, we are not speaking of any proven capacity or attribute of humans, as are Rationalists. Nor are we referring to a proven human need, say the need to avoid suffering or to experience a life of satisfaction. Rather the claim is simply that the human being, *qua* human being, has unqualified underived value, even without the capacity for thought or feeling, and law must reflect this sacred fact.

In a Rationalist and materialist age, in an age of science, when one tends to look for verification and proof, for reasons, this begs the question: why is this so? What is this mysterious human essence and why and how should law seek to make it central to its concept of the person? In the absence of a Christian belief in the soul, this essence seems to have little meaning, nor does its translation into law.

[108] Philosophers Peter Singer and James Rachels have both questioned this distinction between humans and animals. Both argue that species is not a morally significant distinction. For their recent thoughts on this, see Peter Singer 'Ethics Beyond Species and Beyond Instinct' in Cass R Sunstein and Martha C Nussbaum (eds), *Animal Rights: Current Debates and New Directions* (New York, Oxford University Press, 2004) and James Rachels, 'Drawing Lines' in Cass R Sunstein and Martha C Nussbaum (eds), *Animal Rights: Current Debates and New Directions* (New York, Oxford University Press, 2004).

[109] Eg, Raymond Gaita in *A Common Humanity: Thinking about Love, Truth and Justice* (Melbourne, Text Publishing, 1999) insists that the religious word 'sanctity' provides the best expression of innate human value.

8

Human and Non-human Animals: the Implications of Darwin

> [F]rom Darwin we should by now have learned that human history . . . is the natural history of one more animal species.
>
> Alasdair MacIntyre[1]

> The fact is, that each time there is a movement to confer rights onto some new 'entity', the proposal is bound to sound odd or frightening or laughable . . . until the rightless thing receives its rights, we cannot see it as anything but a thing for the use of 'us'—those who are holding rights at the time.
>
> Christopher Stone[2]

What We might have Expected after Darwin

When Charles Darwin was writing *Origin of Species,* he was keenly aware that his theory of the evolution of species, by random mutation and natural selection of the best adapted, might prove deeply offensive to those who saw 'man's' nature and place in the universe as divinely ordered, not as a product of natural biological change.[3] In 1838, he wondered, in his private notebooks, about the sort of creatures we are, reflecting that:

> [m]an in his arrogance thinks himself a great work worthy the imposition of a deity. More humble and I think truer to consider him created from animals.[4]

For a number of years, Darwin kept these thoughts to himself and delayed the publication of *Origin of Species*, the detailed articulation of his theory of the development of species, wary of the reaction he would receive from a solidly Christian English society.[5] Darwin rightly anticipated a

[1] Alasdair MacIntyre, *Dependent Rational Animals: Why Human Beings Need the Virtues* (Chicago, Open Court Publishing, 1999) 11.

[2] Christopher Stone, 'Should Trees Have Standing?' (1972) 45 *Southern California Law Review* 450, 455.

[3] Charles Darwin, *On the Origin of Species by Means of Natural Selection or the Preservation of Favoured Races in the Struggle for Life* (London, John Murray, 1859).

[4] *Charles Darwin's Notebooks,* 300, as quoted in James Rachels, *Created from Animals: the Moral Implications of Darwinism* (Oxford, Oxford University Press, 1990) 1.

[5] Darwin's thinking about the likely responses to *Origin* are nicely documented by his biographers Adrian Desmond and James Moore in *Darwin* (London, Penguin Books, 1992).

strong negative reception to his idea of species development which did not depend on divine intervention. Even then, it was only at the end of *Origin*, almost as a throw-away line, that Darwin hinted at the implications of his theory for the circumstances of our human origins. His *Descent of Man*, the explicit theoretical exposition of our descent from animals,[6] did not appear until 1871 and, as he anticipated, there were hostile responses to his central proposition that we are 'created from animals'. English broadsheets published monstrous images of ape-people and Darwin and his advocates were ridiculed. Darwin's theory, it seemed, threatened to undo the teachings of the Church about our exalted place in Creation and to reduce us to the lowly status of animals. When Darwin was writing, the broadly-accepted view was that the world had been created by God 'in pretty much the same state in which we now find it' in 4004 BC.[7] Darwin was not the first to suggest our kinship with animals, but he was the one to give it a well-reasoned, eloquent and persuasive exposition.

David Hume, a century earlier, had included animals in his moral list of those who matter and had more explicitly questioned that part of Christian theology which ordained otherwise. The thinking of animals, he said, was little different from the thinking of humans but we were unable to accept the simple facts before our eyes. In *A Treatise of Human Nature* he said:

> Next to the ridicule of denying an evident truth, is that of taking much pains to defend it; and no truth appears to me more evident, than that beasts are endow'd with thought and reason as well as men. The arguments are in this case so obvious, that they never escape the most stupid and ignorant . . . The resemblance betwixt the actions of animals and those of men is so entire in this respect, that the very first action of the very first animal we shall please to pitch on, will afford us an incontestable argument for the present doctrine.[8]

And yet the inveterate human tendency was to find reason in men and mere instinct in animals, when the very same actions were to be observed.[9] Hume was convinced that animals and human beings learned about life in the same way. It was simple prejudice that prevented us from seeing this. As he remarked in *An Enquiry Concerning Human Understanding*, it is 'evident, that animals, as well as men learn many things from experience, and

[6] Charles Darwin, *The Descent of Man and Selection in Relation to Sex* (London, John Murray, 1871).

[7] Rachels, above n 4, at 10. This was the date calculated by the Archbishop of Armagh, James Ussher, and was to become the official date stated in the Authorised Bible.

[8] David Hume, *A Treatise of Human Nature* (1739) (London, Penguin Books, 1985) xvi, 226.

[9] 'Nothing shows more the force of habit in reconciling us to any phaenomenon, than this, that men are not astonish'd at the operations of their own reason, at the same time, that they admire the instinct of animals, and find a difficulty in explaining it, merely because it cannot be reduc'd to the very same principles'. *Ibid* 228.

infer, that the same events will always follow from the same causes'.[10] Both humans and animals derived their knowledge of the world from observing the simple laws of cause and effect. Both humans and animals 'learn many parts of their knowledge from observation'.[11] Both humans and animals, he said, also operated from instinct.[12] Thus, Hume accentuated our commonalities with animals. Humans and animals were both creatures of instinct and also creatures capable of experimental reasoning.

As we know, the Darwinian theory of evolution was to take hold in the scientific community. It is now well accepted as the most powerful scientific explanation of how we have come to be. Darwin said, in effect, that we are highly intelligent animals and scientists now broadly agree with him. The modern scientific understanding of our evolved place in nature is essentially Darwinian.

Our commonality with all other forms of life has been further reinforced with the development of the science of genetics. We now know that we share most of our genetic coding not only with other humans but also with non-human animals. We are exceptionally close to the Great Apes. Indeed we have much in common, genetically, with vegetable life. (Scientists enjoy pointing out our genetic similarity to bananas.) Francis Crick, who with James Watson worked out the molecular structure of DNA in 1953, was as keen as anyone to eliminate the belief that somehow we transcend the natural and the material world; that we possess some sort of immaterial essence. In 1966 he wrote 'In recent years molecular biology [has] practically

[10] David Hume, *An Enquiry Concerning Human Understanding* (1777) (Web edn, Leeds Electronic Text Centre, 2000) ix, 104. He cites the 'ignorance and inexperience of the young' animal and compares it with 'the cunning and sagacity of the old'. Humans too acquire wisdom with age. Animals, like humans, learn from experience and so learn to modify their actions. Thus, both animals and humans employ analogous reasoning. This is further demonstrated by 'the effects of discipline and education on animals, who, by the proper application of rewards and punishments, may be taught any course of action' even 'contrary to their natural instincts and propensities' (at 105). Thus, animals like humans are educable. The dog, eg, like the human employs inferences from past experiences. This, however, does not entail reasoning; but nor does it entail reasoning in the case of children, or even 'the generality of mankind'.

[11] *Ibid* 108. Thus, his starting supposition about the reasoning of animals is that it is the same as that of human beings. 'It is custom alone, which engages animals, from every object, that strikes their senses, to infer its usual attendant, and carries their imagination, from the appearance of the one, to conceive of the other, in that particular manner, which we nominate belief' (at 106). And this is also true of 'the higher as well as lower classes of sensitive beings' (at 107). So, consistently, it was the similarity of animals and humans that struck Hume.

[12] Our 'experimental reasoning . . . which we possess in common with beasts, and on which the whole conduct of life depends, is nothing but a species of instinct . . . that acts in us unknown to ourselves . . . Though the instinct be different, yet still it is an instinct, which teaches a man to avoid fire, as much as that, which teaches a bird . . . the art of incubation'. *Ibid* 108.

obliterated the distinction between the living and the non-living'.[13] Crick himself wanted to remove any religious sense we might have of ourselves as other than natural or material beings and effectively dedicated his life to this mission; first with his successful bid to discover the secret of genetic life (and his related work in biochemistry), and then with his later unsuccessful endeavour to discover the material basis of consciousness (a field of science then and now still in its infancy).

With the scientific entrenchment of evolutionary biology (and now with the remarkable and escalating insights into our physical natures provided by the science of genetics), one might have expected a concomitant shift to take place in social and legal thinking about the relative status and value of 'man' and other animals—in the characterisation of humans as creatures, and our relations with other animals and the rest of the natural world. This was something that Darwin himself seemed to anticipate, with some alarm.[14] (Crick, by contrast, embraced a fully natural account of human life and set himself against the world of religion.)

In particular, we might have expected some modification of the legal conceptual divide between persons and property as it applies to humans and animals respectively. But this did not happen to any marked degree. Instead, there remains a firm cultural and legal understanding that humans and animals should be characterised in quite different ways: humans as persons; animals as property. As we saw in the last chapter, the Second World War, and its immediate aftermath, served to consolidate the species divide in the name of natural human rights and to affirm a strong legal metaphysical stance: that law is for humans essentially understood as non-animals—as moral and spiritual persons. As Ben Berger elucidates:

> it was precisely the attempt to treat humans more like animals (in the worst form that that effort can take) that drove the law's sense of human and animal further apart.[15]

There was 'a deepening of species specificity'.[16] A Christian idea of human exceptionality was retained and reinforced.

The scaremongers at the time of Darwin thus proved to be wrong. There was to be no violent or even gradualist shift in thinking about the nature and status of the human, now scientifically understood as descended from animals, as a natural being—at least not within the realm of legal thought. There was to be no great revolution in legal thinking about the nature of being human and the consequent nature of the legal person. There was to be no newly-reconceived human animal.

[13] Quoted in Matt Ridley, *Francis Crick: Discoverer of the Genetic Code* (London, Harper Press, 2006) 125.

[14] See Adrian Desmond and James Moore, *Darwin* (London, Penguin Books, 1992).

[15] Statement by Ben Berger (personal correspondence).

[16] *Ibid.*

Intelligent Design and *Kitzmiller v Dover*

This is perhaps surprising, given that the courts, in other ways, have proven highly receptive to Darwin. Significantly, there has been a consistent refusal to permit the anti-Darwinian theory of Intelligent Design to be taught as science in schools. *Kitzmiller v Dover* is the latest in a long line of American decisions asserting that the Biblical idea of Creation must not be taught in science classrooms.[17] This case was precipitated by a resolution of the Dover Area School Board of Directors in the US State of Pennsylvania in 2004 that students of biology were to be made aware of what it termed 'gaps' and 'problems' in the Darwinian theory of evolution; they were also to be told about the competing theory of 'intelligent design'.[18] In effect, the Board was trying to oust Darwin from the science classroom. These and other similar instructions were challenged by parents of students as unconstitutional, as breaching the constitutionally-mandated separation of Church and State and in December 2005, the US District Court for the Middle District of Pennsylvania agreed with the parents. It affirmed that the state school's policy created 'an excessive entanglement of the government with religion'.[19]

The court was bitingly critical of this endeavour to replace Darwin with the idea of a divine creator and designer of human beings. In a sustained and searing judgment, the court affirmed that the statement of the Dover School Board:

> singles out the theory of evolution for special treatment, misrepresents its statement in the scientific community, causes students to doubt its validity without scientific justification, presents students with a religious alternative masquerading as a scientific theory, directs them to consult a creationist text as though it were a science resource, and instructs students to forego scientific inquiry in the public school class room and instead to seek out religious instruction elsewhere.[20]

In effect, the students were being taught to make a choice between a 'God-friendly' science and an atheistic science.

However, this robust judicial defence of Darwin in the science classroom does not appear to have carried over into other areas of law. As we will see, the broad scientific and legal acceptance of evolutionary theory and its dissemination has not resulted in a concomitant rethinking of law's person and the basis of his value. There has been no observable erosion of the principle of human sanctity nor a correlative reduction of our status in the natural world.

[17] *Tammy Kitzmiller v Dover Area School District*, 400F Supp 2d 707 (MD Pa 2005).
[18] *Ibid* 3.
[19] *Ibid* 115.
[20] *Ibid* 64.

Humans as Animals

This chapter and the next inspect the ideas of those who have pushed for a greater legal recognition of our human animal status and perhaps some form of convergence of humans and animals in law: a narrowing of our relative legal status. I will also consider the arguments of those who resist such a move. The advocates for change are various in their aims. Some, in effect, want animals to be treated more like us and so urge some minimum legal rights for animals. Their primary interest is in the legal status of animals. Others favour greater recognition in law of the moral status of animals, and their fellowship with humans, but without the conferral of rights. Still others want *us* to be treated more like animals. This is not at all to say that they want us to be treated as badly as animals or as somehow debased, as no better than animals, as mere brutes. Rather, they want greater attention to be paid to our own creature natures so that we are viewed more as beings with creature needs and interests and less as abstractly rational or disembodied spiritual beings. By contrast, the opponents of Naturalism say this is not the way to proceed; on moral or legal or scientific grounds, they defend strongly the legal status quo.

Among those who favour a more Naturalistic legal interpretation of human beings, there are at least two distinct arguments advanced. One argument is primarily about the relative legal status of animals (as property) and humans (as persons). This is the subject of this chapter. The suggestion here is that the formal conceptual division between animals and humans should be adjusted, diminished or removed altogether. After Darwin, we should start to see animals and humans as categorically similar in law. Some animals, at least, should be moved into the category of rights-bearing persons and some humans should be moved out of this class of beings. The degree of change advocated depends on the ethical and political leanings of the theorist.

The dramatic import of this line of thinking is that humanity alone is no longer to provide an almost exclusive basis for moral and legal value. Human beings, in this view, are not exceptional; they are not categorically different from other natural beings. The claim is that humanity alone is not a sufficient basis for preferential moral and legal treatment; that our human species is morally insignificant; that we should be morally and legally judged like other animals; that the formal legal divide between humans and animals should be breached.

In law, only a tiny group of thinkers has vigorously pursued this radical line of argument: that we should formally recognise our commonality with other animals and so have animals legally reclassified. Their dramatic aim is to shift at least some animal species into the rights-bearing, and so human, category, and thus alter the conceptual relationship between humans and other animals. But mainly this heroic legal endeavour to reclassify the natural world, and our place within it, is seen as eccentric and misguided; to many jurists, probably the majority, it does not call for serious intellectual engagement. The relatively uncontroversial view is that animals should remain a reasonably well-protected form of property (they are protected by a range of animal welfare laws) and all human beings should remain persons.

More influential in the legal community is the more moderate group of Naturalistic thinkers who urge us to take seriously our natural biological natures but not to abandon the formal legal divide between humans and other animals which sets us apart from the creature world. According to these Naturalistic critics of the legal image of ourselves, the human/animal divide is legitimate, for a variety of reasons. They object to the essentially Kantian idea of ourselves as higher rational beings, defined by our powers of abstract reason. These Naturalists urge an understanding of humans more attuned to our biological natures; some call for a view of us as needy dependent rational animals.

This second argument is therefore less dramatic in its implications for animals, but rather more interesting in its moral and legal implications for us, as we will see in the next chapter when I consider the various efforts to conceptualise humans as natural beings. The idea is that our law pays too little heed to our biological natures and when it does attend to them, it tends to distort or diminish them and so present a false image of human beings. It is said that law still responds to a Kantian imperative that we control and contain that which is animal within us and emphasise the abstractly cerebral. To Kant, the animal was part of us, but it did not and should not define us. As Kant insisted, '[man's] insignificance as a *human animal* may not infringe upon his consciousness of his dignity as a *rational man*'[21] (emphasis added). Such Naturalistic thinkers have urged us to attend more to human beings as natural beings and to review critically the various ways law understands and regulates our physical embodied natures and our physical relations with one another.

My task in these two chapters is thus to reflect on the various ways that law and its interpreters have responded to Darwin's insights, especially in the light of the broad acceptance of those insights within the scientific community. My scholarly focus remains on law's person. To what extent have Naturalistic understandings of the person seeped into law? Do we now think any differently about the relative legal status and nature of 'man' and the other animals?

[21] Immanuel Kant, *The Metaphysics of Morals* (Cambridge, Cambridge University Press, 1991) 230.

Dismantling the Human/Animal Divide

The highly vocal but small group of philosophers and lawyers who wish to challenge the legal and moral partition between animals and humans tend to be philosophical and legal realists: the reality, they say, is that animals are not categorically different from us and law should reflect this reality. It follows that humans and at least some animals should be placed in the same broad legal category. Here, we have the very antithesis of the human rights position, that to be human is to have automatic value. Instead, the idea is that we should value the particular capacities and sentience of any given individual, *whatever its species*. According to these thinkers, we should look to abilities and needs of the particular being; human value is not a given in the absence of both. To retain the current legal position, the treatment of all humans as persons and animals as property, is (in their view) to engage in arbitrary, discriminatory and morally-repugnant practices.

The classical philosophers who provide inspiration for these modern advocates for animals are David Hume and Jeremy Bentham, who also believed that animals were morally significant. Hume, as we saw, believed that we habitually engaged in unwarranted 'speciesism': the same behaviour in humans and animals led to an unwarranted finding of intelligence in the former and of mechanical or instinctive behaviour in the latter. René Descartes, often called the father of modern philosophy, was infamously guilty of just this sort of thinking (which permitted him to engage in startlingly cruel experiments on live dogs).[22] Animals, to Descartes, were simply machines. They were, in the words of his biographer, 'soulless automata, biological machines without consciousness, who experience neither sensations nor emotions . . . mere robots barking and mewing, eating and running'.[23] Bentham put the converse view of animals. '[T]he question', he said, 'is not, Can they reason? Nor, Can they talk? but, Can they suffer?'.[24] Bentham was convinced, as we are today, that animals are capable of immense suffering.

The current generation of animal advocates have quite consciously pursued the logic of Hume, Bentham and Darwin to what *they* see as its natural conclusion. Darwin, in particular, they say, necessarily altered our place in the natural world. He revealed that we are descended from other animals, that we are only animals of a particular species and no more than that, and that our species does not make us significant. There is no longer something exceptional about us and so there is no justification for treating

[22] For a brief description of these experiments, see AC Grayling, *Descartes: the Life of Rene Descartes and Its Place in His Times* (London, Free Press, 2005) 159.

[23] *Ibid* 35.

[24] Jeremy Bentham, *An Introduction to the Principles of Morals and Legislation* (JH Burns and HLA Hart (eds), London, Athlone Press, 1970) 282–3.

other animals as categorically different from us. As James Rachels spells out this conclusion:

> After Darwin, we can no longer think of ourselves as occupying a special role in creation—instead, we must realize that we are products of the same evolutionary forces, working blindly and without purpose, that shaped the rest of the animal kingdom.[25]

And as practical realists, these promoters of animal interests have demanded that law reflect this modern scientific reality about 'man's' relation to other species. Law, they say, must be responsive to nature. Humans must now be considered as individuals, each with their own particular needs and abilities (though some will have none); not as a single species set above the rest of the natural world as a privileged caste.

Peter Singer and the Levelling of Humans

The public intellectual who has done more than any other to ruffle our prejudgments about the relative status of humans and animals is Australian philosopher and ethicist, Peter Singer. In *Animal Liberation*, published in 1975, Singer mounted a bold challenge to the legitimacy of the species divide, declaring species to be morally and therefore legally irrelevant.[26] The species distinction in morality and in law, he said, was arbitrary and unjustifiable. It was equivalent to the distinctions once made about race and sex. It had no good foundation.

Singer has maintained this position over the past 30 years.[27] What still matters or counts, to Singer, for moral purposes is sentience—the ability to suffer—as well as the ability to form a sense of one's self over time. These are abilities shared by humans and animals; they do not generate different moral or legal categories. If a being can experience pain or pleasure, it has some moral value and our society and our law should reflect that value. If that being also has a sense of itself over time and thus the ability to form preferences about its future life, then it has still greater moral value because it now counts as a person.

Because species, of itself, is morally irrelevant, according to Singer, it is the degree of sentience and self-consciousness which determines a being's value. Persons matter most: animal or human. But beings which are sentient also matter. As a utilitarian, Singer believes that a decision that will affect the welfare of a being is morally justified if it causes more pleasure than suffering and for this principle to apply, the being must be sentient. It

25 Rachels, above n 4, at 1.

26 Peter Singer, *Animal Liberation: A New Ethics for Our Treatment of Animals* (New York, Random House, 1975).

27 For an interesting set of critical commentaries on Singer's extensive writings, see Dale Jamieson (ed), *Singer and His Critics* (Oxford, Blackwell, 1999).

is also justified if it satisfies the greatest number of preferences of persons (thus, Singer is known as a preference utilitarian).

Singer remains at his most controversial in his defence of sentient animal interests and his concomitant denial of insentient human interests. He does not baulk at the direct moral comparison of humans and animals. He is willing to say that some animals have more value than some humans and so deserve greater social and legal protection. Perhaps the most provoking application of Singer's philosophy is at the very beginning of human life. The new-born human baby is sentient but lacks a clear sense of itself. 'Infants are sentient beings who are neither rational nor self-conscious'.[28] New-born infants are not persons because they have no continuing sense of themselves. Their potential to become a person, Singer declares, is morally irrelevant. What matters is what they are now:

> No infant—disabled or not—has as strong a claim to life as beings capable of seeing themselves as distinct entities, existing over time.[29]

Singer therefore doubts whether the infant can be said to have an automatic right to life. Infants should be treated in the same manner as we treat any sentient but not rational being, whatever its species. Consistency is called for.

On classic utilitarian grounds, says Singer, it may therefore be right to kill an infant if it is greatly suffering and there are no offsetting benefits to be achieved. Its humanity alone is not a sufficient reason to preserve its life. (Singer shares these views with Michael Tooley, whom we encountered in Chapter 6.) Indeed, it may be positively right to kill a child if there will therefore be another healthy happy child to replace her and this is what the parents want. We already regard children as replaceable, says Singer: women are given the option to abort foetuses with genetic problems. We should therefore be consistent in this attitude and apply it after the birth of a baby. The birth of a human being is not a good enough reason alone to preserve it. Moral significance does not suddenly begin at birth, though legal significance as a person does, at present. Rather, it begins with the ability to form preferences: to care about oneself over time. If 'the total amount of happiness will be greater if the disabled child is killed',[30] then it may be right to kill it.

Singer argues, correlatively, that intelligent and sentient animals should count as individuals with protected interests. As species alone is a morally insignificant moral criterion, one must consider the interests, needs and preferences of the individual being, whatever its species. The sentient intelligent animal can therefore sometimes count for more than the insentient or unthinking human being. Simply and briefly stated, the law has not acceded

[28] 'Justifying Infanticide' in Peter Singer, *Writings on an Ethical Life* (New York, Ecco Press, 2000) 187.

[29] *Ibid.*

[30] *Ibid* 189.

to the demands of Singer, notwithstanding the occasional heroic efforts to have them translated into legal doctrine. Furthermore, there is little sign of law doing so.

The Cases of Baby Theresa and Baby Fae

The 1992 Florida case of Baby Theresa concerned a baby born with the profound birth defect of anencephaly.[31] She had no cerebrum or cerebellum (no higher brain), only a brain stem. Her parents, Laura Campo and Justin Pearson, only learned of her condition in the eighth month of the pregnancy, too late for an abortion. They decided that the birth should proceed by way of Caesarean section to enable the baby's organs to be healthy and available for transplantation. (Anencephalic babies are likely to have large heads and so vaginal births can kill them and their organs.) The firm desire of the parents was to donate her organs to other babies so that some positive benefit should come from the birth of their child. They were driven by the principle of utility endorsed by Singer. However, because Baby Theresa had some brain function, she was declared to be legally alive and the Florida Court of Appeals confirmed the decision of the circuit court judge that her organs could not be removed. A few months after the death of Theresa by organ failure, the Florida Supreme Court ruled that anencephalic babies are not considered to be brain dead for the purposes of organ donation. There was no question of killing the baby to save others because she remained a protected legal person. This remains clear, uncontroversial law.

By contrast, in the case of Baby Fae, a healthy heart was removed from a non-consenting donor and given to another. However, this did not give rise to a criminal prosecution because the being whose life was sacrificed, though sentient and of very modest intelligence, was a female baboon, named Goobers, not a human baby. The recipient of the heart was Baby Fae who was born in California in 1984 with a serious heart syndrome: the left side of her heart was underdeveloped. After strong persuasion from a paediatric surgeon, the parents consented to the transplant of a baboon heart into their baby. Fae's defective heart was removed and Goober's healthy heart was connected. Not surprisingly, given the highly experimental nature of the surgery and the inexperience of the surgeon (he had never performed a human heart transplant before), Fae died three weeks later. Although the operation was strongly condemned by animal rights activists, it did not and could not result in a criminal prosecution for the murder or manslaughter of Goober, because Goober was not a person.[32] This remains the law and there is no serious suggestion that it should change.

[31] *In re TACP*, 609 So 2d 588, 589 (Fla 1992). The case is discussed in Steve J, 'Casenote: Personhood and Death' (2003) 62 *University of Cincinnatti Law Review* 1227.

[32] The case is discussed at length in Gregory E Pence, *Classic Cases in Medical Ethics* (3rd edn, Boston, McGraw Hill, 2000) 340.

Animal Lawyers and the Elevation of Animals

Peter Singer is the most prominent philosopher writing today about the moral status of animals and advocating an end to 'speciesism'. Steven Wise and Gary Francione are perhaps the two most prominent legal advocates for the changed status of animals, and implicitly the changed status of human beings. Like Singer, both confront, head-on, our most fundamental presuppositions about human exceptionality.

These unflinching legal advocates of both animal rights and interests can find little that is good in law for non-human species. They depict a great partition between humans and the rest of the natural world. On the one side, the human side, the side of persons, everything is for the human good; on the other side, the animal side, the side of property, all is exploitation and abuse. In this account of our legal relations with animals, only humans are legal subjects; animals are only and always objects. We are legal beings and they are legal things. Therefore, it cannot really be said that they relate to us at all in law. They are the objects of legal relations between human beings; they are not parties to those relations. Implicitly, this way of dividing up natural beings in law is based on a false premise (in their view) in that it both denies our animal nature and thingifies sentient and thinking beings that are not human. The division is therefore based on a fundamental lie and it neglects the lessons of Darwin.

This legal bifurcation of the world of natural beings into persons and property, it is said, is absurdly at odds with the accepted scientific view that we are on a continuum with other animals and that that continuum is an animal continuum. There is no such progressive or continuous view of our status in law: one that runs from lower to higher animals. The legal divide between the human and animal world is not only scientifically false; it is also (in their view) morally impoverished. It is based on lazy, misguided and uncaring legal thinking. It is simply the *sine qua non* of much of our legal thought that humans matter simply because we are humans (who are somehow not thought of as animals). Normally it goes without saying, because there is no real concern, within the broader legal community, about the classification of non-human animals as things for use. The fundamentally different legal regimes for humans and animals are taken as given because they are implicitly acceptable. Normally they give scant cause for concern. Animals are simply a rather lively form of property; they are not moral beings like us.

Steven Wise describes the human/animal divide in law in just these terms. He observes:

> a thick and impenetrable wall [which] has separated all human from all nonhuman animals. On one side, even the most trivial interests of a single species—ours—are jealously guarded. We have assigned ourselves, alone among the million

> animal species, the status of 'legal persons'. On the other side of that wall lies the legal refuse of an entire kingdom . . . They are 'legal things'. Their most basic and fundamental interests . . . are intentionally ignored, often maliciously trampled, and routinely abused.[33]

As we will see, Wise is a passionate animal rights activist given to strong prose. It has been suggested that he describes too starkly the legal distinction between humans and animals; that animals are not quite reduced to 'legal refuse'. Extensive animal welfare provisions proscribe cruelty to animals. The legal treatment of animals is a concern of many: witness the passionate debates in Britain about the abolition of fox-hunting.[34] And yet it is true that the fundamentally different legal regimes for humans and animals are generally taken for granted. Indeed, the very idea that an animal might be endowed with a legal right, and so personified, remains anathema to most lawyers, who are nevertheless well disposed to the personification of inanimate abstract entities, such as corporations. So it would seem that the non-personification of animals is doing important cultural work.

There are two obvious legal ways to improve upon this situation. We can use the animal welfare law that we have at present, but press for better, stronger anti-cruelty provisions and for greater vigilance in the enforcement of existing legislation. That is, we can insist that the interests of animals, especially their interest in avoiding suffering and also in leading lives more in sympathy with their animal natures, are best preserved by existing or improved law. This approach tends to be conservative and incremental. It builds on what there is and it does not pose a serious challenge to the existing legal classification of animals; nor does it threaten the legal classification of humans. It still appears to consign animals to the category of property or things, though admittedly heavily-protected property. But perhaps not completely so.[35]

Or, we can press for animal rights. We can argue that animals should not be treated as legal things: rather they should be rights holders, like us. They should be removed from the category of property and shifted into the category of persons. This move is much more threatening to human status and has been strongly opposed by most lawyers. To Wise and Francione, however, the current welfare/property approach does too little for animals.

[33] Steven Wise, *Rattling the Cage: Towards Legal Rights for Animals* (Cambridge, Mass, Perseus Books, 2000) 4.

[34] Cass Sunstein in particular has put the view that animals are already the beneficiaries of many laws which take seriously their interests (see discussion below).

[35] To the extent that such laws are designed for the benefit of animals themselves, and not just for their owners, or for the sensibilities of other humans, and to the extent that they impose duties on others to preserve those animal interests, there is a case to be made for the quasi-personhood of animals. The reason is that laws that protect the interests of a being or an entity and impose duties on others may be said to generate rights. As we will see, Cass Sunstein argues for this interpretation of animal welfare legislation.

It leaves them vulnerable to abuses and helpless to defend themselves from extreme and systematic cruelty of human beings. Welfare reform has not changed this; its record is poor. This is why, in their view, the property status of animals is no longer acceptable and more swingeing changes are required.

Steven Wise and the Intelligent Apes

Steven Wise pioneered the practice of animal law. He is a legal practitioner representing animals, a political activist, a law teacher on a number of American campuses offering the relatively-new subject of animal law and author of two influential volumes on 'animal rights'. To Wise, law employs a human measure in all respects. It is all about and for human beings. For the moment, Wise accepts the inevitability of this human-centrism: that as creatures of intelligence and imagination, we understandably form the focus of law. But the focus should not be exclusive, he says. Our nearest non-human relatives, who possess the capacity for a modest amount of reason, should also be persons.

Wise builds his case for the rights of certain clever animals with a variety of lawyerly techniques and types of evidence. He has resort to standard legal method and argumentation. He deploys some well known rhetorical and narrative devices of the courtroom lawyer and he marshals a considerable body of scientific evidence about the nature of animals.

Wise asserts that common law reasoning is essentially analogous reasoning and that our fundamental common law principles of equality and fairness are best honoured by treating like cases alike and unlike cases differently. This much is uncontroversial. Where the controversy arises is in Wise's characterisation of the like and unlike. Certain animals, he insists, are uncannily like human beings and it is only ignorance and bigotry which has concealed this fact from us. And so he sets out to show that certain primates are, on current evidence, so like us that legal consistency and fairness demand that they be treated like us.

It is the mental abilities of certain animals, rather than their capacity to suffer, which, to Wise, singles them out for preferred legal treatment.[36] In this sense he is a Rationalist. Chimpanzees and bonobos, he believes, possess a sufficiently sophisticated mental life to qualify them for basic human dignity-rights. Such creatures are like human children; they possess naturally a very basic form of autonomy, in the form of certain preferences and

[36] Wise says that if he were 'Chief Justice of the Universe, I might make the simpler capacity to suffer, rather than practical autonomy, sufficient for personhood and dignity-rights . . . But the capacity to suffer appears irrelevant to common-law judges in their consideration of who is entitled to basic rights . . . And so I present a legal, and not a philosophical argument for the dignity-rights of nonhuman animals. *Drawing the Line: Science and the Case for Animal Rights* (Cambridge, Mass, Perseus Books, 2002) 34.

desires, likes and dislikes, and this autonomy, he says, should be reflected in law:

> Whether we call it self-determination, autonomy or volition, it is sufficient for basic legal rights. Things don't act autonomously. Persons do. Things can't self-determine. Persons can. Things lack volition. Persons don't. Persons have wills.[37]

To make his case for basic animal intelligence, Wise turns to a variety of sciences. Primatology supplies him with evidence of the mental life of certain primates. Wise points to the intelligence of chimpanzees and bonobos, in particular. These apes are capable of doing many of the things regarded as quintessentially human: they employ language; they have mental representations, a sense of self and also a sense of other minds; they employ humour; they lie and deceive. He describes in such animals 'a theory of mind', an ability to pass the mirror self-recognition test and 'to share joint attention'.[38] They have particular personalities and brought up by humans in a human manner, they become family members: non-human children.

Wise turns to evolutionary biology for evidence of our genetic and taxonomic similarity with the higher primates. From immunology he draws the point that 'humans and chimpanzees are as similar as "two subspecies of gophers living on opposite sides of the Colorado River"'.[39] Again, because like should be treated alike, chimpanzees and bonobos should be treated like us.

For Wise, animal rights should be seen as a logical and natural extension of human rights. He analogises the current plight of animals with the former plight of slaves, and of women. In both cases, abuses arose from the consignment of intelligent and sentient beings to the status of property. Slaves became persons; women became persons; it is time that intelligent animals became persons. Wise believes that there is an inexorable logic to this endowment of rights. Law has steadily expanded its circle of concern as it has come to appreciate the natural attributes of excluded beings and each expansion has meant a growing enlightenment. Now we should draw the circle larger still and include the non-human primates.

Wise does not confine himself to impersonal legal logic. He appeals also to our sympathy and our empathy, as a good courtroom lawyer should, by depicting the interior lives of animals and showing us their distinctive human-like personalities. *Rattling the Cage* thus begins with the tale of Jerom, a tortured young man—imprisoned, injected with disease-bearing serum over many years and reduced to a state of ultimate despair:

> Jerom died on February 13, 1996, ten days shy of his fourteenth birthday. The teenager was dull, bloated, depressed, sapped, anaemic and plagued by diarrhoea.

[37] *Ibid* 30.
[38] Wise, above n 33, at 268.
[39] Vincent Sarich as quoted in *ibid* 2–3.

> He had not played in fresh air for eleven years . . . Throughout the Iran-Contra hearings, almost to the beginning of the Gulf War, he sat in the small, windowless, cinder-block Infectious Disease Building . . . Throughout the war and into Bill Clinton's campaign for a second term as president, he languished in his cell.[40]

Jerom, it transpires, is a chimpanzee employed in medical research: his prison is a research laboratory; his torturers are medical scientists. Implicitly, an analogy has been drawn with slave owners and their human property and with Nazi doctors and their human subjects. Jerom has been cast as a sentient and intelligent human innocent.

In his second book, *Drawing the Line*, Wise describes the great impediments to the grant of personhood for animals. Perhaps the greatest obstruction, he believes, is that of mentality. It is utterly alien to the current mindset of most of us to regard animals in such a manner. 'The idea that everything exists for the sake of humans remains one of our "core beliefs"'.[41] No less than a shift of world view is demanded of us.

Wise emphasises our strong vested interests in thinking as we do, hence our resistance to change. We have broad-ranging investments in animals as products: as meat, as clothing, as research subjects, as the ingredients of 'plastic, tires, crayons, cosmetics . . . ink, shaving cream . . . textiles' and so on.[42] It seems that in almost all parts of our lives, we use animals as things. How could we possibly afford to regard them as persons? And yet such economic arguments were made about slavery, according to Wise, but finally our better natures prevailed. Once again, we should rise to the moral challenge; this time we should extend rights to animals.

Gary Francione and the Abolition of Property in Animals

Gary Francione, like Wise, is a practitioner lawyer, a teacher, a scholar and a legal activist.[43] Also like Wise, he advocates the rights of animals, but on different grounds and to different ends. To Francione, it is the sentience of animals that matters, morally and legally, not their cognitive abilities. Francione is, in this respect, with Jeremy Bentham for whom the capacity for suffering entitled animals to moral and legal respect. Where Francione is at odds with Bentham, and with his political successors, such as Peter Singer, is in his rejection of the principle of utility as a means of elevating the moral and legal status of animals. The principle of utility means that a decision is warranted if it increases the utilities and decreases the disutilities

[40] Wise, above n 33, at 1–2.

[41] Wise, above n 36, at 19.

[42] *Ibid* 10.

[43] His two major scholarly works are Gary Francione, *Animals, Property and the Law* (Philadelphia, Temple University Press, 1995); Gary Francione, *Introduction to Animal Rights: Your Child or the Dog?* (Philadelphia, Temple University Press, 2000).

of those affected. The utilitarian calculus can employ different measures of utility, such as happiness or preferences, and it can incorporate the interests of the non-human as well as the human. Francione's concern is that whenever the interests of animals are factored into utility's calculus, and placed alongside the interests of humans, animals invariably lose.

The reason why the interests of animals will always be found inferior to those of humans, no matter how much we reform animal welfare laws, is that animals remain property within this legislative regime. Admittedly, animals are a special type of property: on paper, at least, some are highly protected and it might even seem that duties are owed them. But, nevertheless, they remain a species of property. And because they are a form of property, not persons, animals are cast outside the legal and moral community. As property, they cannot bring legal actions in their own name in order to protect their own interests. Despite the repeated efforts of animal activists, animals continue to be denied standing in all legal matters which directly concern their own interests. Always, animal interests must be allied to the affected interests of a human being, who therefore has standing, if animal interests are to be protected in court. Never can animals be party to a legal action in their own right, on their own behalf, in defence of their own interests.

As Francione insists, 'the institution of property is still a means of serving human ends'[44] and it is an institution which is fundamental to our law. Our law deeply respects the rights of the property owner; it is not concerned about the interests of the property itself. Damage to property is not an infringement of the interests or rights of the property; rather it is a diminution of the value of the property to the owner. Animals are therefore not legally recognised as beings of inherent or intrinsic value, as having value in their own right; always their value is derived from human interests and typically from the interests of their owner. Consequently, the rights of the human property owner, or of other relevant humans, will always trump the interests of the property itself, even when that property is heavily protected. If humans stand to derive a strong enough benefit from the injury or killing of animals, say as research subjects or as animal products, then the injury or killing is thought to be justified. Even small benefits to humans are permitted to justify considerable animal abuse. There is no ethical equilibrium here. Rather, there is a gross imbalance of interests between animals and humans, which is endemic to the entire meat industry. Eating meat is unnecessary; it is also unnecessary to employ animals as ingredients in the many thousands of products we use on a daily basis.

Animal welfare legislation does little to stop these ordinary practices of cruelty, according to Francione. At best it limits them. Even sustained torture of animals is thought to be morally and legally justified if humans stand

[44] Gary Francione, *Animals Property and the Law* (Philadelphia, Temple University Press, 1995) 102.

to benefit. Often, animal protections laws, ostensibly designed to minimise cruelty, endow the property owner who stands most to gain from the cruelty with the power to decide whether cruelty to her property is present and justified. By way of illustration, Francione points out that under federal American animal welfare legislation, 'the primary source of regulation of laboratory animals is by those who own and use the animals'.[45]

A fair and objective assessment of animal abuse is unlikely in these circumstances, according to Francione. Rather, the instrumental value of animals to humans, especially to the humans who own them, will count for more than their own suffering. The calculus will never be in their favour. Francione describes our legal and moral thinking about animals as:

> a 'hybrid' system because we juxtapose the interests of a rightholder with that of a nonrightholder who, in addition to not being a rightholder, is also the object of the rightholder's exercise of right.[46]

Francione's solution is far more dramatic than that proposed by Wise, who demands only two basic rights for a tiny number of highly-intelligent animals which he regards as quasi-human. The less intelligent animals remain property in Wise's scheme. Francione is unimpressed by such line-drawing between different types of animals, according to their cognitive capacities: to him, it is simply a means of making new oppressive hierarchies. Francione demands nothing less than the total abolition of property in animals. Thus, the one right he demands for animals is the right not to be property. And so he calls himself an abolitionist, implicitly allying himself to those who opposed human slavery. The implications are breathtaking. Domesticated animals would cease to be brought into existence. Millions of animals would quickly disappear from the face of the earth. We would all become vegans. There is a deliberate provocation in this stand as it demands a change of world view.

Legal Response

Wise and Fracione both press for a dramatically different legal world from the one we now inhabit, with a very different cast of characters. Wise, an implicit Rationalist, would have intelligent animals recognised as persons who can act in law. Francione, who is perhaps closer to the Religionists, in that he finds innate value (perhaps even a divine spark) in all living beings, would see his idea of the intrinsic value of sentient beings extended to animals and consequently the abolition of property in animals. Essentially, their pleas have fallen on deaf legal ears.

[45] Gary Francione, *Animals, Property and the Law* (Philadelphia, Temple University Press, 1995) 5.

[46] *Ibid* 107.

Wise and Francione accurately identify an enduring legal problem for animals which they have yet to rectify. The problem is that animals cannot become parties to an action concerning injury done to themselves because they are not legal persons. And because they are not persons, they can never achieve legal standing to intervene in a legal matter in which their interests are directly affected. As one American judge suggested in a remarkable proposal to extend rights to nature itself:

> The critical question of 'standing' would be simplified and also put neatly in focus if we fashioned a federal rule that allowed environmental issues to be litigated before federal agencies or federal courts in the name of the inanimate object about to be despoiled, defaced or invaded by roads and bulldozers.[47]

Because animals are not persons and can never qualify for standing, often the only legal recourse for those who object to animal cruelty is to demonstrate that they, as humans, are adversely affected by the observation of cruelty; the harm to the animals themselves, the animals' own suffering, is not directly in issue. This problem was brought into stark relief in *Animal Legal Defense Fund, Inc v Glickman*.[48] Here, the District of Columbia Full Court of Appeals had to decide whether the plaintiff, Marc Jurnove, had legal standing to bring an action against the Secretary of Agriculture for failure to promulgate and enforce adequate regulations under the Federal Animal Welfare Act. Jurnove objected to the inhumane treatment to animals he observed as a regular visitor to the Long Island Game Park and Zoo. He particularly opposed the enforced isolation of certain primates, which he knew to be highly social animals. To obtain legal standing, Jurnove had to demonstrate that he was the one who suffered an 'injury in fact'.[49] The real injury was, of course, to the animals themselves who were being kept in inhumane conditions.

The Full Court of Appeals supported a broad interpretation of 'injury in fact' and found that through witnessing animals being kept in such harsh conditions, Jurnove had himself suffered a concrete, specific emotional injury which directly impaired his 'aesthetic interest' in observing, studying and enjoying animals. There was no question, however, of the animals themselves bringing an action in their own name for the injury done to them, though this would have been the preferred option of the animal advocates involved in the case and would have more accurately reflected the identity

[47] *Sierra Club v Morton*, 405 US 727, 741 (1972) (Douglas J).

[48] 154 F3d 426 (DC Cir 1998); 119 S Ct 1454 (1999).

[49] In the United States, standing to sue is governed by Art III of the Constitution and by the requirements of Ch 7 of Title 5 of the US Code (formerly part of the Administrative Procedure Act). Article III of the Constitution requires three elements to be satisfied: the plaintiff must have suffered an injury in fact; there must be a causal connection between the injury and the conduct complained of; and it must be 'likely' that the injury will be redressed by a favourable decision.

of the injured parties. The case remained formally human centred, about human interests, although it was really all about the suffering of animals.

Cass Sunstein: Questioning the Species Divide

In his analysis of the current legal status of animals, American constitutional lawyer Cass Sunstein makes an interesting suggestion. It is that animals may already possess some of the rights which we associate with persons even though we do not tend to think of them as such.[50] Accordingly, the property status of animals is not absolute and certainly it does not, conceptually, have to be absolute. Sunstein therefore questions the accuracy of the stark dichotomy between human persons and animal property depicted by the animal advocates. These two founding legal concepts, persons and property, he suggests, do not operate in this rigid inflexible manner. The legal wall dividing humans from animals is therefore not as high and as thick as we might think.

Sunstein acknowledges the sustained cruelty administered to millions of animals on a daily basis in the United States. He says this is deeply unacceptable both to himself and to most Americans. It does not comport with the average American's attitude to animals which is typically characterised by compassion and, for very many, a direct and close relationship with a domestic animal. Sunstein further acknowledges that there are in place federal laws which regulate the treatment of animals not bred for food, laws which are ostensibly intended to secure animal welfare. The conspicuous problem is that they do not. Sunstein identifies 'a large gap between statutory text and real-world implementation'.[51] Animals are routinely unlawfully mistreated, the Federal Animal Welfare Act is routinely violated, and nothing happens to the offenders.

Animals welfare laws, per se, do not just treat animals as the means to human ends, as Wise and Francione suggest.[52] The problem with animal welfare laws lies in their enforcement not their letter, says Sunstein. In fact, the current laws dedicated to animal welfare already endow animals with some formal legal rights, on paper at least. They not only prohibit beatings but they also impose positive duties on people to care for animals. Thus, '[a]nyone who has impounded or confined an animal is obliged to provide good air, water, shelter and food'.[53] To Sunstein, this establishes an animal right.

Animals therefore have a mixed legal status. They are a heavily-protected form of property, endowed with some basic rights. Within their current status, they could therefore receive quite good protection, but the laws as

[50] Cass Sunstein, 'Standing for Animals (with Notes on Animal Rights)' (2000) 47 *UCLA Law Review* 1335.

[51] *Ibid* 1334.

[52] *Ibid* 1364.

[53] *Ibid* 1338.

they are currently administered, Sunstein believes, are largely ineffectual. It follows that mainly-property status is not, in itself, a bad thing for animals and it is not essential to think of animals as full persons to improve their lives significantly. Indeed, rights in themselves are not a guarantee of protection. In this analysis, animals are already modest rights holders who are receiving too little benefit from those rights. It is effective rights that animals need, without necessarily becoming full legal persons, conventionally understood.

Sunstein concedes that, at present, animals are primarily non-persons who therefore lack legal standing to bring an action on their own behalf, in their own name, and in their own interests. They depend utterly on an interested human with standing to proceed for them. When the human government official charged with the responsibility of enforcing animal welfare legislation does not perform their task responsibly, it is up to other interested humans with the relevant standing to step in. This may be difficult to achieve, especially (and perhaps paradoxically) if the sole motivation for the legal intervention is a moral objection to animal cruelty. (For someone to achieve standing in an animal rights case, they must establish that their human interests are directly affected.)

Rather than effect a dramatic shift in the status of animals, Sunstein recommends that private actions by interested humans be permitted to ensure that animal welfare laws are properly enforced. He further suggests that animals themselves be permitted such an action in order to protect their own interests. This sounds very much like a recommendation of personhood, although Sunstein seems not to think that he is going this far.[54]

Buttressing Humanity

This chapter has, in the main, displayed a sympathetic attitude towards the animal advocates and their endeavours to bring about some convergence of the legal characterisation of animals and humans. But the case would not be balanced if we were to neglect the significant philosophical and legal literature on the dangers of abandoning the species divide. The animal advocates have their strong detractors.

Philosopher Cora Diamond defends the exceptionality of humans and our continuing distinction from other animals on conceptual grounds. In a deep way, she believes, humans are defined as that which is not food and animals are defined as that which is food (she ignores cannibal practices).[55] For Diamond, the difference we assert between humans and animals is central to the very meaning of what it is to be human. We define the human

[54] *Ibid* 1367.

[55] Cora Diamond, 'Eating Meat and Eating People' in Cass Sunstein and Martha Nussbaum (eds), *Animal Rights: Current Debates and New Directions* (New York, Oxford University Press, 2004) 93.

negatively against the animal. Humans sit at the table and animals are on the table, and we learn this from a very young age. The privilege that we give to certain animals as pets does not alter this fundamental conceptual truth. Humans are not food (again ignoring cannabilism). Animals are (perhaps ignoring those cultures which do not regard animals in this way). Not being food (not being animal) is fundamental to the definition of the human being.

To Diamond, 'it is not respect for our interests which is involved in our not eating each other'.[56] Rather, this is something that goes 'to determine what sort of concept "human being" is'.[57] This is also true of our naming, not numbering human beings, and the fact that we accord special significance to human sexuality, birth and death. These practices are all part of the concept of the human:

> And so too . . . with the idea of the difference between human beings and animals. We learn what a human being is in—among other ways—sitting at a table where *we* eat *them*. We are around the table and they are on it . . . The difference is . . . a central concept for human life and is more an object of contemplation than observation.[58]

Diamond is also concerned that the treatment of humans as just another species of animal neglects that which is most important in humans; it erodes the very foundations of human value which are to do with human agency and responsibility: so there is a moral as well as conceptual point here. If we think of ourselves as just one more species of animal, 'there is no footing left from which to tell us what to do, because it is not members of one among species of animals that have moral obligations to anything'.[59] She clarifies: '[t]he moral expectations of other human beings demand something of me as other than an animal'.[60] It is not as an animal that an appeal is made to me to treat well those who can suffer (including animal beings). It is as a human being with moral agency. This, of course, is precisely the thinking of the legal Rationalists.

Mary Midgley is another philosopher who explains the exceptionality of human animals on conceptual grounds, but she is more critical of the work being done by the diminution of our animal status:

> [O]ur view of man . . . has been built up on a supposed contrast between man and animals which was formed by seeing animals not as they were, but as projections of our own fears and desires.[61]

[56] Cora Diamond, 'Eating Meat and Eating People' in Cass Sunstein and Martha Nussbaum (eds), *Animal Rights: Current Debates and New Directions* (New York, Oxford University Press, 2004) 98.

[57] *Ibid.*

[58] *Ibid.*

[59] *Ibid* 106.

[60] *Ibid.*

[61] Mary Midgley, *Beast and Man: the Roots of Human Nature* (Ithaca, Cornell University Press, 1978) 25.

Thus, the conceptual job being done by the human/animal divide is to assign to animals the human vices: they are disgusting; they are what we are not.

Martha Nussbaum has defended the distinction on moral and humanitarian grounds.[62] The line between animals and us entails a vital assertion that we cannot be treated like animals. Humanity alone is sufficient to secure non-animal treatment. We cannot be treated like or as brutes. Nussbaum maintains that human rights will be diluted and diminished if animals are extended the sort of legal consideration currently only extended to humans. A sustained commitment to the uniqueness of human life, she believes, is essential for our own human protection. We should not equate human and animal suffering 'lest we lose our moral footing utterly':[63]

> Throughout history it has seemed important in morals and politics to say that there is something special about the human species—its capacity for moral judgment, its possession of reason—that generates ethical, political and legal obligations unlike those generated by the mere presence of animal life.[64]

The moral and legal divide between humans and animals ensures that all humans, whatever their ability, are endowed with a special status. Gross physical or mental ability make no difference. We have value simply because we are human. Nussbaum, in effect, defines us negatively as not-animals. It is our distinction from animals, that which is not animal in us, which gives us value and ensures that there are minimally-decent ways we must all be treated. Our humanity, and not that which we share with animals, must be treasured and preserved. We dare not blur the divide between animals and us: for then we might license the treatment of humans as animals. Nussbaum asks:

> Would the recognition of greater commonality between ourselves and the animals have the consequence of improving morality or, instead, of removing its main prop?[65]

She reminds us that the Nazis lost sight of the distinction between animals and ourselves; that Hitler loved animals.

Those who would do away with the human/animal divide in law may therefore be missing something highly significant about its nature and meaning and implications. The moral and legal debasement of animals may

[62] But it must be added that she has since adjusted her thinking and now regards animals as agents capable of inclusion within a theory of justice. See 'Beyond "Compassion and Humanity": Justice for Nonhuman Animals' in Cass Sunstein and Martha Nussbaum (eds), *Animal Rights: Current Debates and New Directions* (New York, Oxford University Press, 2004) 299.

[63] Martha Nussbaum, 'Animal Rights: the Need for a Theoretical Basis' (2001) 114 *Harvard Law Review* 1506, 1511.

[64] *Ibid.*

[65] *Ibid* 1511.

be critical to the defence of 'human' dignity. If animals cease negatively to define us, then we are no different from the swine of the world, which we implicitly despise. As Mary Midgley reminds us, we use animals to absorb all our negative characterisations. If animals define the moral and legal limits of humanity, if it is unacceptable, morally and legally, to treat humans as animals, then perhaps we must retain this conviction. Otherwise we erode the very concept of the human. In short, for humans to be moral and legal persons we need animals to be property; then we know precisely what we are not. We are on sure moral and legal ground.[66]

[66] Midgley, above n 61, describes the rich symbolism of animals in our thinking about what we are and this is directly reflected in law: animals represent that which is debased, the vices, etc. The human by contrast has inherent dignity. Thus, we eat animals, we bury humans; we buy and own animals, we relate to humans as subjects. Everything that we do to animals is disallowed for ourselves. Feminists have suggested that women play an equivalent negative role in defining men.

9
Embodiment: Humans as Biological Beings

[A] human is a biological entity, like other animals.

Mary Warnock[1]

Traditional Western philosophical and religious traditions routinely assume the transcendence of the mind over the body. They assume that our inmost essence is mental and spiritual, which they regard as distinct from the bodily. To live in our culture is to unwittingly soak up the metaphysical mind/body dualism that pervades our commonsense views of cognition, knowledge, language and values.

Mark Johnson[2]

This chapter gathers together the implications of Rationalism, Religionism and Naturalism for our understanding of the embodied human being in law. It considers what view of the human being, as a natural corporeal animal being, as a body, is necessarily implied by these various interpretations of the person and their relative influence in law. Darwin pressed for an understanding of ourselves as 'created from animals', as part of the natural world and as one more kind of animal. But this is not a view of human beings which has been generally endorsed by law, as we saw in the last chapter. The more pervasive legal idea is that reason or spirit most defines us; much less so our animality or physicality. The idea is that we are intrinsically valuable and that this value somehow derives either from our present, past or future capacity for reason or from our enduring human spirit, not from our creature natures.

As the Catholic Compendium expresses it, man is a person, a 'someone', not just a 'something'.[3] In this view, the human person 'is superior to the material world'.[4] He is not just 'a speck of nature' for he possesses 'a spiritual and immortal soul'.[5] These are also the implications of the philosophical

[1] Mary Warnock, *Imagination and Time* (Oxford, Blackwell Publishing, 1994) 146.

[2] Mark Johnson, 'Mind Incarnate: from Dewey to Damasio' (2006) 135 *Daedalus* 46.

[3] Pontifical Council for Justice and Peace, *The Compendium of the Social Doctrine of the Church* (Strathfield NSW, St Paul's Publications, 2004) 56.

[4] *Ibid.*

[5] *Ibid* 64. Of course, this is a view of our natures which is hotly disputed by religious sceptics, such as Richard Dawkins. See *The God Delusion* (Boston, Houghton Mifflin, 2006) for an exposition of the view that the religious position is preposterous and flies in the face of science.

and religious traditions referred to by Johnson in the quote above: that for much of the time we can transcend the natural body and operate as minds or as souls.

But the human is embodied; we are animals in fact, not freely-floating minds or souls. So what does the law make of our corporeality in view of its general commitment to a higher view of us as abstract reasoners, or as sanctified and spiritual beings, but certainly not as animals, which remain consigned to the non-human legal category of property?

The legal understanding of the human body in law is far from straightforward. The influential ideas of the legal person as either mature reasoner or as spirit seem implicitly, though in rather different ways, to play down the person as a body. One might say that law does not generally provide a fleshed-out view of the person. And yet there are to be found in law certain interpretations of our physical natures.

The person imagined as a reasoner seems to be only incidentally, rather than essentially, embodied and certainly he is not defined by the body, for the legal focus is on the mind (as opposed to brain function). To the extent that the rational legal person is made flesh, he seems to be imagined with a rather well-controlled, able and healthy body, which does not pose a problem for the free and effective exercise of reason. It can be safely got out of the way. Several negative implications can be drawn about law's physical person. Implicitly, his reason is not clouded by sickness or pain; his mind is not impaired by mental illness or disability; he is not pregnant and he is certainly not in labour; he is not a baby or a child (for then he could not reason at a sufficiently sophisticated level); he is not even explicitly sexed.

This diminution of our embodied natures conforms well with philosophical Rationalism. Indeed, Kant insisted that we are the sort of beings who can and should contain and possess our physical selves and concentrate on higher matters of the mind. It follows that legal actors should relate in a seemly and contained manner and at a distance. They should be capable of governing and analysing their own thoughts, and reining in their emotions and their bodies. They should not be interfered with and they should not interfere with others. As we will see, Kant specifically called for a subduing of the human body in order to preserve the proper uses of the faculty of reason; the body was to be acknowledged but contained. It should not become unruly.

By contrast, the human being understood as spirit is often explicitly examined in law in a variety of dramatically-impaired physical forms, in which the mind is dull or inactive and the body is basically all that there is to the being in question, as with the dying or the comatose or the foetus. Legal cases about such abject or neophyte beings tend to represent the battleground of the hardline Religionists as they oppose abortion (regardless of the wishes of the woman) and withdrawal of medical treatment or euthanasia (regardless of the wishes of the patient and their suffering). They declare that all human life is sacred, whatever the condition of the body. But here there is hardly a naturalistic or scientific inquiry into the precise character of our physicality and the great physical variability which marks all of our lives and how these facts should bear on law. Instead, the soul and human sanctity are thought to provide the human constant (indeed, this is their specific function in human rights law) and the immense variety of physical conditions in which humans exist over the course of a human lifetime, and sometimes barely exist at all, is considered morally and legally irrelevant. It seems that the soul or sanctity iron out physical differences among human beings in the sense that we are all thought to be similarly and equally sacred as moral and legal persons, whether we are only a tiny cluster of cells (as with the embryo) or we are physically mature humans but in a comatose state.

It is the body implied by Rationalism which will form the chief focus of this chapter because it has exerted such a strong influence on legal thinking, though one not always made explicit. But I will also consider religious efforts to factor in the spirit and so produce an account of the physical human person which asserts his unwavering value (even in the absence of reason) and also ensures his dominion over the rest of the animal world. I will further examine the counter-arguments of those who say that humans in law should be treated as essentially natural creature beings, with creature needs and interests. To some of these Naturalists, we are getting above ourselves when we think that we are more than mere animals (recall that the animal rights lawyers tended to think this way about us). To others, we are highly complex mental *and* physical beings whose rich diversity of being is poorly and thinly represented by Rationalism. In this view, law should pay much greater attention to the great variety of human beings, as we are embodied; it should attend to our fluctuating and highly diverse physical natures.

Kant and the Body in Law

I begin this account of the body in law with Kant because he wrote eloquently, extensively and influentially about what we, as rational beings, should do about the fact that our rational minds are located in often quite troubling bodies. And, in essence, his strong message was that the body should be recognised but contained and subdued. It should not be permitted to interfere with the cool and moral exercise of reason. For Kant, the capacity for independent reason gave us our essential natures and our inherent dignity. 'Autonomy of the will', said Kant, 'is that property of it by which it is a law to itself independent of any property of the objects of its volition'.[6]

[6] Immanuel Kant, 'Foundations of the Metaphysics of Morals' in LW Beck (ed), *Kant Selections* (New York, Macmillan, 1988) 281.

All concepts of a moral nature had 'their seat and origin entirely a priori in reason'.[7] Kant contrasted the autonomous individual, whose actions are self-willed through the power of reason, with the less fortunate heteronomous being, whose will was subjected to that of another.[8] As Scruton puts it, such persons had retreated into slavery:

> having failed to achieve that autonomy which alone commands the respect of rational beings, he stands outside the moral order, unfree, subservient, diminished in his very personhood, and in his respect for himself.[9]

In *The Metaphysics of Morals*, Kant distinguished clearly between man 'as a *sensible being*, that is, as man (a member of one of the animal species), and . . . as an *intelligible being*'[10] and went on to deal at length with the nature and duties of man 'as an animal being'.[11] Sensible man's first duty to himself was self-preservation. His second duty was not to defile himself by lust. Kant was also concerned that man should show his respect for self and others by not reducing others to the objects of his animal pleasure. To Kant it was wrong for man to:

> make use of another person to get this [animal] pleasure apart from a special limitation by a contract establishing the right, by which two persons put each other under obligation.[12]

Here, he was referring to the marriage contract between a man and a woman which, in his view, had the legitimate sexual purpose of procreation. Kant spoke out against 'carnal lust':

> The vice engendered through it is called lewdness; the virtue with regard to this sensuous impulse is called chastity, which is to be represented here as a duty of man to himself.[13]

The only rightful 'bodily union' was, therefore, heterosexual and within the confines of marriage. Everything else represented:

> unnatural lust . . . [which] makes man not only an object of enjoyment but, still further, a thing that is contrary to nature, that is, a loathsome object, and so deprives him of all respect for himself.[14]

[7] Immanuel Kant, 'Foundations of the Metaphysics of Morals' in LW Beck (ed), *Kant Selections* (New York, Macmillan, 1988) 261.

[8] *Ibid* 282.

[9] RA Scruton, *A Short History of Modern Philosophy: from Descartes to Wittgenstein* (London, Routledge, 1989) 155.

[10] Immanuel Kant, *The Metaphysics of Morals* (Mary Gregor (tr), Cambridge, Cambridge University Press, 1991) 215.

[11] *Ibid* 218.

[12] *Ibid* 220.

[13] *Ibid* 220.

[14] *Ibid* 221.

In other words, Kant conceived of embodied or sensible man as a bounded, separate and distinct subject who bore a duty to respect the physical space between himself and other bounded physical beings. The vital respect that Kant required man to show man demanded that men 'keep themselves at a distance from one another'.[15] Respect for bodily self and bodily other also meant 'taking care of one's body, but not to the point of effeminacy'.[16]

As one commentator summarises this Kantian view of the rational autonomous person: '[He] is a distinct, individual entity who enters into a compact with other individuals for benefits he expects to gain thereby'.[17] For this 'complete and autonomous individual', his 'relations are conceived . . . to be merely external links';[18] or as Kant himself explained the need for individuation and physical separation from one's fellow man:

> The principle of mutual love admonishes men constantly to come closer to one another; that of the respect they owe one another, to keep themselves at a distance from one another; and should one of these great moral forces fail, 'then nothingness (immorality), with gaping throat, would drink up the whole kingdom of (moral) beings like a drop of water'.[19]

Kant emphasised the need to contain the body for the benefit of reason. We should be masters of our bodies and others should not subordinate us to their physical desires. He recognised the threat that the unconstrained body could pose to reason and the moral will and so he instructed us to keep ourselves apart physically and to ensure that we are not brought down by the demands of our bodies. And this idea of a potentially disruptive body, which must be contained and managed so as not to interfere with the exercise of reason, is implicit in much of our law. Also present within this legal understanding of the body is an element of disgust with many bodily functions: they are associated with the baser dimensions of being human; they are the functions which bring us closer to animals and so must be carefully directed and controlled.

Principle of Bodily Integrity

The term 'bodily integrity', often invoked in legal judgments which touch on our physical natures, contains this Kantian idea of a managed, distinct, intact body which is not debasing us and is not getting in the way of the proper dispassionate exercise of reason and which is sufficiently wholesome

[15] *Ibid* 244.

[16] *Ibid* 246.

[17] WT Jones, *Kant and the Nineteenth Century* (New York, Harcourt Brace Jovanovich, 1952) 137.

[18] *Ibid.*

[19] Kant, above n 10, at 244, quoting Haller.

to permit us to relate to others at a distance.[20] But there is also a religious idea of the body running through law. It is thought by some that the body as the housing for the soul (though Finnis called it the very form of the soul) is also somehow sacred and the term used by some jurists to invoke this characteristic is 'inviolate' or 'inviolable'.[21] Here, there is connoted a more respectful approach to the body because it is that which is melded with or houses the soul. And after all, in the religious view of us, we are made in the image of God. It is therefore important to respect and not to debase the body. Also implicit in the religious view is that the body carries the strong potential to debase us if used in the wrong ways. (By strong religious tradition, sexual relations outside of marriage and also between the same sex have been regarded as improper and debasing uses of the body. Finnis makes this quite clear and (unfortunately) endorses it.)

These Rationalist and Religionist ideas of our physical persons are both evident in criminal law and also tort law for which the starting assumption is that it is unlawful for one person intentionally to touch another without their consent; this is, in essence, the basic crime of assault and the tort of battery. Physical distance and separation, bodily integrity, is our basic right (implicitly a Kantian requirement) and it is said to be our right because our bodies are 'inviolate' (a religious idea). The initial point of such law is a liberal one of assumed bodily autonomy. Human separation, human distinctness, is what law must protect and preserve. As Lord Justice Goff explained in *Collins v Wilcock*:

> The fundamental principle, plain and incontestable, is that every person's body is inviolate. It has long been established that any touching of another person, however slight, may amount to a battery.[22]

In the same judgment, William Blackstone is cited as the basis of the rule. To Blackstone:

> the law cannot draw the line between different degrees of violence, and therefore totally prohibits the first and lowest stage of it; every man's person being sacred and no other having a right to meddle with it, in any the slightest manner.[23]

The inviolacy of the body is clearly asserted here as a well-established common law principle of general application.

[20] Eg the idea of 'bodily integrity' is repeatedly invoked by the English Court of Appeal in *In Re A (Children) (Conjoined Twins: Surgical Separation)* [2001] Fam 147.

[21] See, eg *Re F (Mental Patient: Sterilisation)* [1990] 2 AC 1: 'I start with the fundamental principle, now long established, that every person's body is inviolate' (Lord Goff). This principle was strongly reaffirmed by the English Court of Appeal in *In Re A (Children) (Conjoined Twins: Surgical Separation)* [2001] Fam 147.

[22] [1984] 3 All ER 374, 378.

[23] William Blackstone, *Commentaries on the Laws of England* (17th edn, London, Sweet and Maxwell, 1830) vol 3, 120.

A person's integrity therefore depends on a legally enforceable right to police the boundaries of their body. Full legal personhood is equated with full and effective control of one's own body and an unqualified right to exclude others from it, unless of course one is a married woman, in which case the husband is to be permitted sexual access. As Sir Matthew Hale explained, a:

> husband cannot be guilty of a rape committed by himself upon his lawful wife, for by their mutual matrimonial consent and contract the wife has given up herself in this kind unto her husband, which she cannot retract.[24]

This rule held firm until the 1990s.

In an effort to ensure that the body is used in a seemly and acceptable manner, marital and homosexual relations have been and remain carefully regulated by family and criminal law. There has been strong, sustained and successful legal resistance to the idea that there can be lawful marriage between a man and a man or a woman and a woman.[25] And it is only very recently that homosexual relations have ceased to be criminal. For both the Rationalists and the Religionists, there are proper and improper uses of the body and these views of our corporeality and how we should relate to one another as physical beings have found clear expression in law. It was not long ago that homosexual acts between men were described as 'abominable'.[26] Now it seems they are grudgingly tolerated.

In the jurisprudence arising from legal relations between doctors and patients, we also find repeated statements about the legal significance of the body. In particular, we find consistent affirmations of the Kantian right to keep others away from us, and to keep our bodies intact. The classic statement of this right is to be found in *Schloendorff v Society of New York Hospital* where Justice Cardozo declared that:

> Every human being of adult years and sound mind has a right to determine what shall be done with his body; and a surgeon who performs an operation without his patient's consent commits an assault.[27]

Consent is therefore needed before there is any physical touching and without that consent there is both a tort and a crime. It is thought that we have a fundamental right to bodily separation from others and that without it we cannot exercise our most basic legal right to autonomy. We saw this right

[24] Matthew Hale, *History of the Pleas of the Crown* (Sollom Emlyn (ed), London, E and R Nutt and R Gosling, 1736) 629.

[25] For a recent collection of essays on the denial of the legal right of gay people to marry, see (2006) 37 *Victoria University of Wellington Law Review*.

[26] See Richard Davenport Hines, *Death and Punishment: Attitudes to Sex and Sexuality in Britain Since the Renaissance* (Glasgow, Fontana Press, 1991).

[27] *Schloendorff v Society of New York Hospital*, 211 NY 125 (1914). In *Malette v Shulman* (1990) 67 DLR (4th) 321, Robins JA affirmed that '[t]he right of a person to control his or her own body is a concept that has long been recognised at common law'.

to bodily autonomy asserted, for example, in the cases concerning the right of pregnant women to refuse medical treatment. This right of the pregnant woman to stop others touching her was said to be more fundamental, more important, than the interests of the foetus.

So entrenched is the legal idea of 'bodily integrity' that it is regarded as beneficial, even if the achievement of that integrity is at the cost of the life of the person involved. In the case of *In Re A (Children)* (discussed in Chapter 6), the English Court of Appeal was asked to consider the legality of the surgical separation of conjoined twins, an operation which would definitely kill the weaker twin, Mary. Although there was a number of legal bases for the court's decision that the surgery would be lawful, the judges consistently affirmed the right of Mary to her 'bodily integrity' and the 'human dignity' which was thought to come with it.[28] Clearly, the court was influenced in its decision by the sad fact that Mary had only a 'primitive brain' and multiple physical afflictions and that she depended for her life on her attachment to Jody who was thought to have a normal brain and the prospect of a relatively normal life if detached from her twin. Nevertheless, it was affirmed by Lord Justice Ward that, if successful, the operation would 'give Mary the bodily integrity and dignity which is the natural order for all of us';[29] or as Lord Justice Walker concluded:

> Every human being's right to life carries with, as an intrinsic part of it, rights of bodily integrity and autonomy—the right to have one's own body whole and intact and (on reaching an age of understanding) to take decisions about one's own body.[30]

Making Sense of the Legal Body: The Compromised Naturalism of Ronald Dworkin

I now turn to consider what prominent legal and moral thinkers have made of the body in law and the broader culture. I start with Ronald Dworkin who makes a concerted effort to come to terms with our physical natures and to accept the lessons of evolutionary biology—to naturalise the human being. However, as a committed Rationalist, Dworkin refuses to abandon the Kantian idea that it is our capacity for reason which most defines us and endows us with dignity. Recall that Dworkin believes that when the individual loses all capacity for reason, then effective personhood is lost. All that is left is a creature of need with no coherent view of its own life. Dworkin is also reluctant to abandon religion as another legitimate source of human value, with its idea that it is the immaterial soul which can make us innately

[28] *In Re A (Children)* [2000] 4 All ER 148.
[29] *Ibid* 182 (Ward LJ).
[30] *Ibid* 258 (Walker LJ).

valuable, not our embodied human natures. Hence, we do not cease to be protected legal persons when our reason is lost.

To Dworkin, we are animals but of a very special sort. We have been brought to such a point of excellence by evolutionary processes that we have become intrinsically valuable rational moral individuals; in short, we may still be animals but we have become exceptional. We are the high point of evolution. The discoveries of Darwin do not dislodge us from our elevated moral and legal position. Non-human animals remain lesser creatures and are only valuable as a species, not as individuals, as we are. We may be rational animals, as Kant put it, but we are still extraordinary. It is only when we are reduced to unthinking creatures, say by dementia, that our personhood, according to Dworkin, is in doubt. But our human value never completely disappears; our human sanctity is somehow retained.

For Dworkin, evolution therefore points to our natural dominion over the rest of the natural world: we are the wonderful culmination of evolutionary processes and hence intrinsically worthwhile. Our evolved nature does not put us at one with other animals (as Wise and Francione contend). Rather, we have evolved well beyond other creatures. We have made it. We are utterly exceptional natural beings. We are 'a triumph of . . . evolutionary creation'.[31] We are 'the highest product of natural creation'.[32] We are 'special among natural creations'.[33] The problem is that Darwin did not say this. He wrote instead about the impersonal forces of evolution and maintained that evolutionary success simply meant successful adaptation to prevailing circumstances, whatever they might be. We could say that cockroaches have excelled in this Darwinian adaptation, and yet we hardly revere the cockroach for its evolutionary prowess.

There is a secure line in Dworkin's thinking to the Rationalism of Kant who said that we are animals but that to achieve our true humanity—that which we really are—we must rise above our base animal natures and ascend to the plane of reason. We must define ourselves against our animal natures, conceding them, but then containing them and moving on. As Kant remarked, 'man's insignificance as a human animal may not infringe upon his consciousness of his dignity as a rational man'.[34]

Dawkins v Dworkin

Dworkin's interpretation of Darwin is therefore highly problematic. Dworkin may seem to embrace evolutionary biology and to accept our animal status but he does not abandon the idea of human exceptionality.

[31] Ronald Dworkin, *Life's Dominion: an Argument about Abortion and Euthanasia* (London, Harper Collins, 1993) 83–4.

[32] *Ibid* 82.

[33] *Ibid.*

[34] Kant, above n 10, at 230.

Indeed, he insists that as natural beings we are 'nature's masterpiece'.[35] This is hardly a coming to terms with our creature natures. Rather, Dworkin holds on to what Richard Dawkins has called:

> the vanity of the present: of seeing the past as aimed at our time, as though the characters in history's play had nothing better to do with their lives than foreshadow us.[36]

Dworkin retains what Dawkins has called 'the conceit of hindsight, the idea that the past works to deliver our present'.[37]

This leads to what is arguably an overblown view of our natures and certainly it badly distorts the work of Darwin. It tells a false evolutionary tale, one which conjures up:

> a shambling file of simian ancestors, rising progressively in the wake of the erect, striding majestic figure of Homo sapiens: man as evolution's last word (and in this context it always is man rather than woman); man as what the whole enterprise is pointing toward.[38]

But to Dawkins this is a hubristic and human-centred account of evolution, which dishonours Darwin:

> It makes no sense (and no less) to aim our historical narrative towards Homo sapiens than towards any other modern species—Octopus vulgaris, say, or Panntera leo or Sequoia sempervirens. A historically minded swift, understandably proud of flight as self-evidently the premier accomplishment of life, will regard swiftkind—those spectacular flying machines with their swept-back wings . . . as the acme of evolutionary progress.[39]

If we are intellectually honest, as Dawkins demands of us, we should appreciate that it is an act of faith, a human preference, to regard ourselves as naturally superior and when we seek scientific support for this view of ourselves as the natural culmination of evolutionary progress—as rational man, master of his fate, the person—it entails a particular skewing of the scientific evidence and a particular reading of history which logically ends with us and favours us: the supposed evolutionary high point.

Dawkins asks us to consider the swift's view of history. If we valued flight, then humans would fare badly. Our emphasis on reason, or rather what we think is our capacity for reason as that which makes a person and demands respect, is itself a preference. So too is our emphasis on the human spirit as humanity defining. It is not innately or objectively true or valuable; it is a cultural choice.

[35] Dworkin, above n 31.

[36] Richard Dawkins, *The Ancestor's Tale: a Pilgrimage to the Dawn of Evolution* (Boston, Houghton Mifflin, 2004) 1.

[37] *Ibid.*

[38] *Ibid* 2.

[39] *Ibid* 6.

Humbling Naturalism of Gray and Fernandez-Armesto

As Dawkins makes clear, we humans represent the end point of only one of many evolutionary lines. We endow human characteristics with particular value because this exalts us as a species. Were we to value other characteristics, as we could, we humans would fare less well. We would not be the special ones among nature's evolved creatures. It follows that the Rationalist preference for human reason is simply that: a preference, not a deep, enduring, cosmic truth. Others have gone further and positively put the case against human beings as a special case: as the logical and necessary centre of law and culture. Accepting that we are animals, these thinkers have suggested that we have no good reason to think well of ourselves, especially on Rationalist or religious grounds.

In *Straw Dogs*,[40] Gray offers a sustained reply to what he decries as the vestige of Christianity still implicit in Enlightenment humanism. This is our unfounded belief that we are intrinsically important and that we have special powers of reason which place us above the rest of the natural world. Implicitly, Gray takes issue with Dworkin's account of human nature:

> In Kant's time the creed of conventional people was Christian, now it is humanist. Nor are these two faiths so different from one another. Over the past two hundred years, philosophy has shaken off Christian faith. It has not given up on Christianity's cardinal error—the belief that humans are radically different from other animals . . . Philosophy has been a masked ball in which a religious image of mankind is renewed in the guise of humanist ideas of progress and enlightenment.[41]

Gray insists on our ordinary animal status and our error in thinking that we are other than this. We may have surrendered 'an irrational belief in God' but we have retained a false creed: 'an irrational faith in mankind':[42]

> Other animals are born, seek mates, forage for food, and die. That is all. But we humans—we think—are different. We are *persons*, whose actions are the results of their *choices*. Other animals pass their lives unawares, but we are conscious. Our image of ourselves is formed from an engrained belief that *consciousness*, *selfhood* and *free will* are what define us as human beings, and raise us above all other creatures.[43]

All of this is human invention, says Gray, which is self-advancing and self-inflating. We place ourselves at the centre of everything: the world is for us because only we are truly worthwhile:

> If humans are to be believed, the Earth . . . had no value until humans came onto the scene. Value is only a shadow cast by humans desiring or choosing. Only

[40] John Gray, *Straw Dogs: Thoughts on Humans and Other Animals* (London, Granta Books, 2002).

[41] *Ibid* 37.

[42] *Ibid* 38.

[43] *Ibid.*

> *persons* have any kind of intrinsic worth. Among Christians the cult of personhood may be forgiven. For them, everything of value in the world emanates from a divine person, in whose image humans are made. But once we have relinquished Christianity the very idea of the person becomes suspect.[44]

Felipe Fernandez-Armesto is similarly sceptical about our special place in the natural world and the distinctiveness and superiority of our human attributes. He describes 'our obsessive urge to classify ourselves apart from the rest of creation'.[45] To Fernandez-Armesto, '[w]e have, it seems, never ceased to be apes; yet we aspire to be angels'.[46] Implicitly, Gray and Fernandez-Armesto both strike at the very foundations of the argument of Dworkin for human exceptionality.

To Dworkin, we are either God's children or evolution's 'masterpiece', a fact which law quite rightly recognises with its principle of human sanctity. But to Fernandez-Armesto:

> [m]ost of the attributes on which we humans congratulate ourselves seem, in short, to be evolutionary compensations for physical feebleness. Well-developed brainpower is a competitive advantage in a struggle for survival with more powerful rival predators. Tool-making suits species under-equipped in tooth and claw. Language is useful for creatures compelled to huddle in large groups for security and for hairless apes who need a substitute for grooming.[47]

A problem with the thinking of Gray and Fernandez-Armesto is that it implicitly shares the Rationalists' and even the Religionists' disgust with our animality, even though they are set on disputing both philosophies of life. Both thinkers argue that we are only animals, believing this to be a sorry reality, especially as we do not even seem to be very impressive animals. Here we are, huddling together as pathetic hairless apes. However, there is little endeavour here to attend positively and in detail and without the moralistic overtones to our creature natures. Implicitly the message is that animals are disgusting and so are we.

Embracing our Creature Status: Moral Philosophers and Legal Feminists

Gray and Fernandez-Armesto believe that we are animals who do not want to see ourselves as brutes but as something far more exalted. Both believe that our creature status is and should be humbling. We are *only* animals. Let's not inflate ourselves.

[44] John Gray, *Straw Dogs: Thoughts on Humans and Other Animals* (London, Granta Books, 2002) 58.

[45] Felipe Fernandez-Armesto, *So You Think You're Human?: a Brief History of Humankind* (Oxford, Oxford University Press, 2004) 11.

[46] *Ibid* 8.

[47] *Ibid* 54.

Other moral and legal thinkers have also embraced our creature status but have sought to find a more constructive realism within it. They call for greater philosophical and legal honesty about the limits of our creature being; but they also believe that such realism can itself prove therapeutic, for it will enable us to come to grips with what we really are. Agency, dignity and animality, some say, are not necessarily antithetical. In fact, an acceptance of our species nature can lead to greater self-knowledge and self-direction. We should not despise ourselves as animals; instead we should know ourselves as creatures; we should know our human powers and our human limits. And we should abandon the false idea that abstract rationality most defines and dignifies us. We should reject the idea that we are most ourselves when we are high-level reasoners and least like animals. In law, this argument has been most fully developed by legal feminists.[48]

A persistent concern of feminist legal writers has been the strong legal Rationalist tendency to normalise a being defined by mental and often physical ability and by rights-bearing, by thc personal ability to define and defend their own interests, rather than by needs and interests and duties owed by others and enforced by others.[49] The social contract creation story has this autonomous being as its central character: the person who is already an independent rational agent at the moment of deciding to enter civil society. A number of feminists has decried this legal preoccupation with the adult, rational, self-governing, rights-enforcing individual, which has rendered exceptional and odd those who are weak and vulnerable: those who cannot achieve this rugged degree of physical self-sufficiency.[50] In an influential series of articles, Jennifer Nedelsky in particular has described what she sees as the 'pathological conception of autonomy' to be found in our Rationalist liberal law which entails 'boundaries against others'.[51]

[48] See, eg Nicola Lacey, *Unspeakable Subjects: Feminist Essays in Legal and Social Theory* (Oxford, Hart Publishing, 1998) esp ch 4; Kristen Savell, 'The Mother of the Legal Person' in Susan James and Stephanie Palmer (eds), *Visible Women: Essays on Feminist Legal Theory and Political Philosophy* (Oxford and Portland, Hart Publishing, 2002) 29; Ngaire Naffine and Rosemary J Owens (eds), *Sexing the Subject of Law* (North Ryde, LBC Information Services and Sweet and Maxwell, 1997) esp Ngaire Naffine, 'The Body Bag' (at 79).

[49] See, eg Ngaire Naffine, *Law and the Sexes: Explorations in Feminist Jurisprudence* (North Sydney, Allen and Unwin, 1990).

[50] A similar charge has been levelled at philosophy by Alisdaire MacIntyre who argues that '[t]here are only passing references to human vulnerability and affliction and to the connections between them and our dependence on others . . . And when the ill, the injured and the otherwise disabled are presented in the pages of moral philosophy books, it is almost always exclusively as possible subjects of benevolence by moral agents who are themselves presented as though they were continuously rational, healthy and untroubled'. *Dependent Rational Animals: Why Human Beings Need the Virtues* (Chicago, Open Court Publishing, 1999) 2.

[51] Jennifer Nedelsky, 'Reconceiving Autonomy' (1989) 1(1) *Yale Journal of Law and Feminism* 7, 13. See also 'Law, Boundaries and the Bounded Self' (1990) 30(1) *Representations* 162 and 'Reconceiving Rights as Relationships' (1993) 1(1) *Review of Constitutional Studies* 1. See also Ngaire Naffine, 'The Body Bag' in Naffine and Owens, above n 48.

Jennifer Nedelsky and the Bounded Self

Over a number of years, Nedelsky has developed her argument that law's implicitly bounded conception of the body is misguided and also biased towards men against women. To Nedelsky, '[t]he image of humans as self-determining creatures . . . remains one of the most powerful dimensions of liberal thought'.[52] Our liberal law, she says, tends to treat each of us as distinct and separate and autonomous and 'the central symbol for this vision of autonomy', she suggests, is property and the related legal idea of privacy.[53] Property permits us to secure distance from others, to build walls around ourselves, both literally and metaphorically and so secure our perfect privacy. In this legal property-driven vision of the human being, '[t]he most perfectly autonomous man is thus the most perfectly isolated'.[54] He is one who has fully secured 'an inviolable sphere' of perfect seclusion.[55]

Nedelsky believes that the idea of the boundary has become 'a central metaphor in the legal rhetoric of freedom'.[56] Within Anglo-American legal theory, she suggests, boundary images proliferate.[57] Strong boundaries are seen as 'essential to the integrity and autonomy of the self'.[58] And it is this bounded model of human autonomy which she denounces as 'pathological', with its emphasis on the importance of 'boundaries against others', rather than enabling, caring and connecting human relations.[59]

The idea of the bounded self is particularly unfortunate for women, suggests Nedelsky, because it carries with it the implication that normal heterosexual intercourse is a form of violation: sex appears to be a breaching of the woman's boundary walls and a consequent breaching of her very self.[60] If our human dignity in law is thought to depend on retention of human wholeness and human separation, as Kant insisted (and the court in *Re A (Children)* affirmed), then the sexually-penetrated woman is a reduced person. She is not the sort of being who can contain and defend her creature nature; she cannot keep it intact. Nedelsky makes plain that her:

> point is not that the boundary metaphor is apt for men but destructive for women. Rather it is misleading about the nature of human selfhood and thus about the institutions and concepts that will foster the flourishing of that selfhood.[61]

[52] Nedelsky, 'Reconceiving Autonomy', above n 51 at 8.
[53] *Ibid* 12.
[54] *Ibid.*
[55] *Ibid* 20.
[56] Nedelsky, 'Law, Boundaries and the Bounded Self', above n 51..
[57] *Ibid* 167.
[58] *Ibid* 168.
[59] Nedelsky, 'Reconceiving Autonomy', above n 51, at 12.
[60] This is an idea I have explored in 'Possession: Erotic Love in the Law of Rape' (1994) 57 *Modern Law Review* 10.
[61] Nedelsky, above n 51, at 171.

This bounded view of our bodies necessarily creates an existential problem for all of us at some point in our lives, for we all go through stages in which we are utterly dependent creatures. And, as we saw in Chapter 5, it creates an existential problem for *all* pregnant women because they so poorly conform to the bounded, individualistic model of being. The evidence that law finds pregnant women distinctly odd is clear and strong. The medical jurisprudence, in particular, typically talks about the 'special' nature of pregnancy and of the difficulties of making just and satisfying decisions about the legal treatment of pregnant women and their foetuses, as if human beings came into existence, more typically, in some other manner. Not far behind this legal thinking lies the story of contract, where relations are achieved through explicit agreement, and at a distance, not through physical intimacy and where human beings are reproduced, who knows how.[62]

To legal feminists there is something seriously wrong with a law and legal theory which treats pregnancy as an unusual and awkward condition; when the pregnant cannot conform to the prevailing legal model of the separate, distinctive, intact autonomous agent. To state the obvious, every human life begins with a pregnancy. When one ponders the matter, it is surely far odder to think of life beginning with a manly handshake with strangers in the public sphere, as we each agree to cede power to the state and to live together in civil society, than life beginning in the womb and then the crib.

There is now a substantial corpus of feminist writing committed to exposing the failures of law to make sense of pregnancy which is, to repeat, utterly unexceptional.[63] To this end, feminists have applied an especially critical eye to a line of cases on the right of pregnant women to refuse medical treatment, especially Caesarian sections. What is plain is that the courts are struggling to make sense of a pregnant, rational, legal actor because rational legal actors are not supposed to be pregnant. Indeed, the embodied condition of all of us is meant to assume but a minor role in our legal relations. We are supposed to be able to operate at arm's length, even from our doctors, when we want to: to operate as minds (as decision-makers) rather than as bodies. The result is some awkward legal reasoning when it comes to affording to the pregnant person the rights of the non-pregnant.

On the one hand, the courts in cases involving pregnant women who refuse medical intervention have repeatedly affirmed the Rationalist emphasis of our law, the priority it accords to individual reason and to individual choice and the right to conduct relations at arm's length. With reasonable

[62] For a recent discussion of Nedelsky and the bounded self, see Margaret Davies, *Property: Meanings, Histories, Theories* (Abingdon, Routledge, 2008) 45–6.

[63] See especially Mary Ford, '*Evans v United Kingdom*: What Implications for the Jurisprudence of Pregnancy' (2008) 8(1) *Human Rights Law Review* 171; Mary Ford, 'A Property Model of Pregnancy' (2005) 1 *International Journal of Law in Context* 261; and Emily Jackson, *Regulating Reproduction: Law, Technology and Autonomy* (Oxford, Hart Publishing, 2001).

consistency, women have been treated as contractual individuals with an absolute right to keep their doctors at a distance, even when the life of their foetus is at risk.[64] On the other hand, there have been persistent endeavours to undermine the perceived capacity for reason of women who would endanger a foetus (who is not at a distance), to question her competence.[65] And a religious principle of foetal sanctity, quite antithetical to the autonomy of women, has also been invoked, further queering the pitch.[66]

The continuing bind, according to legal feminists, is that the prevailing theory of the rational legal actor tends to be highly abstracted and to accommodate poorly our embodied humanity; and it is especially poor at dealing with pregnant humanity. Indeed, in much conventional medical jurisprudence, pregnant women emerge as 'special' cases and as human oddities. As Mary Ford has observed:

> [m]odels which emphasise the 'uniqueness' of pregnancy threaten to 'strand' pregnant women out of reach of the protection of law by depriving them and their advocates of analogies.[67]

The thing is that pregnant women are conspicuously embodied and, when in labour, they are highly vulnerable beings. But this is not special; all of us are embodied and, for some of our lives, we are all vulnerable, dependent human creatures.

A further point made by some legal feminists is that women are still being consigned to the creature dimensions of life so that men can relate to each other at a dignified distance, as rational agents.[68] Women, who are thought to be naturally closer to nature, are the ones to give birth, to care for the young and the old. True legal actors are not like this: they are healthy, self-sufficient, rational, adult men who are relating to one another at arm's length, not changing nappies or cuddling a child. The legal actor, they say, is rarely thought of as a suckling baby or a woman giving suck; he is not the frail aged, the heavily dependent on the good offices of others. The emphasis is on reason and contract, on autonomous beings operating at a distance.

[64] Eg Butler-Sloss LJ in R*e MB (Medical Treatment)* [1997] 2 FLR 426 clearly confirmed the right of pregnant patients to refuse treatment. See also Rebecca Bailey-Harris, 'Pregnancy, Autonomy and Refusal of Medical Treatment' (1998) 114 *Law Quarterly Review* 550 on the confirmation of pregnant patient autonomy in *St George's NHS Trust v S* [1997] 2 FLR 426.

[65] See Jane Weaver, 'Court-ordered Caesarean Sections' in Andrew Bainham, Shelley Day Sclater and Martin Richards (eds), *Body Law and Laws* (Oxford and Oregon, Hart Publishing, 2002) 229.

[66] These cases are discussed in Emily Jackson, *Regulating Reproduction* (Oxford, Hart Publishing, 2001) and also in John Seymour, *Childbirth and the Law* (Oxford, Oxford University Press, 2000).

[67] Mary Ford, 'A Property Model of Pregnancy' (2005) 1 *International Journal of Law in Context* 261, 285.

[68] See especially Katherine O'Donovan, *Sexual Divisions in Law* (London, Weidenfeld and Nicolson, 1985).

This is not to say that the dependent young and old do not find their way into law and receive law's protection. But they tend to be treated as abnormal, not as typical. They are special or diminished cases of legal persons (as we saw in Chapter 6).

It follows also that the physically disabled are tacitly regarded as defective legal persons. They demonstrate a palpable failure to keep their bodies intact, to demonstrate bodily integrity with its associated dignity. (Recall that integrity and dignity were explicitly linked in *In Re A (Children)*.) Law, with the broader culture, therefore participates in a subtle degradation of the individual who cannot control her limbs or is even missing a limb; who is wheelchair- or bed-bound.[69] Law's concentration on the whole and the self-sufficient can be fruitfully contrasted with an alternative thesis of human being that has 'man' as 'a creature of need and not of plenitude, of lack rather than fullness'.[70] In this antithetical view of human beings, offered by Michael Ignatieff, we are 'naturally insufficient, incomplete, at the mercy of nature and of each other'.[71]

To Mary Midgley, the antidote to the prevailing way of thinking about our creature natures is to admit that:

> [w]e are not just rather like animals; *we are animals*. Our difference from other species may be striking, but comparisons with them have always been, and must be, crucial to our view of ourselves.[72]

Or as Alisdaire MacIntyre expresses it, we are not 'exempt from the hazardous condition of "mere" animality'.[73] To understand our human nature, we must therefore understand our species nature. And this is where human freedom realistically must reside, not in transcending our creature nature but in understanding it and developing it.

Midgley maintains that we are started with nature and finished in culture but remain natural and remain agents. Her point is that an agent should be possessed of a nature and instincts and it is from these natural dispositions that we develop choice. But choice is not effaced by nature; rather it provides the basic dispositions which provide a reason for choosing one way of life over another.

If law were to take seriously our human embodiment, if it were to attend to the specific needs and interests that arise because of it, it would be more

[69] For an eye-opening collection of essays on the treatment of the disabled around the world, see Benedicte Ingstad and Susan Reynolds Whyte (eds), *Disability and Culture* (Berkley, University of California Press, 1995). In this collection, see especially the essay by Robert Murphy on the American treatment of the disabled: 'Encounter: the Body Silent in America'.

[70] Michael Ignatieff, *The Needs of Stangers* (New York, Viking, 1984) 57.

[71] *Ibid.*

[72] Mary Midgley, *Beast and Man: the Roots of Human Nature* (Cornell University Press, Ithaca, 1978) xiii.

[73] MacIntyre, above n 50, at 4.

responsive to the rich variety of embodied humanity and it would therefore be more representative. It would track our lives in a more fitting manner and accept the great multiplicity of human beings. And it would find women to be just as fitting as legal subjects as men. As Jennifer Nedelsky has observed:

> The justification for leaving the body aside was to find some core commonality that was truly universal, unvaried and free of contingency.[74]

But we are contingent creatures and we have ages and sexes and various degrees of mental and physical ability and disability. We need to know what sort of creatures we are, how we differ from one another and how we change over the course of a lifetime, in order to build suitable legal institutions for ourselves. As Nedelsky explains, 'once we bring in the body, we must confront difference'.[75] And further:

> if we fully incorporate a sense of ourselves as embodied in the picture of human beings we theorize about and design institutions for, it will be much harder to ignore bodily differences.[76]

Reconciling Agency and Animality

If Midgley and Nedelsky are right, our physical dependence and our animality are not necessarily at odds with our agency and our dignity, though this was the view of Kant. As Owen Flanagan similarly reflects:

> [o]nce the story is in place that says we sit above animals but below angels and God, the alternate story that says we are animals seems (and is) unflattering. But it is unflattering only in contrast to the story that says we humans are not animals, and that it is unflattering to be compared with animals, let alone to be one.[77]

What would be the implications of treating ourselves in a manner which is genuinely consistent with evolutionary biology (that is, on a continuum with the rest of nature, not something of a fundamentally different order) but which is neither romanticised (as with Dworkin) or coloured by feelings of disgust (as with Gray)? As Flanagan observes, we are so unaccustomed to viewing ourselves in this manner that we are yet to have a coherent account of ourselves as moral and free animals. To be animal is almost by definition not to be moral and not to be free. As Kant said, we must rise above our animal natures. The fear engendered by seeing ourselves as natural beings is that somehow we will lose both our agency and our spiritual value. If we

[74] Jennifer Nedelsky, 'Embodied Diversity and the Challenges of Law' (1996–1997) 42 *McGill Law Journal* 91, 103.

[75] *Ibid.*

[76] *Ibid.*

[77] Owen Flanagan, *The Problem of the Soul: Two Visions of Mind and How to Reconcile Them* (New York, Basic Books, 2002) 10.

are animals, admittedly highly intelligent animals, how can we be moral agents?

Flanagan, in cautiously optimistic spirit, reflects on this problem that we face:

> We could, I claim, get used to thinking of ourselves as animals, as fully embodied, and thus as soulless and without prospects for an afterlife in the company of spirits, without experiencing discomfort or fear at the very idea. But it will not be easy. A full century after Darwin, most people, including most intellectuals who pay homage to the idea that we are animals, don't really accept that we are animals.[78]

And, as we have seen, nor does our law. As Flanagan continues, in a manner that also well describes law's complex attitude to our physical natures:

> The problem is that we have not yet found a way to tell a story about what it means to be a human animal that isn't in some way disquieting. This has as much to do with negative views about what it means to be an animal as with what it means to be a person. It certainly is not based on any objective fact that being an animal is inherently unseemly. If we were to pay more than lip service to the idea that we are animals by devoting careful and sustained attention to the kind of animal we are, I believe we could get used to the idea and embrace it. This shift will require adjustments, including disposing of various myths, illusions, and delusions about our natures, but a frank and honest understanding of ourselves as animals needn't produce existential horror or unremitting nausea.[79]

[78] *Ibid.*
[79] *Ibid.*

10
The Myths We Live By

> [T]he climate of a society's legal system is ultimately determined by the kind of people by whom it is dominated . . . It makes a difference whether a legal system is dominated, as that of classical Rome, by gentlemen of leisure and high-ranking administrators, or, as the Islamic, by theologians, or, as the classical Chinese, by philosopher-bureaucrats.
>
> Rheinstein[1]

> It is simply that the generative ideas of the seventeenth century . . . have served their term. The difficulties inherent in their constitutive concepts balk us now: their paradoxes clog our thinking.
>
> Susanne K Langer[2]

Cash Value

We have examined a variety ways of thinking about ourselves as legal subjects: in terms of our capacity for reason, our supposed sanctity and our biological and species nature. To employ a term coined by William James, what is the 'cash value', in law, of characterising and evaluating a being one way rather than another?[3]

How we view ourselves makes a great practical difference to law and its application. If it is thought that reason is most important, then its diminution or absence will mean the erosion or the end of our legal being. If sanctity is the thing which most defines us, then reason may be irrelevant and legal personality may even exist well before birth, when we are only a tiny cluster of cells. If it is our creature natures which matter, then we may be most interested in the capacity for pain and pleasure: what may matter is our creature needs, and their proper nurture, and when there is no longer a capacity to think and feel, then there is no one there who truly counts in law.

[1] Rheinstein, M 'Legal Systems' in David Sills (ed), *International Encyclopaedia of the Social Sciences* (New York, Macmillan-Free Press, 1968) vol ix, 208 quoted in HK Lucke, 'Good Faith and Contractual Performance' in P Finn (ed), *Essays on Contract* (Sydney, Law Book Co, 1987) 170.

[2] Susanne K Langer, *Philosophy in a New Key: a Study in the Symbolism of Reason, Rite and Art*, extracted in Mary Warnock (ed), *Women Philosophers* (London, Everyman JM Dent, 1996) 119.

[3] William James, *Pragmatism* (New York, Dover Publications, 1995) 21.

These fundamental philosophical differences about what makes us what we are have been most conspicuous in the big life-and-death cases. Not surprisingly, legal decisions about abortion, about pregnant women in or near labour, about the treatment of the profoundly intellectually disabled and about the dying, have flushed out the most passionate advocates of each position.

When a decision had to be made about the legality of withdrawing life support from the unthinking and insensate Tony Bland, believers in Bland's sanctity said that life support must continue because Bland was still a person. The Rationalist sceptics said that there was no person left, while the Naturalists said that there was no sensate creature there, who could feel pain or pleasure. The latter two views supported termination of life support. The court itself tried to juggle and balance all three views. It thought about what the rational Tony would have wanted; it reflected on the intrinsic value/sanctity of a human life; and it considered Tony as a creature of pain and pleasure. It concluded that there was no creature life left in Tony, no pleasure to be had and no pain to suffer; there was nothing which mattered to him. He had no interests left.

Case law which considers the rights of pregnant women to refuse treatment thought necessary to save the life of their foetus has attracted the same debaters and debates. With great consistency, the judiciary has formally supported the rights of the rational woman, as a full legal person, to determine what is done to her own body. However, the creature needs of the foetus, often characterised as an 'unborn child', as a needy dependent being, as well as its supposed sanctity have played an important part in legal thinking.

Abortion remains one of the most disputed issues. Despite very broad democratic support for its legal availability for women, as rational persons, it remains an absolute (not a necessary) evil to those who believe that, from conception, the embryo is itself a sacred person.

Debates about euthanasia attract the same card-carrying cast of philosophical and legal thinkers. The believers in human sanctity have, to date, largely won this battle, to the despair of those who believe that as suffering creatures we should be permitted to end our misery; and to the despair, also, of those who believe that as rational beings we should have the right to govern our own lives, to be our own authors.

The small body of jurisprudence on animal 'rights' and standing has attracted less attention, less public notoriety, no doubt because the problem of human sanctity does not arise here, except in a negative sense. There are those who are concerned that animal rights might erode human rights. Those who care deeply about the supposed sanctity of humans, however, tend not to enter these legal frays.

And throughout all of these debates, there has run a dispute about what makes someone or something a legal person. The legal device of the person therefore has great creative and humanitarian potential, but it is also highly divisive and it is also prone to abuse. As the Legalists insist, personality-creating rights and duties can be distributed in an immense variety of ways, depending on legal purpose and legal relation. There appears to be no natural or legal limit to them. Rights can be richly present in a given individual, barely present in another; rights will fluctuate over a human lifetime as a host of legal relations are entered and left. So too will duties.

Precisely because it is so manipulable, the legal device of the person has been used and can still be used, quite lawfully, in almost violently opposing ways: to enrich or to impoverish legal lives. In the most egregious cases it has been used to 'unperson' altogether.[4] This was essentially the fate of the Jewish people in the Holocaust and the reply to it was the international demand for a basic set of rights for all human beings. The idea of human sanctity, variously expressed, formed an important component of this reply to Nazi Germany.

If human beings cannot gain a purchase within a legal system, if they are not permitted to exercise the most basic legal rights, if they are not allowed a basic legal existence, then their plight is dire. The border protection laws of Australia are precisely designed to ensure that those seeking entry to Australia by boat, without visa, cannot acquire access to the basic rights of persons seeking refugee status. The edges of Australia are defined, creatively, as not Australia for these specific purposes, the 'boat-people' are kept legally offshore, and so they are denied access to refugee rights within the Australian legal system.

For a rather different example of how status can be manipulated and personality denied, we can look to marriage laws. The rights and duties associated with married persons, until recently, have been available only to men and women in relation to one another. And although many jurisdictions now recognise the registration of civil partnerships between gay people, it generally remains the case that gays cannot enter the legal sphere of marriage; they can not get a purchase on marriage; they are legally invisible within this set of legal relations, effectively outlaws. For another well-used example of how personality can be explicitly denied and individuals excluded from law: until the early part of the twentieth century, women could not enter public offices designed for 'persons'. This was done quite lawfully, with law and by law.

Recent American animal welfare legislation provides yet another illustration of the manner in which law admits and excludes beings from beneficial laws by ukase. The original Federal Animal Welfare Act of 1966 required the Secretary of Agriculture to protect, in various ways and for certain purposes, creatures who were defined as 'animals' and this meant dogs, cats, monkeys, guinea pigs, hamsters, rabbits and 'such other warm-blooded

[4] George Orwell, *Nineteen Eighty-Four* (London, Secker and Warburg, 1949).

animals'. But the law specifically excluded 'horses not used for research purposes and other farm animals . . . used . . . for food'.[5] As James Rachels observes: 'Of course this is not intended as a proper definition of animals, but only a specification of which animals are included within the scope of the act'.[6] The definition of 'animal' was later changed to exclude mice, rats and birds, the sort of creatures commonly used in research experiments. This did not, of course, stop them being sentient warm-blooded creatures; it did stop them being animals for the purposes of this welfare law and so eased the lives of research scientists.

In an important sense, the Legalists are right. The legal concept of the person can be metaphysically neutral. It is not necessarily tied to any particular philosophical, religious or scientific understanding of what we really are and therefore it can be used in any which way, to endow and deny rights; to impose and remove duties. A favourite example of this great legal freedom to personify, almost it would seem on a whim, is the Idol case.[7] In the 1920s, the Privy Council agreed that a wooden idol could be regarded as a legal person. The legal deeming of dogs as cats at Oxford, to bring them within the class of animals not excluded from Oxford rooms, is another illustration often used to show that law can assign status in whatever ways it pleases, and in the face of ordinary views of what makes a person a person or an animal an animal.

But legal rights and duties are not typically dispensed and imposed arbitrarily and they are certainly not randomly distributed. There are distinctive patterns of legal relations which have great consistency over time, and change only with great legal reluctance. And it is these patterns which the Legalists have been unwilling to acknowledge as fundamental to personality. This book has largely been about the reasons for these patterns: about the ways in which strong metaphysical views of what makes a person a person have determined the nature of legal personality—how they have entered law and become part of law. These metaphysical views are responsible for the relative stability of personality, which is not to deny its complexity and its capacity for change.

These metaphysical views have been for good or ill, depending on one's outlook on life. But there is no escaping them. There is no way that legal rights and duties can be assigned in a metaphysically-neutral fashion because they can only ever be assigned by those with certain belief systems about what we are. We all operate within a world view conditioned by our accident of birth. As the cultural anthropologist Clifford Geertz observed:

[5] James Rachels 'Drawing Lines' in Cass R Sunstein and Martha C Nussbaum (eds), *Animal Rights: Current Debates and New Directions* (New York, Oxford University Press, 2004) 162, 163.

[6] *Ibid.*

[7] *Pramatha Nath Mullick v Pradyamna Kumar Mullick* (1925) L Rep 5.

> the image of a constant human nature independent of time, place and circumstance, of studies and professions, transient fashions and temporary opinions, may be an illusion, that what man is may be so entangled with where he is, who he is, and what he believes that it is inseparable from them . . . men unmodified by the customs of particular places do not in fact exist, have never existed, and most important, could not in the very nature of the case exist.[8]

What makes a 'man', or more pointedly what makes a 'person', is subject to time and place and circumstance. And as Geertz insists, this:

> makes the drawing of a line between what is natural, universal, and constant in man and what is conventional, local, and variable extraordinarily difficult. In fact, it suggests that to draw such a line is to falsify the human situation, or at least to misrender it seriously.[9]

This was also the view of John Dewey who thought that there were no eternal properties of the non-legal person upon which jurists could confidently rely. Instead, 'the history of western culture showed a chameleon-like change' in its understanding of what it was to be a person.[10]

Four Metaphysical Approaches

We have examined four ways of thinking about the legal person, law's subject: four ways in which thinkers have sought to tie the device of personality to a particular metaphysic: Legalism, Rationalism, Religionism and Naturalism. For each approach, for each world view, there are those who subscribe to a strong metaphysical position and those of a more moderate outlook—those who are more typically open-minded in intellectual disposition. In its stronger variety, the thinker concludes that there is an underlying metaphysics to law's person, a true nature that we all possess, and when these true characteristics of our person are not properly reflected in law's subject, law is inauthentic or impaired. In its more muted form, the thinker concludes that the legal person does and should have certain characteristics, but these are not all encompassing; they do not exclude other attributes; and law's person remains a person even if law fails properly to recognise these qualities in its subject. Strong metaphysicians tend to communicate poorly with those of different mentalities.

It is perhaps unusual to regard Legalists as metaphysicians. But among the Legalists, there are those who adopt an aggressively *anti*-metaphysical position which necessarily represents a strong and negative response to those who believe that law has a natural legal subject. In its negative dependency on natural law, it represents a metaphysical stance. The idea is that law's person can

[8] Clifford Geertz, *The Interpretation of Cultures* (New York, Basic Books, 1973) 35.

[9] *Ibid* 36.

[10] John Dewey, 'The Historic Background of Corporate Legal Personality' (1926) 35 *Yale Law Journal* 655, 658.

be and should be fully independent of natural persons and moral persons; the true legal person is purely legal; she is not defined by her natural human characteristics; she should be uncontaminated by metaphysics if she is to maintain her legal purity. This can well be regarded as a dogmatic form of legal metaphysics: a commitment to a purely virtual legal person.

The more modest Legalist position entails a commitment to a *non*-metaphysical or a-metaphysical rather than anti-metaphysical stance. The view here is that law can go about its business of constituting legal persons, of assigning personality-creating rights and duties, in a relatively autonomous manner and often this is the best way for it to proceed, that is, technically and legally and without resort to a theory of human nature.

By contrast, Rationalists of a strong sort maintain that the rational moral person and the legal person are one and the same. The true legal person is the rational human person and indeed the rational human person is the true human person. Reason is the metaphysical essence of the person, legally and morally conceived. This is strong Rationalism. There is also a more moderate variety which accepts that law's persons are not always rational, legally or morally, but that the benchmark of law's person is the rational person. It is the capacity for reason which is thought to dignify the legal individual and also legitimise assignments of legal responsibility. But it is conceded, pragmatically, that many laws do not entail this requirement and should not do so.

Religionists, too, come in strong and more moderate varieties. A strong religious metaphysical stance is adopted by Finnis and by orthodox Catholics generally. Here, the true person is the spiritual sacred person. Our essence is our sanctity and law must recognise our truly sacred natures. A more moderate religious position was adopted by Roosevelt and by other human rights supporters. In their view, law should acknowledge human sanctity but other considerations may be brought to bear and these may be in tension with sanctity. Respect for autonomy and a liberal respect for difference of belief are probably the most significant competing considerations.

Naturalists also draw a variety of metaphysical implications from Darwin and they too come in strong and moderate varieties. To some, we are essentially animals. We are not special ensouled or distinctively rational beings and law should reflect this metaphysical fact about our animal material nature, though it has yet to do so. Whether this elevates us or demotes us is open to dispute. Some say that a greater Naturalism can only prove beneficial and therapeutic. Others fear that it might prove to be debasing.

A Fifth Approach: the Relational Person

We have seen that the legal concept of personality can be regarded as inherently relational and that Legalists make much play of this fact. The legal person, they insist, is defined by their legal relations and only by their legal relations. Legal persons do not bring their own inherent character to law, for it to be stamped and approved by law. Rather, they have their legal character constituted by law within constellations of changing legal relations. One's legal nature, in this view, is always reliant on a relation with another (thus, a right in one person represents a duty in another). This might suggest one further metaphysical approach to law's person, which pays particular attention to the manner in which law constitutes persons, which is relationally. This fifth metaphysical approach is one that sees the person both in law and society as formed by their relations, rather than by their inherent characteristics, be it the capacity for reason or sanctity or some other characteristic. It entails a social understanding of the person. In this view, the way that law forms the person—relationally—directly reflects the way that the person is formed in society, likewise relationally; that is to say, the nature and form of legal relations, which make legal persons, mirror or picture (in an early Wittgensteinian sense) the nature and form of real human relations, which turn us into human subjects: into human persons.

This social relational view of the person has been theorised and defended in various ways by philosophers and by lawyers. For example, the moral philosopher Charles Taylor describes the person as an interlocutor. To Taylor:

> we accede to the status of human subjects through being taken up as interlocutors in an exchange that pre-exists us . . . And this may help to explain the importance of personae and names . . . Being given a name is being inducted into a linguistic exchange, being designated as an interlocutor . . . To have the name, or perhaps the mask, is to be the interlocutor.[11]

American lawyer Drucilla Cornell provides another account of the relational person, one that she would like to see reflected in law. 'Transformation', she says, 'is demanded of us precisely because there is no self-enclosed subject who can truly cut herself off from the Other'.[12]

Emmanuel Levinas has described a relational self which comes into being through openness to the other.[13] Jennifer Nedelsky has theorised a legal person whose freedoms positively derive from enabling relations.[14] William James also emphasised the composite, transient and relational nature of the person. He said that 'we are dealing with fluctuating material'.[15] James saw

[11] C Taylor, 'The Person' in Michael Carrithers, Steven Collins and Steven Lukes (eds), *The Category of the Person* (Cambridge, Cambridge University Press, 1985) 279.

[12] D Cornell, 'Convention and Critique' in D Cornell, *Transformations* (New York, Routledge, 1993) 15.

[13] E Levinas, *Otherwise than Being or Beyond Essence* (A Lingis (tr), The Hague, Martinus Nijhoff, 1981).

[14] Jennifer Nedelsky, 'Reconceiving Autonomy: Sources, Thoughts and Possibilities' in A Hutchinson and L Green (eds), *Law and the Community: the End of Individualism?* (Toronto, Carswell, 1989) 230.

[15] William James, *The Principles of Psychology* (Chicago, William Benton, 1952) 188.

no sharp distinction between what is me and what is you. Our social selves, he declared, are as many as there are individuals who recognise us and 'carry an image' of us in their minds. If any of these images are wounded, so too is the individual.[16] Our social being is therefore dependent on the perspective of the other.

For James, the self was to be understood as a 'stream' rather than as a substance or entity. The word 'stream' conveys movement and change; there is no stable identity. The subject self is not something which can be identified, pinned down or known. We have knowing, certainly, within the 'stream of thought', but 'this knowing is not immediately known'.[17] To James 'the existence of the thinker', our thinker of rationalist philosophy, that which has the thoughts, is better regarded as 'a logical postulate'.[18]

A mutable identity is only fully realised, however if, from moment to moment, I am not committed to a single persona but can be a particular being-in-process and in-relation. I must be permitted to respond to you, as a particular human being, and you, in a like manner, must be allowed to make your mark on me. Only then do I have the sort of freedom of identity in relation that these writers describe. In this account of being a person, I am constantly in transformation as I commune with others. However, if I cannot thus engage with others, if my self-understanding is not allowed to shape, and be shaped by, others, if I am isolated from the transforming effects of the social world on me, then there is a certain unacceptable fixity to my person. I am denied access to the multiple characters which might otherwise form and enrich my public personae.

Perhaps it is the case that law's relational person (as understood by the Legalists) directly pictures this social relational understanding of the person as existing in relation. It is even possible to add a normative element to this legal conception of the person and to see this relational legal model of the person as a positively desirable one for human relations generally. Especially if one favours a Jamesian, communitarian or even a Buddhist approach to human relations, then the legal relational model of the person is perhaps one we should aspire to. After all, the legal approach to personality admits of a multiplicity of personae depending on who we are with and why. Legal personality always looks to another; there is no stable or essential legal person; rather we come into and out of being according to our relations and without them there is only the smile of the Cheshire Cat. It might also seem that the legal understanding of the person implicitly contains within it an important measure of respect for others, in that any right or duty always looks to another for its exercise.

[16] William James, *The Principles of Psychology* (Chicago, William Benton, 1952) 190.
[17] *Ibid* 196.
[18] *Ibid.*

The problem with this way of looking at legal personality—as relational and always open to others—is that it is heavily idealised, even romanticised. It neglects the fact that the effective exercise of any person-constituting right depends always on a prior legal (and political) decision that a given individual should be permitted to exercise that beneficial right and a legal decision as to the form that right should take. Legal relations do not develop spontaneously and freely (as many social relations seem to do) according to the wishes of the parties involved, even if those wishes are noble and altruistic and mutually respectful. Rather, legal relations must assume a legal form and the parties to the relation must be recognised by law. To repeat a simple example, a man who loves another man cannot choose to enter a marital relation with that man in order to endow him with the benefits of marriage. Law regards him as the wrong sort of person for this sort of relation. Legal relations always depend on a prior legal decision about what legal relations are to be permitted and who should be allowed to enter those relations and who should not. Always, legal relations depend on the dictates of law, which are inevitably evaluative—some would say political. They are certainly not about free love, nor even about free respect for the rights of another if the law itself does not recognise those rights.

Personality has always operated by inclusion *and* exclusion and the decision as to who should be included or excluded has depended on social evaluations of who are fit and proper persons. Women were once thought not to be fit and proper persons to hold public office. Now they are, because social evaluations (or rather the evaluations of the legally influential) have altered. Sometimes racial considerations have dominated; sometimes patriarchal beliefs; sometimes Christian sentiments. Now we put particular store by individual reason. Thus, an idealised view of personality as somehow embodying Buddhist or communitarian values tends to leave out these vital practical, social and political considerations at the heart of law and also neglects the manner in which law formulates and controls the nature of legal relations.

An idealised relational view of the legal person also neglects some perhaps less attractive features of our legal system. While it may be the case that the relational nature of personality offers the possibilities for such an open, even loving, view of persons, it by no means demands it. Cornell and MacIntyre seek a recognition in human relations (and Cornell in legal relations) of the particularity, the distinctiveness, of the other party to that relation. They also tend to look for some basic warmth and concern for that other person in those relations. But this is not required by law and legal personality is no less effective when it entails a direct denial of the particular characteristics and needs of a person. Nor does it depend on kindness or compassion or even a cold respect for the other party to the relation.

Our adversarial system is in fact premised on the idea that it is as adversaries that we relate in a court of law. It assumes that people are unlikely to embrace relations which are not thought to be to their direct advantage, and that they will do their level best to deny the interests of the other person which are thought to conflict with their own. This is not a law of loving respectful relations, where it is assumed that the needs of the other will spontaneously be put before one's own. It is trite law that we are not obliged to care for or rescue those who are weak and dependent and who could do with our help. It is only if we assume a positive legal obligation that we can be required to do the right thing by those who need us. This is hardly a law of love or a law of respect for the particular needs and interests of the other person. It is a law of minimal obligations to others, which is not to say that law should do more than this. There are good liberal reasons for this view of us as persons who only grudgingly assume relations of obligation.

Finally, the persons that we are permitted to be in law do not depend on our free and loving choices; they do not depend on our individual desire to undertake duties to others if those duties are not already recognised by law. To repeat, the qualifications for personality and the consequent exercise of rights and duties in any given legal relations are determined by law and (generally speaking) not the parties. A failure to satisfy those qualifications may simply preclude one from any legal existence within those legal relations. Hence, my desire to assume legal as well as moral duties to my cat will not bring those duties into existence and somehow turn my cat into a rights-bearing person. It is not up to me to determine how the law views my cat. Nor does my belief that as citizens we should assume greater responsibility for those who are grossly disadvantaged bring those obligations into legal being. Nor is it up to me, for that matter, to choose my legal sex and then operate as a legal man or woman, depending on my inclinations within any particular relation. The consequences of my sexuality are also legally, not personally, determined (to invoke the heterosexual marriage law example once again). Perhaps it would be a good thing if the law were more flexible and open to the particular needs and desires of others than this; but this is not how it is. This is not the current meaning of legal personality.

Legal Philosophies as Acts of Faith and Incommensurable World Views

The metaphysical approaches to the person described in this book entail a view of what we are, in essence, and our place in the natural and to some supernatural world. (And each asserts an obligation on the part of law to reflect that nature.) Each is founded on an act of faith: an assertion, a belief, that this is the case. That is, each starts from a profound conviction rather than proof, which I suspect is not available. Each of us, coming to this subject of the person, will be more in tune with one approach than another. And it may well be that one or more approach canvassed here seems inherently preposterous. The great intellectual feat, and perhaps moral requirement, is to understand one's own world view as well as the world view of the other: to see both.

Necessarily, we all occupy a place inside or outside of any given system of belief, which creates an intellectual and ethical problem of trying to understand it (both the other and our own) and render it faithfully and respectfully. From the inside, it is our world view. We are persuaded by it because it is how things seem to us. From the outside it is alien or wrong. If world views are incommensurable, if they lack a common ground, the problems of understanding and mutual respect are considerable or insuperable. Kuhn gave currency to the idea of incommensurability. This is an idea which belongs to philosophy of science but can equally be applied here. Thus:

> theories which, in a radical sense, cannot be compared are often said to be incommensurable . . . Scientific revolutions, which involve wholesale discarding of one set of theories in favour of another, are thought typically to produce such radical shifts of meaning that the concepts employed in the theories propounded after revolution simply cannot be expressed in terms of the concepts of pre-revolutionary theory.[19]

The Rationalist philosophy of liberal individualism—the idea of the unitary autonomous moral agent—is one which any academic necessarily participates in. We write about it from the inside and so its rightness can seem indisputable. As people whose task it is to reason, we are in a sense the central characters of Rationalism. It is ourselves who are dignified within this world view and so we engage in a critique from within (which as a consequence may mean that our critical edge is blunted by familiarity).

The belief in a supernatural being who defines our natures is one which has very little meaning for non-believers, or religious sceptics such as myself. Those who believe in God and those who do not could be said to have incommensurable mentalities. The sceptic can perhaps understand the striving to find meaning in our lives, but faith in a personal God may be entirely alien. The believer and non-believer have incommensurable positions.

One's world view dictates the implications of that outlook and one's disposition to those of another system of belief. World view is not so much a matter of persuasion as a matter of belief or conviction. And within the conviction, the way of seeing things seems wise or right or natural. Simply what is. One is always already inside a variety of systems of belief which means that it may be difficult to regard them as social and historical ways of thinking: as dependent on time, place and circumstance. As Richards Rorty observes, 'even when we have justified true belief about everything we want to know, we may have no more than conformity to the norms of the day'.[20]

[19] J Logue, 'Incommensurability' in T Honderich (ed), *The Oxford Companion to Philosophy* (Oxford, Oxford University Press, 1995) 397.

[20] Richard Rorty, *Philosophy and the Mirror of Nature* (Princeton, Princeton University Press, 1979) 367.

Systems of thought have their advocates and their detractors. In this book, I have concentrated on those thinkers who have spoken on behalf of one belief system or another: who have become the voice of a particular belief or thought system. Thinkers such as Wise and Francione emphasise our animal status and seek to change the status of animals to make it more commensurate with our own. Finnis defends a religious world view in which the foetus is a full person. Moore speaks for our rational natures and believes that the irrational are not truly persons.

Some thinkers try to iron out differences of belief and to say that they are reconcilable. Dworkin declares that no one really believes that foetuses are persons, but clearly they do. Finnis makes it quite plain that he regards the foetus as a human being and as a person. Most lawyers take as a given the importance of our species over others but Wise, Francione and Singer manifestly do not share these automatic assumptions. These are variously denials of different belief systems or endeavours to trump one by another. Finnis simply and openly asserts that the others are wrong. Certain thinkers are passionate advocates of a certain metaphysical approach and passionately denounce those who think differently. The Rationalist individualist Moore is one. The religious thinker Finnis is another. By contrast, Dworkin invokes moral intuitionism: we all just feel this way, he says. We can each caricature the views of those who have quite foreign outlooks and this has often occurred within debates about the legality and morality of abortion, euthanasia and the property status of animals. But this is not 'edifying philosophy' or philosophy as conversation.[21]

All the approaches to life and the person that I have considered are in currency, whatever the denials. They all still exist at the same time, now, though some are compatible and some are inimical or incommensurable. All influence legal thinking. The story of the move from status to contract is that of the individual eventually triumphing over the group, of one mentality replacing another. So, too, we have the story of the rise of scientific Rationalism. And yet the religious order is retained in current thought, especially on the nature of the foetus and the nature of animals and on our non-animal nature. The idea of human sanctity remains secure in law. It relies on supernaturalism, not Naturalism and science.

The concept of the person, in use, therefore takes its meaning, variously and fluctuatingly, from all four metaphysical positions. Those who argue vehemently that one approach is the only and the right one deny these competing positions. They are trying to fix meaning, linking it to only one world view, and so achieve certainty and security and relieve confusion and anxiety. They see the opposite view as dangerous, as impure, as taboo, as evil, or irrational. There appears to be an obsessive, denying and controlling

[21] Richard Rorty, *Philosophy and the Mirror of Nature* (Princeton, Princeton University Press, 1979) 367.

instinct in those who insist that only one way of thinking is true and must be applied.[22]

Both the Legalists and the Metaphysicians (that is the Rationalists, the Religionists and the Naturalists), especially when in deep oppositional mode, are neglecting something important in their analysis of the person. Both omissions are to do with fixity of orientation. The Metaphysicians are staring outwards, from their legal eerie, into what they take to be the essential heart of the real non-legal world and trying to 'name' or 'picture' this natural or supernatural reality of what we are. The Legalists are staring inwards, their faces towards law and their backs towards the social world outside, where their concepts must also do their work. And to the extent that the Legalists refuse to go beyond law and its conventions in their analysis of legal terms, to the extent that they stick doggedly to the view that legal terms derive their meaning fully from distinctively legal principles and techniques, they strip legal concepts of their metaphysical meaning, even though that broader meaning still has real effects on law. They refuse also to acknowledge, for example, that judges who believe that the concept of the person refers to a real metaphysical person will import that supposed metaphysical meaning into law in their interpretation of the concept, thus making that meaning part of the legal concept.

When these competing mentalities are brought together in a single legal problem, a single case, there can be a deeply unsatisfactory, illogical, incoherent result or resolution. We cannot think it because it relies on two or more incommensurable world views. We have seen such inconsistent mentalities operating within the beginning and end-of-life cases.

Distinctive Nature of the Legal Enterprise

All this is not to deny the central point made by those who adhere to the more Legalistic view of the person: that law and its basic concepts are also meaningfully analysed and understood as a (semi)autonomous system, well away from metaphysics. Although law may have (historically determined) metaphysics, law is not the same as philosophy and it is not a form of natural science and it is not theology. The highly practical and diverse tasks of social regulation and dispute resolution, which are given to law, also give it its own distinctive nature.

In relation to dispute resolution and adjudication, the way of the (common) law is to problem solve, case by case. A problem arises and it is put to a court of law for resolution and disposition. The court finds a solution and makes a holding. A right or duty is ascribed, without a total theory of the right or duty holder being espoused.

[22] See Mary Douglas, *Purity and Danger: an Analysis of Concepts of Pollution and Taboo* (New York, Routledge, 2002).

Parliamentary law-making is also always directed to a specific human problem rather than trying to divine the metaphysical basis of existence (though some laws get the law-makers thinking along metaphysical lines, especially when it involves embryos or foetuses or the dying who want help to die more swiftly). Thus, parliamentary law-making and judicial dispute resolution are inherently pragmatic in the philosophical sense. They are directed at specific problems and demand specific outcomes; legal meaning is determined by its cash value—by the actual resolution of a legal problem for particular people.

Moreover, law imposes itself on the individual, often regardless of the wishes of the individual. It employs and operates by way of force and compulsion which is why it does not subscribe to a free relational view of its subject, one in which personae, arising out of legal relations, are assumed and discarded at the whim of the individual. Law imposes its categories, its standards and its obligations. It can render invalid an activity (the sale of an organ, same-sex marriage, sex change). It can punish for infraction. Equally, it can enable legal relations, turning an agreement into a legally enforceable commercial contract or a marriage. Thus are legal words performatives. Law imposes itself in a highly practical and forceful way on the non-legal world. It is not in the power of individuals dissatisfied with law's classifications simply to assert that they are wrong and to refuse to recognise them or comply with them. This forceful, regulatory and also enabling nature of law is distinctive to it and distinguishes it from the theological, the scientific and the philosophical.

Philosophy, for example, does not have this practical demand placed on it nor therefore does the discipline, because it does not have to work in this sense. Philosophical determinations are not necessarily determinations about real people. They are not obliged to produce practical resolutions of human differences.

Why Law is Still Flexible

We have seen a variety of legal theorists endeavouring to tie the legal person to their particular conception of a human being. But in truth, for much of the time law does not even endeavour to be consistent in its view of its legal subject and it would be harsh on most of us if it did. It would mean a departure from some of the most basic principles of justice which relate to the equality of all before the law. A central feature and an important virtue of law is its dynamism: its flexibility, its creativity, its ability to respond to fresh problems and to new circumstances. Legal judgments could not respond to the specific needs and demands of each new case if they always kept referring back to a fixed idea of what it is to be a proper legal being. The legal person does not compel the judge to think in a singular manner about personality; or as Nekam puts it, 'the question which is really crucial for legal understanding is when and from what point of view a thing is taken as a legal entity'.[23]

The common law is well known for its pragmatism and its impurity of principle. It is known for its common sense. Nekam, for example, observes that 'Anglo-Saxon jurists' have given 'nominally ardent lip-service' to the idea that the legal person should assume a certain form, but have felt 'little or no concern . . . at disregarding the theory altogether should situations warrant it'.[24]

So, for much of the time our common law does not keep faith with the idea that there is an essential set of attributes possessed by the legal person, such as an ability to reason and assert one's interests against the rest of the world, and this is not a cause of legal angst. Although jurists frequently expound the importance of autonomy and reason, law in fact does not consistently demand of its subject a rational will. Consequently, law is much more inclusive than it should be, were it to stay faithful to the demands of the Rationalists. As Wise observes: 'Paradoxically, courts . . . recognize the dignity-rights of humans who lack the capacities for autonomy and self-determination'.[25] Wise invokes an idea of 'realistic autonomy' to help explain this.[26] He argues that while the ideal is a rational being, the reality is something much less than this. Notwithstanding its emphasis on will, law does not in fact demand reason in an individual to endow rights.

This considerable realism, even pragmatism, of law was evident in the case of *Gillick v West Norfolk Health Authority*[27] which recognised the organic and gradual development of rationality and gradually moved the power to enforce the child's claims from a responsible adult to the child. However, there was no question that the immature child, even one who would never acquire rationality, would be regarded as a non-person. Law's treatment of the irrational (as we saw in *Re A (Children)* in Chapter 6) is very different from the approach of those who say that personhood requires reason and that philosophical purity demands it. While Singer would diminish the size of the moral and legal community in some cases (for example, for profoundly disabled human beings) and extend it in others (to include intelligent animals), law continues to protect all live human beings.[28]

[23] Alexander Nekam, *The Personality Conception of the Legal Entity* (Cambridge, Mass, Harvard University Press, 1938) 118.

[24] *Ibid* 99.

[25] Steven Wise, 'Hardly a Revolution: the Eligibility of Nonhuman Animals for Dignity-Rights in a Liberal Democracy' (1998) 22 *Vermont Law Review* 793, 909. (However, Wise has no real philosophical explanation of this, as he remains wedded to a naturalised and Rationalist view of the legal person.)

[26] But this modification also allows him to retain autonomy as the key idea of law and he wants to do this as it is central to his argument that certain animals should have rights.

[27] *Gillick v West Norfolk and Wisbech Area Health Authority* [1986] 1 AC 112.

[28] A continuing problem is that it still leaves all live animals with insufficient protections and either no or diminished personhood depending on the analysis.

Non-legal philosophers often assume that legal personhood depends on the inflexible Rationalist model of the legal subject, the idea that legal subjects are typically and ideally rational human beings, and so they endeavour to fit beings to this conception of the person.[29] But this is not essential: law can and does embrace a wide variety of ways of being which makes for a broad community of persons including those who do not comply with the Rationalist model. And it can do this because of the way that personality is conceived in law which allows for the remarkable versatility of legal personality, and enables law to respond to the immense array of human interests.[30] This is not to deny the compelling, controlling, even violent nature of legal personality. If a court or legislature does not believe that a being is of the right kind to be a person, then they can make it so. Belief, including political belief, is very much at the heart of personification.

Should Personality be Severed From Human Beings?

According to Nekam, we should sever the philosophical or metaphysical concepts of the person from the legal concept. The connection between the two causes endless confusions and problems. He goes so far as to say that we should eliminate the words 'person' and 'personality' from law and replace them with the term 'legal entity':

> The use of the idea of personality to explain the subject-of-rights character of a thing, and the consequent use of the word 'person' to designate the legal entity, are both as inappropriate as they are dangerous. While from one point of view they say too much, from another they say too little.[31]

To Nekam the term 'person' says too much when it conveys the idea that a natural human subject necessarily stands behind the legal entity. It misleadingly carries all the metaphysical and psychological connotations of 'personality'. It also tends to conceal the fact 'that the world of law is always an artificial, abstract world'.[32] The term says too little in that it fails to communicate anything about why or when something will be regarded as a legal entity. It says nothing about 'the existing gradation among the legal entities':[33] that some have but a few rights, while others are amply endowed. It fails also to tell us from whose perspective it can be said that something has a right and so can be counted as a person.

[29] Thus, when animal rights lawyers insist on the intelligence of the higher primates in order to gain them access to the community of legal persons, they assume that law necessarily models its legal person on a particular conception of a human subject. Wise, for one, employs this logic. So do will theorists and many natural lawyers.

[30] Michael Ignatieff, *The Needs of Strangers* (New York, Viking, 1984) 52.

[31] Nekam, above n 23, at 67.

[32] *Ibid.*

[33] *Ibid.*

Nekam further argues that the expressions 'person' and 'personality' tend to suggest:

> because of their constant allusion to human personality and to all those rights with which in our society the human being is invested, that all subjects of rights must be fundamentally similar in character, that they all must have a certain minimum amount of rights attributed to them, that it is a necessary part of the definition of a legal entity that it should be such for at least a minimum group of rights.[34]

In other words, the terms imply that there is a certain basic agglomeration of rights that is due to every legal person, when this is manifestly not the case. This humanising terminology makes the concept seem more monolithic than it is. It therefore serves little good. In short, the theoretical category of the person is 'too-narrowly and too-dogmatically conceived'.[35]

However, the connection between the natural person and law's person, a connection which Legalists want to deny, and the Metaphysicians want to entrench, may in fact serve a valuable moral purpose. If we were to lose the sense of the legal person as an inherently valuable type of natural being, then we might well dilute our moral concern. We might lose that sense of a minimum threshold of what can be done in law to human beings. There might be a dissipation or dissolution of the person. If, as the Legalists insist, we are only dealing with abstractions of great flexibility, we may lose our sense of limits—what it is right and wrong to do to a person. This was the central concern of Eleanor Roosevelt.

Human rights discourse and human rights instruments have provided a vital means of improving the treatment of human beings. They assert that there are threshold requirements for the humane treatment of all human beings. The dangers they respond to are eloquently expressed in the Preamble to the Universal Declaration of Human Rights (1948):

> Whereas recognition of the inherent dignity and of the equal and inalienable rights of all members of the human family is the foundation of freedom, justice and peace in the world,
>
> Whereas disregard and contempt for human rights have resulted in barbarous acts which have outraged the conscience of mankind, and the advent of a world in which human beings shall enjoy freedom of speech and belief and freedom from fear and want has been proclaimed as the highest aspiration of the common people,
>
> Whereas it is essential, if man is not to be compelled to have recourse, as a last resort, to rebellion against tyranny and oppression, that human rights should be protected by the rule of law.[36]

[34] *Ibid.*

[35] *Ibid* 87.

[36] GA Res 217(III), UN GAOR, 3rd sess, Supp No 13, UN Doc A/810 (1948) 71.

Indeed, if one examines the moral tone of the Legalists, one can perhaps detect this loss of moral dimension: the absence of real people whom we care about, whatever their physical or mental ability. Legalists who believe they can analyse law without a working concept of humanity amputate the human being from law, in effect depopulating it. By contrast, lawyers who insist that rights are natural to human beings, and that laws which abuse such rights are not true law, are explicitly replying to human rights abuses. They are replying to the abuses implicit in Nazi law and in the law of apartheid in the former South African regime.[37]

By retaining a link between legal persons and real human beings (variously understood) and also by insisting that real human beings demand certain minimum moral treatment, it may be that law and judges retain their humanity. They retain a core idea of a person as a naturally moral, and hence valuable, being. This connection (often inexplicit) means that judges and other legal officials can legitimately employ a moral language of human sanctity or human dignity when they are analysing the concept of the legal person; and it is thus that they can assert that there are certain things that simply cannot be done to us because we have this moral quality. There is a moral benchmark.

This is perhaps the ingredient sometimes missing in Peter Singer's work and which turns out to be so provocative. That is, there is an important moral reason for preserving a connection between the legal person and human being. The worst-case scenario is the treatment of people as things, as in Nazi Germany.

Implications for Justice

What has all this to do with legal equality and justice? Perhaps the greatest concern generated by this analysis is that law's idea of 'man' can be discriminatory and arbitrary and so undermine the principle of equality. The human being who best approximates this character has the best set of abilities as a legal person and is regarded as the most complete person. Concessions are made for children, the mentally ill and the pregnant because by necessary implication they are not complete persons. The social and political nature of these concessions is concealed by their naturalisation.[38]

This is the critical legal and social justice dimension of this book: the observation that law's various ideas of what we truly are can operate unequally and inequitably. Those who most approximate law's valued

[37] See discussion in Mark Tebbit, *Philosophy of Law* (London and New York, Routledge, 2000) 5.

[38] Henry Maine made this clear when he said that there are only remaining the natural differences between persons as reasons for legal differentiation of persons. And thus he made explicit what usually remains implicit: that there are still thought to be 'normal cases of legal personality' and then the exceptions. See *Ancient Law* (London, John Murray, 1930).

characters do best in law. There are human ideal types or norms and greater and lesser departures from those norms. This is most glaringly apparent in relation to animals. Because animals are perceived to have none of the qualities of the legal person, they do not even gain entry into legal personhood. They are property, not persons. There is also a moral freight which comes with the concepts of person and property: that which is a full flourishing legal actor because of his perceived wholeness as a person and rational will is given greater moral value. Those who are defective legal actors have less. And, of course, that which is property is stripped of moral status.

Even jurists who accept that law's person is most importantly a legal device concede that legal personification serves a social and expressive function and is therefore not fully internal to law. It sends a message to the community and expresses, on behalf of the community, who or what is to count—who matters. Thus, it expresses value. And in this view it is also entirely appropriate that law be responsive to what the community regards as valuable.

Because the adult, rational, autonomous, non-pregnant human tends to be the paradigmatic person, this being possesses not only the best set of rights, but also the personal power to enforce them. This being fares best in law, is best-suited to law. Will theorists are explicit about this, saying that you must have a will to have rights. Those who depart from the model are perceived as deteriorations and consequently special cases requiring special provision.

The Myths We Live by

There is a delicate balancing act to be achieved here. We need to understand and inspect the 'myths we live by' about the sort of beings that we are, and about what gives us value.[39] We need to appreciate that they are myths or mentalities or systems of belief and that there are competing beliefs about our essential natures. But this is not to say that the myths are false or meaningless or ineffectual or without social and moral value. We live our legal lives according to them and they may well be doing very good work for us.

A strictly Legalistic view that they are all foolish metaphysics and have nothing to do with law is to ignore the fact that we live the myths and to leave us not knowing how and why we think and act as we do and whether it is good for us to think this way. If lawyers do not understand their own person, they are lawyering in the dark. They cannot criticise or evaluate that which they cannot understand.

This book has sought a critical understanding of our most fundamental systems of beliefs about our subject in order to appreciate their true complexity.

[39] See Mary Midgley, *The Myths We Live By* (London and New York, Routledge, 2003).

This has been a difficult undertaking because there is no Archimedean point from which to study what is going on. Nor is there a firm epistemological foundation upon which to stand. We are always already immersed in a way of thinking about our subject and from this imperfect position we must try to understand more than our own narrow set of attitudes. There is no way of completely stepping behind or beyond our situation in life and the concepts that our life gives us to understand our situation. There is no way of getting outside of all belief systems and looking in.

On this problem of clear seeing, Brian Leiter invokes usefully 'Neurath's boat':

> Neurath analogizes our epistemological situation to sailors who are trying to rebuild their ship while at sea. Since they cannot rebuild the whole ship at once—they cannot step outside the ship, as it were, and rebuild it from scratch—they must choose to stand firm on certain planks in the ship while reconstructing others. They will, of course, choose to stand firm on the planks that work the best—a pragmatic criterion—while rebuilding those that are less dependable or useful or necessary. Of course, at a later date, the sailors may choose to rebuild the planks they had stood on previously, and in so doing they will again stand on some other planks that serve their practical ends. Our epistemic situation, for Neurath, is the same: we necessarily stand firm on certain planks of our theoretical conception of the world—hypotheses, epistemic norms, and the like—while evaluating other claims about the world. The planks we choose to rest our epistemic edifice upon are just those that have worked the best for us in the past; but nothing precludes the possibility that at some point in the future, we will rebuild those planks as well, while relying on a new theoretical conception.[40]

If we consider, clearly and bracingly, the way our legal meanings work and how they are always derived from a system of belief, then we begin to understand how we really think and what work we are willing to let our concepts do in their various guises. If we take, for example, the legal treatment of the foetus, we discover that we do not assign it a fixed meaning and certainly that we do not regard it as consistently sacrosanct or as consistently simply a collection of cells (in a naturalistic fashion). We learn about the complexity and variability of how we think about it; or we may say that we learn how those with legal influence think about it. When we know what we think, we are better placed to evaluate that way of thinking.

We can do this for all the instances of persons and non-persons in law: for animals or for rational individuals or for persons in a persistent vegetative state. Instead of looking for the core of essential meaning of the entity, its supposed kernel of truth, we ask instead: How does the concept really do its work in law? And the way it does its work is likely to turn out to be quite varied; our meanings are more nuanced and less dogmatic than perhaps we first thought.

[40] Brian Leiter, 'Rethinking Legal Realism: Toward a Naturalized Jurisprudence' (1997) 76(2) *Texas Law Review* 267, note 172, 307.

This does not leave us bereft of a means of criticising our myths about the person. The rightness of the application of a concept can be judged either according to the extent of its fidelity to that concept in nature to which it should correspond (the metaphysical approach) or, say, according to its utility. It may be, as Leiter suggests, 'that some beliefs have to be accepted simply because they "work" relative to various human ends'.[41] It may be, for example, that the concept of 'human sanctity' as a metaphysical dimension of legal personality has important utilities: it sets a bottom threshold of treatment of humans; it entails an assertion of human dignity; it is all inclusive (of humans)—Jews, women, the profoundly disabled. But it may also have disutilities in pinning concepts to what I would regard as unfortunate applications: for example, it may disallow abortion and embryonic stem cell research but countenance cruelty to animals. Traditional and repressive meanings can change if they are not regarded as fixed but conventional and open to critical assessment. The concern of universalists, such as Dworkin, is that we lose an external non-cultural relative criterion of judgment of value. But to acknowledge that meaning and value are always within a community of epistemic and moral meaning is not to exclude strongly reasoned argument.

Perhaps a better means of evaluating the appropriateness of a legal characterisation of the person is not how well it captures reality, or how well it satisfies scientific or philosophical understandings of the person, but rather how well it serves a *just* legal purpose. This obliges us to look at the work done by the characterisation of the person and the results achieved. To achieve these purposes, law may variously invoke human types and variously abandon them. One is obliged to consider what meaning best advances those ends.

In this view, it is not nature driving law but rather legal and social purpose driving nature. To understand why any particular entity is offered legal protection through a particular legal definition, one must consider many things: what and who the particular law is for; its social consequences; its regulative purpose; the role of that law vis-à-vis other laws; how those affected by that law are valued in that society. And to evaluate a law we need to consider the same complex of factors. The merit of a law does not derive from its ability to establish the best possible correspondences with real life but from its ability to achieve its ends, and of course from the merit of those ends. And the thinking lawyer should be perfectly able to see all this.

As Bernstein remarks, '[o]nce we give up the quest for certainty, once we recognize the impossibility of an "absolute" justification, and the fallibility of all beliefs, including our moral beliefs, we need not despair'.[42] We are not obliged to rely on the dominant conventional view of meaning. It does

[41] *Ibid* 305.

[42] Richard J Bernstein, *Praxis and Action* (London, Duckworth, 1972) 227.

not follow that meaning is acceptable simply because it derives from that of the dominant community. Nor is meaning acceptable simply because it accords with narrow legal purposes. It should not be a matter of legal decree. It is incumbent on us to reflect on how and why we think as we do, and whether we can think otherwise and whether we should do so, in the interests of justice.

Bibliography

Journal Articles

Bailey-Harris, Rebecca, 'Pregnancy, Autonomy and Refusal of Medical Treatment' (1998) 114 *Law Quarterly Review* 550

Berger, Benjamin L, 'Law's Religion: Rendering Culture' (2007) 45 *Osgoode Hall Law Journal* 277

Dawson, John, 'The Changing Legal Status of Mentally Disabled People' (1994) 2 *Journal of Law and Medicine* 41

Dewey, John, 'The Historic Background of Corporate Legal Personality' (1926) 35 *Yale Law Journal* 655

Dworkin, Ronald, 'Unenumerated Rights: Whether and How *Roe v Wade* Should be Overruled' (1992) 59 *University of Chicago Law Review* 381

—— 'Politics, Death and Nature' (1996) 6(2) *Health Matrix* (Summer) 201

—— 'Euthanasia, Morality and Law Transcript' (1998) 31 *Loyola LA Law Review* 1147

—— 'In Praise of Theory' (1997) 29 *Arizona State Law Review* 353

—— 'Tyranny at the Two Edges of Life: a Liberal View' (2004) *New Perspectives Quarterly* (Winter) 16

Finnis, John, 'The Rights and Wrongs of Abortion: a Reply to Judith Jarvis Thomson' (1973) 2 *Philosophy and Public Affairs* 117

—— 'The Legal Status of the Unborn Baby' (1992) 43 *Catholic Medical Quarterly* 5

—— 'Bland: Crossing the Rubicon?' (1993) 109 *Law Quarterly Review* 329

—— 'Euthanasia, Morality, and Law' (1996) 31 *Loyola LA Law Review* 1123

—— 'Public Reason, Abortion and Cloning' (1998) *Valparaiso University Law Review* 32

Ford, Mary, 'A Property Model of Pregnancy' (2005) 1 *International Journal of Law in Context* 261

—— 'Evans v United Kingdom: What Implications for the Jurisprudence of Pregnancy' (2008) 8(1) *Human Rights Law Review* 171

French, Peter, 'The Corporation as a Moral Person' (1979) 16(3) *American Philosophical Quarterly* 207

Friedman, Lawrence, 'Is there a Modern Legal Culture?' (1994) 7 *Ratio Juris* 117

Gardner, John, 'The Mark of Responsibility' (2003) 23(2) *Oxford Journal of Legal Studies* 157

Grear, Anna, 'Challenging Corporate Humanity: Legal Disembodiment and Human Rights' (2007) 7 *Human Rights Law Review* 511

Harris, John, 'Human Beings, Persons and Conjoined Twins: an Ethical Analysis of the Judgment in Re A' (2001) 9 *Medical Law Review* 221

James, Nicholas, 'Separate Legal Personality: Legal Reality and Metaphor' (1993) 5 *Bond Law Review* 217

Johnson, Mark, 'Mind Incarnate: from Dewey to Damasio' (2006) 135 *Daedalus* 46
Kramer, MH, 'Do Animals and Dead People Have Legal Rights?' (2001) 15(1) *Canadian Journal of Law and Jurisprudence* 29
Lacey, Nicola, 'Responsibility and Modernity in Criminal Law' (2001) 9 *Journal of Political Philosophy* 249
Lawson, FH, 'The Creative Use of Legal Concepts' (1957) 32 *New York University Law Review* 907
Leiter, Brian, 'Rethinking Legal Realism: Toward a Naturalized Jurisprudence' (1997) 76(2) *Texas Law Review* 26
Lymburner, JA and Roesch, R, (eds), 'The Insanity Defense: Five Years of Research (1993–1997)' (1999) 22 *International Journal of Law and Psychiatry* 213
Moore, Michael, 'The Relevance of Philosophy to Law and Psychiatry' (1984) 6 *International Journal of Law and Psychiatry* 177
Naffine, Ngaire, 'Possession: Erotic Love in the Law of Rape' (1994) 57 *Modern Law Review* 10
—— 'In Praise of Legal Feminism' (2002) 22(1) *Legal Studies* 71
Nedelsky, Jennifer, 'Reconceiving Autonomy' (1989) 1(1) *Yale Journal of Law and Feminism* 7
—— 'Law, Boundaries and the Bounded Self' (1990) 30(1) *Representations* 162
—— 'Reconceiving Rights as Relationships' (1993) 1(1) *Review of Constitutional Studies* 1
—— 'Embodied Diversity and the Challenges of Law' (1996–1997) 42 *McGill Law Journal* 91
Notes, 'What We Talk About When We Talk About Persons: the Language of a Legal Fiction' (2001) 114 *Harvard Law Review* 1746
Nussbaum, Martha, 'Animal Rights: the Need for a Theoretical Basis' (2001) 114 *Harvard Law Review* 1506
Poole, Ross, 'On Being a Person' (1996) 74 *Australian Journal of Philosophy* 38
Scruton, Roger, 'Corporate Persons' (1989) *The Aristotelian Society*, Supplementary vol LXIII, 239
Shestack, Jerome J, 'The Philosophical Foundations of Human Rights' (1998) 20 *Human Rights Quarterly* 201
Smith, Bryant, 'Legal Personality' (1928) 37 *Yale Law Journal* 283
Steve J, 'Casenote: Personhood and Death' (2003) 62 *University of Cincinnatti Law Review* 1227
Stith, Richard, 'The Right to Death', Reply by Ronald Dworkin, 38(6) *New York Review of Books*, 28 March 1991
Stone, Christopher, 'Should Trees Have Standing?' (1972) 45 *Southern California Law Review* 450
Sunstein, Cass, 'Standing for Animals (with Notes on Animal Rights)' (2000) 47 *UCLA Law Review* 1335
Watt, H, 'Conjoined Twins: Separation as Mutilation' (2001) 9 *Medical Law Review* 237
Weitzenboeck, Emily M, 'Electronic Agents and the Formation of Contracts' (2001) 9(3) *International Journal of Law and Information Technology* 204
Wise, Steven, 'Hardly a Revolution: the Eligibility of Nonhuman Animals for Dignity-Rights in a Liberal Democracy' (1998) 22 *Vermont Law Review* 793

Books and Chapters

Ashworth, Andrew, *Principles of Criminal Law* (4th edn, Oxford, Oxford University Press, 2003)

Atiyah, PS, *The Rise and Fall of Freedom of Contract* (Oxford, Clarendon Press, 1979)

Austin, John, *Lectures on Jurisprudence* (R Campbell (ed), 5th edn, London, John Murray, 1885)

Bentham, Jeremy, *An Introduction to the Principles of Morals and Legislation* (JH Burns and HLA Hart (eds), London, Athlone Press, 1970)

Bernstein, Richard J, *Praxis and Action* (London, Duckworth, 1972)

Blackstone, William, *Commentaries on the Laws of England* (17th edn, London, Sweet and Maxwell, 1830)

Cane, Peter, *Responsibility in Law and Morality* (Oxford, Hart Publishing, 2002)

Carter, Rita, *Consciousness* (London, Weidenfeld and Nicolson, 2002)

Catechism of the Catholic Church (Homebush NSW, St Pauls Society of St Paul, 1994)

Cornell, D, 'Convention and Critique' in D Cornell, *Transformations* (New York, Routledge, 1993)

Dan-Cohen, Meir, *Harmful Thoughts: Essays on Law, Self and Morality* (University of Chicago Press, 2003)

Darwin, Charles, *On the Origin of Species by Means of Natural Selection or the Preservation of Favoured Races in the Struggle for Life* (London, John Murray, 1859)

—— *The Descent of Man and Selection in Relation to Sex* (London, John Murray, 1871; 2nd edn, London, John Murray, 1874)

Davies, Margaret, *Asking the Law Question: the Dissolution of Legal Theory* (3rd edn, Pyrmont, Law Book Co, 2008)

—— *Property: Meanings, Histories, Theories* (Abingdon, Routledge-Cavendish, 2008)

Davies, Margaret and Ngaire Naffine, *Are Persons Property? Legal Debates about Property and Personality* (Aldershot, Ashgate, 2001)

Dawkins, Richard, *The God Delusion* (Boston, Houghton Mifflin, 2006)

—— *The Ancestor's Tale: a Pilgrimage to the Dawn of Evolution* (Boston, Houghton Mifflin, 2004)

Dennett, Daniel, *Freedom Evolves* (New York, Viking, 2003)

Derham, DP, 'Theories of Legal Personality' in Leicester Webb (ed), *Legal Personality and Political Pluralism* (Melbourne, Melbourne University Press, 1958)

Descartes, René, *Mediations of First Philosophy* (John Cottingham (ed), Cambridge, Cambridge University Press, 1992)

Desmond, Adrian and James Moore, *Darwin* (London, Penguin Books, 1992)

Diamond, Cora, 'Eating Meat and Eating People' in Cass Sunstein and Martha Nussbaum (eds), *Animal Rights: Current Debates and New Directions* (New York, Oxford University Press, 2004)

Douglas, Mary, *Purity and Danger: an Analysis of Concepts of Pollution and Taboo* (New York, Routledge, 2002)

Duff, PW, *Personality in Roman Private Law* (Cambridge, Cambridge University Press, 1938)

Duff, RA, *Trials and Punishments* (Cambridge, Cambridge University Press, 1986)
Dworkin, Ronald, *Life's Dominion: an Argument about Abortion and Euthanasia* (London, Harper Collins, 1993)
—— *Freedom's Law: the Moral Reading of the American Constitution* (New York, Oxford University Press, 1996)
Fernandez-Armesto, Felipe, *So You Think You're Human?: a Brief History of Humankind* (Oxford, Oxford University Press, 2004)
Fingarette, Herbert, *The Meaning of Criminal Insanity* (Berkley, University of Californian Press, 1972)
Finnis, John, *Natural Law and Natural Rights* (Oxford, Clarendon Press, 1980)
—— 'A Philosophical Case Against Euthanasia' in J Keown (ed), *Euthanasia Examined: Ethical, Legal and Clinical Perspectives* (Cambridge, Cambridge University Press, 1997)
—— 'The Priority of Persons' in Jeremy Horder (ed), *Oxford Essays on Jurisprudence* (4th series, Oxford, Oxford University Press, 2000)
—— 'Abortion, Natural Law and Public Reason' in Robert P George and Christopher Wolfe (eds), *Natural Law and Public Reason* (Washington, DC, Georgetown University Press, 2000)
—— 'Natural Law: the Classical Tradition' in Jules Coleman and Scott Shapiro (eds), *The Oxford Handbook of Jurisprudence and Philosophy of Law* (Oxford, Oxford University Press, 2002)
—— '"The Thing I Am": Personal Identity in Aquinas and Shakespeare' in Ellen Frankel, Fred D Miller Jr and Jeffrey Paul (eds), *Personal Identity* (Cambridge, Cambridge University Press, 2005)
Flanagan, Owen, *The Problem of the Soul: Two Visions of Mind and How to Reconcile Them* (New York, Basic Books, 2002)
Fletcher, George, *Rethinking Criminal Law* (Boston, Little Brown & Co, 1978)
Ford, Norman M, *When Did I Begin? Conceptions of the Human Individual in History, Philosophy and Science* (Cambridge, Cambridge University Press, 1988)
Francione, Gary, *Animals Property and the Law* (Philadelphia, Temple University Press, 1995)
—— *Introduction to Animal Rights: Your Child or the Dog?* (Philadelphia, Temple University Press, 2000)
Fuller, Lon, *Legal Fictions* (Stanford, Stanford University Press, 1967)
Gaita, Raymond, *A Common Humanity: Thinking about Love, Truth and Justice* (Melbourne, Text Publishing, 1999)
Gardner, John and Stephen Shute, 'The Wrongness of Rape' in J Horder (ed), *Oxford Essays in Jurisprudence* (Oxford, Oxford University Press, 2000)
Garrett, Brian, *Personal Identity and Self-Consciousness* (London, Routledge, 1998)
Geertz, Clifford, *The Interpretation of Cultures* (New York, Basic Books, 1973)
Gilligan, Carol, *In a Different Voice* (Cambridge, Mass, Harvard University Press, 1981)
Glendon, Mary Ann, *A World Made New: Eleanor Roosevelt and the Universal Declaration of Human Rights* (New York, Random House, 2001)
Gray, John, *Straw Dogs: Thoughts on Humans and Other Animals* (London, Granta Books, 2002)
Gray, John Chipman, *The Nature and Sources of the Law* (2nd edn, New York, Macmillan, 1921)

Gray, K and P Symes, *Real Property and Real People: Principles of Land Law* (London, Butterworths, 1981)
Grayling, AC, *The Life of Rene Descartes and Its Place in His Times* (London, Free Press, 2005)
Hale, Matthew, *History of the Pleas of the Crown* (Sollom Emlyn (ed), London, E and R Nutt and R Gosling, 1736)
Harel, Alon, 'Theories of Rights' in William Edmundson and Martin Golding (eds), *Blackwell Guide to the Philosophy of Law and Legal Theory* (Cambridge, Blackwell, 2005)
Hart, HLA, *Definition and Theory in Jurisprudence* (Oxford, Clarendon Press, 1953)
Hohfeld, WN, *Fundamental Legal Conceptions as Applied in Judicial Reasoning* (New Haven, Yale University Press, 1934)
Honore, AM, 'Ownership' in AG Guest (ed), *Oxford Essays in Jurisprudence* (Oxford, Oxford University Press, 1961)
Honore, Tony, *Responsibility and Fault* (Oxford and Portland, Hart Publishing, 1999)
Hume, David, *A Treatise of Human Nature* (1739) (London, Penguin Books, 1985)
—— *An Enquiry Concerning Human Understanding* (1777) (Web edn, Leeds Electronic Text Centre, 2000)
Ignatieff, Michael, *The Needs of Strangers* (New York, Viking, 1984)
Ingstad, Benedicte and Susan Reynolds Whyte (eds), *Disability and Culture* (Berkley, University of California Press, 1995)
Jackson, Emily, *Regulating Reproduction: Law, Technology and Autonomy* (Oxford, Hart Publishing, 2001)
James, Susan and Stephanie Palmer (eds), *Visible Women: Essays on Feminist Legal Theory and Political Philosophy* (Oxford and Portland, Hart Publishing, 2002)
James, William, *The Principles of Psychology* (Chicago, William Benton, 1952)
—— *Pragmatism* (New York, Dover Publications, 1995)
Jamieson, Dale (ed), *Singer and His Critics* (Oxford, Blackwell, 1999)
Jones, WT, *Kant and the Nineteenth Century* (New York, Harcourt Brace Jovanovich, 1952).
Kant, Immanual, *Grounding for the Metaphysics of Morals* (James W Ellington (tr), Indianapolis, Hackett Publishing Company, 1981)
—— 'Foundations of the Metaphysics of Morals' in LW Beck (ed), *Kant Selections* (New York, Macmillan, 1988)
—— *The Metaphysics of Morals* (Mary Gregor (tr), Cambridge, Cambridge University Press, 1991)
Kass, Leon R, *Life, Liberty and the Defense of Dignity: the Challenge for Bioethics* (San Francisco, Encounter Books, 2002)
Keeton, GW, *The Elementary Principles of Jurisprudence* (London, Sir Isaac Pitman and Sons, 1930)
Kelsen, Hans, *General Theory of Law and State* (New York, Russell and Russell, 1945)
—— *Pure Theory of Law* (Berkley, University of California Press, 1967)
Kinley, D (ed), *Human Rights in Australian Law: Principles, Practice and Potential* (Sydney, Federation Press, 1998)
Kocourek, A, *Jural Relations* (2nd edn, Indianapolis, Bobbs-Merrill Company, 1928)

Kramer, Matthew H, 'Rights Without Trimmings' in Matthew H Kramer, NE Simmonds and Hillel Steiner, *A Debate Over Rights: Philosophical Enquiries* (Oxford, Clarendon Press, 1998)
Lacey, Nicola, *Unspeakable Subjects: Feminist Essays in Legal and Social Theory* (Oxford, Hart Publishing, 1998)
—— '"Philosophical Foundations of the Common Law" Social not Metaphysical' in Jeremy Horder (ed), *Oxford Essays in Jurisprudence* (4th series, Oxford, Oxford University Press, 2000)
Langer, Susanne K, 'Philosophy in a New Key: a Study in the Symbolism of Reason, Rite and Art' extracted in Mary Warnock (ed), *Women Philosophers* (London, Everyman JM Dent, 1996)
Levinas, E, *Otherwise than Being or Beyond Essence* (A Lingis (tr), The Hague, Martinus Nijhoff, 1981)
Lloyd, Genevieve, *The Man of Reason: 'Male' and 'Female' in Western Philosophy* (London, Methuen, 1984)
Locke, John, *An Essay Concerning Human Understanding: an Abridgement* (John W Yolton (ed), reissue, London, Everyman's Library, London, 1991)
—— *An Essay Concerning Human Understanding* (John W Yolton (ed), London, Everyman and JM Dent, 1993)
Lodge, David, *Consciousness and the Novel* (London, Penguin Books, 2002)
Logue, J, 'Incommensurability' in T Honderich (ed), *The Oxford Companion to Philosophy* (Oxford, Oxford University Press, 1995)
Lucke, HK, 'Good Faith and Contractual Performance' in P Finn (ed), *Essays on Contract* (Sydney, Law Book Co, 1987)
MacIntyre, Alasdair, *Dependent Rational Animals: Why Human Beings Need the Virtues* (Chicago, Open Court Publishing, 1999)
Maine, Henry, *Ancient Law* (London, John Murray, 1930)
Malik, Charles, *Verbatim Record from the More Important Speeches and Interventions of Charles Malik*, Papers of Charles Malik (Library of Congress, Manuscript Division, 1946)
Malik, Maleiha, 'Faith and the State of Jurisprudence' in Peter Oliver, Sionaidh Douglas Scott and Victor Tadros (eds), *Faith in Law: Essays in Legal Theory* (Oxford, Hart Publishing, 2000)
Merton, Robert, *On Theoretical Sociology* (New York, Free Press, 1967)
Midgley, Mary, *Beast and Man: the Roots of Human Nature* (Ithaca, Cornell University Press, 1978)
—— *Science and Poetry* (London and New York, Routledge, 2001)
—— *The Myths We Live By* (London and New York, Routledge, 2003)
Mill, JS, *On Liberty* (London, Longman, Roberts & Green, 1869)
Moore, Michael, *Law and Psychiatry: Rethinking the Relationship* (Cambridge, Cambridge University Press, 1984)
—— *Placing Blame: a General Theory of the Criminal Law* (Oxford, Clarendon Press, 1997)
Mosley and Whiteley's Law Dictionary (10th edn, Sydney, Butterworths, 1988)
Naffine, Ngaire, *Law and the Sexes: Explorations in Feminist Jurisprudence* (North Sydney, Allen and Unwin, 1990)
—— 'The Body Bag' in Ngaire Naffine and Rosemary J Owens (eds), *Sexing the Subject of Law* (North Ryde, LBC Information Services and Sweet and Maxwell, 1997)

Naffine, Ngaire and Rosemary J Owens (eds), *Sexing the Subject of Law* (North Ryde, LBC Information Services and Sweet and Maxwell, 1997)
Nedelsky, Jennifer, 'Reconceiving Autonomy: Sources, Thoughts and Possibilities' in A Hutchinson and L Green (eds), *Law and the Community: the End of Individualism?* (Toronto, Carswell, 1989)
—— 'Law, Boundaries and the Bounded Self' in Robert Post (ed), *Law and the Order of Culture* (Berkeley, University of California Press, 1991)
Nekam, Alexander, *The Personality Conception of the Legal Entity* (Cambridge, Mass, Harvard University Press, 1938)
Nussbaum, Martha, *Love's Knowledge: Essays on Philosophy and Literature* (New York, Oxford University Press, 1990)
—— 'Beyond the Social Contract: Toward Global Justice' in *The Tanner Lectures on Human Values* (Salt Lake City, University of Utah Press, 2003)
—— 'Beyond "Compassion and Humanity": Justice for Nonhuman Animals' in Cass Sunstein and Martha Nussbaum (eds), *Animal Rights: Current Debates and New Directions* (New York, Oxford University Press, 2004)
O'Donovan, Katherine, *Sexual Divisions in Law* (London, Weidenfeld and Nicolson, 1985)
Orwell, George, *Nineteen Eighty-Four* (London, Secker and Warburg, 1949)
Pence, Gregory E, *Classic Cases in Medical Ethics* (3rd edn, Boston, McGraw Hill, 2000)
Pontifical Council for Justice and Peace, *Compendium of the Social Doctrine of the Church* (Strathfield NSW, St Paul's Publications, 2004)
Pound, Roscoe, *Jurisprudence* (St Paul, Minn, West Publishing, 1959)
Rachels, James, *Created from Animals: the Moral Implications of Darwinism* (Oxford, Oxford University Press, 1990)
—— 'Drawing Lines' in Cass R Sunstein and Martha C Nussbaum (eds), *Animal Rights: Current Debates and New Directions* (New York, Oxford University Press, 2004)
Rawls, John, *A Theory of Justice* (Cambridge, Mass, Belknap Press, 1971)
Rheinstein, M 'Legal Systems' in David Sills (ed), *International Encyclopaedia of the Social Sciences* (New York, Macmillan-Free Press, 1968)
Ridley, Matt, *Francis Crick: Discoverer of the Genetic Code* (London, Harper Press, 2006)
Rogers, Lesley J and Gisela Kaplan, 'All Animals are Not Equal' in Cass Sunstein and Martha Nussbaum (eds), *Animal Rights: Current Debates and New Directions* (New York, Oxford University Press, 2004)
Roosevelt, Eleanor, 'Making Human Rights Come Alive' in Allida Black (ed), *What I Hope to Leave Behind: the Essential Essays of Eleanor Roosevelt* (Brooklyn, Carlson Publishing Inc, 1995)
Rorty, Richard, *Philosophy and the Mirror of Nature* (Princeton, Princeton University Press, 1979)
Sachs, A and JH Wilson, *Sexism and the Law: a Study of Male Beliefs and Legal Bias in Britain and the United States* (Oxford, M Robertson, 1978)
Salmond, John, *Jurisprudence* (Glanville L Williams (ed), 10th edn, London, Sweet and Maxwell, 1947)
Savell, Kristen, 'The Mother of the Legal Person' in Susan James and Stephanie

Palmer (eds), *Visible Women: Essays on Feminist Legal Theory and Political Philosophy* (Oxford and Portland, Hart Publishing, 2002)
Scruton, RA, *A Short History of Modern Philosophy: from Descartes to Wittgenstein* (London, Routledge, 1989)
—— *Animal Rights and Wrongs* (3rd edn, London, Metro Books, 2000)
Seymour, John, *Childbirth and the Law* (Oxford, Oxford University Press, 2000)
Singer, Peter, *Animal Liberation: a New Ethics for our Treatment of Animals* (New York, Random House, 1975)
—— 'Justifying Infanticide' in *Writings on an Ethical Life* (New York, Ecco Press, 2000)
—— 'Ethics Beyond Species and Beyond Instinct' in Cass R Sunstein and Martha C Nussbaum (eds), *Animal Rights: Current Debates and New Directions* (New York, Oxford University Press, 2004)
Stone, A, *Mental Health and Law: a System in Transition* (Rockville, Md, National Institute of Mental Health, 1975)
Tamanah, Brian, *A General Jurisprudence of Law and Society* (Oxford, Oxford University Press, 2001)
Taylor, C, 'The Person' in Michael Carrithers, Steven Collins and Steven Lukes (eds), *The Category of the Person* (Cambridge, Cambridge University Press, 1985)
Tebbit, Mark, *Philosophy of Law* (London and New York, Routledge, 2000)
Thomas, JAC, *Textbook of Roman Law* (Amsterdam, North Holland, 1976)
Tonnies, Ferdinand, *Community and Association* (London, Routledge and Kegan Paul, 1955)
Tooley, M, *Abortion and Infanticide* (Oxford, Clarendon Press, 1983)
Tur, Richard, 'The "Person" in Law' in Arthur Peacocke and Grant Gillett (eds), *Persons and Personality: a Contemporary Inquiry* (Oxford, Basil Blackwell, 1987)
Wacks, Raymond, *Understanding Jurisprudence: an Introduction to Legal Theory* (New York, Oxford University Press, 2005)
Waldron, Jeremy, *Law and Disagreement* (Oxford, Clarendon Press, 1999)
Waller, L and CR Williams, *Criminal Law: Text and Cases* (9th edn, Chatswood, NSW, Butterworths, 2001)
Warnock, Mary, *Imagination and Time* (Oxford, Blackwell Publishing,1994)
Warren, Mary Ann, *Moral Status* (Oxford and New York, Oxford University Press, 2000)
Weaver, Jane, 'Court-ordered Caesarean Sections' in Andrew Bainham, Shelley Day Sclater and Martin Richards (eds), *Body Law and Laws* (Oxford and Oregon, Hart Publishing, 2002)
Weber, Max, *Economy and Society: an Outline of Interpretive Sociology* (New York, Bedminster, 1968)
Wise, Steven, *Rattling the Cage: Towards Legal Rights for Animals* (Cambridge, Mass, Perseus Books, 2000)
—— *Drawing the Line: Science and the Case for Animal Rights* (Cambridge, Mass, Perseus Books, 2002)
Wittgenstein, L, *Philosophical Investigations* (GEM Anscombe (tr), Oxford, Blackwell, 1953)
Wolgast, Elizabeth, *Ethics of an Artificial Person: Lost Responsibility in Professions and Organizations* (Stanford, Stanford University Press, 1992)

Other Sources

Barnes, Simon, 'Living with Eddie', *The Weekend Australian Magazine*, 14–15 April 2007, 31

Davis, Dena, 'Genetic Dilemmas and the Child's Right to an Open Future' in *Hastings Center Report* (March-April 1997)

National Health and Medical Research Council, *Ethical Guidelines on the Use of Assisted Reproductive Technology in Clinical Practice and Research* (Australian Government, September 2004)

'Statement by Mrs Franklin D Roosevelt', Department of State Bulletin (December 1948)

Index

www.ingramcontent.com/pod-product-compliance
Ingram Content Group UK Ltd.
Pitfield, Milton Keynes, MK11 3LW, UK
UKHW020141290926
15471UKWH00004B/626

9 781841 138664